"In *Experiential Marketing*, Wided Batat offers a review of ways in which the consumption expe tions for marketing practice. I especially appreciate the book experiential marketing mix and its scholarly grounding in an insightfully elaborated formulation of the essential experiential concepts via case examples and reviews of the relevant literature (including a timely awareness of the emerging physical-&-digital or 'phygital' consumption context)."

Morris B. Holbrook, *W. T. Dillard Professor Emeritus of Marketing,*
Graduate School of Business Columbia University

"It's very clear that in today's experience economy marketing must change. The old ways of thinking, while good for their time, no longer cut it. It is, therefore, great to see Wided Batat's new book take on the 7Ps of the old marketing mix and replace them with the 7Es, each one focused on thinking experientially. All marketers should read this book and then change their approach to generating demand that fits in with a time when experiences have become the predominant economic offering."

B. Joseph Pine II, *co-author of* The Experience Economy

"Definitely one of the most powerful treatments of the subject to date. A book full of wisdom. Anyone who is serious about customer experience will find it indispensable. Wided Batat's book is an incredibly valuable resource for anyone seeking to navigate the complexities of the customer experience."

Markus Giesler, *Director, Big Design Lab, York University*

"As both a journalist and a consumer, I find it difficult to keep up with the many changes taking place in the business world and specifically in marketing. I appreciate that Wided Batat has decided to explore those changes head on in her new book *Experiential Marketing*. So much of what we hear about these days is 'experience over product,' so the timing couldn't be better for a book on this topic. I look forward to adding it to my reference collection for future stories."

Elizabeth Garone, *journalist,* The Wall Street Journal
and BBC Capital

"Nice structure. The content is certainly relevant for the digital age. The overall concepts seem right and seem to be useful for managers."

Bernd Schmitt, *author of* Customer Experience Management

EXPERIENTIAL MARKETING

Why do some brands make us feel good, while others frustrate us? What makes us engage with certain brands, rebuy the same products, return to the same store or revisit the same destination over and over again? Is there a framework underlying how past and lived shopping experiences can affect our future experiences, our buying decisions, and our brand loyalty?

In this exciting new book, Wided Batat introduces readers to the new customer experience framework and the era of the "Experiential Marketing Mix." She explores the concept of the 7Es (Experience, Exchange, Extension, Emphasis, Empathy, Emotional touchpoints, Emic/Etic process); a tool that focuses on the consumer as a starting point in marketing strategies. By using these, companies can design suitable, emotional, and profitable customer experiences in a phygital context (physical place and digital space) including both offline and online digital experiences. Batat argues that a traditional product-centric approach should be replaced by the appropriate mix of 7Es, based upon a more consumer/experience-centric logic.

Experiential Marketing is a guide to building experiences consumers cannot forget. It will be of interest for CEOs, brand managers, marketing and communication professionals, students, and anyone eager to learn more about how to design the ultimate customer experience in a new phygital. In this book, Professor Batat combines theory and practice and gives readers an overview of: the origins and the rise of the customer experience logic, the 7Es of the new experiential marketing mix, and the challenges for the future.

Wided Batat is a marketing professor and an internationally renowned expert and speaker on experiential and digital marketing specialized in the fields of retail, luxury, food, well-being, youth cultures, generation Z&Y, Millennials and post-Millennials, and tourism. She has published dozens of books in English and French, and articles in top-tier academic journals that have received several awards. Professor Batat introduced an innovative and disruptive approach to global and digital customer experience by providing a strategic framework of the customer experience offline and online and the new experiential marketing mix (7Es). Entrepreneur, Professor Batat is also a bilingual (French and English) international professional trainer and the founder of B&C Consulting Group, an innovative market research and consumer insights company specialized in global and digital customer experience design, buying behavior, and consumer trends.

EXPERIENTIAL MARKETING

Consumer Behavior, Customer Experience and The 7Es

Wided Batat

Routledge
Taylor & Francis Group

LONDON AND NEW YORK

First published 2019
by Routledge
2 Park Square, Milton Park, Abingdon, Oxon OX14 4RN

and by Routledge
52 Vanderbilt Avenue, New York, NY 10017

Routledge is an imprint of the Taylor & Francis Group, an informa business

© 2019 Wided Batat

British Library Cataloguing-in-Publication Data
A catalogue record for this book is available from the British Library

Library of Congress Cataloging-in-Publication Data
Names: Batat, Wided, author.
Title: Experiential marketing : consumer behaviour, customer
    experience and the 7Es / Wided Batat.
Description: Abingdon, Oxon ; New York, NY : Routledge, 2019. |
    Includes bibliographical references and index. |
Identifiers: LCCN 2018025521 (print) | LCCN 2018028987
    (ebook) | ISBN 9781315232201 | ISBN 9781138293151
    (hardback : alk. paper) | ISBN 9781138293168 (pbk. : alk. paper)
Subjects: LCSH: Marketing. | Consumer behavior. | Customer
    relations. | Relationship marketing.
Classification: LCC HF5415 (ebook) | LCC HF5415 .B375 2019
    (print) | DDC 658.8/342—dc23
LC record available at https://lccn.loc.gov/2018025521

ISBN: 978-1-138-29315-1 (hbk)
ISBN: 978-1-138-29316-8 (pbk)
ISBN: 978-1-315-23220-1 (ebk)

Typeset in Bembo
by Swales & Willis Ltd, Exeter, Devon, UK

Visit the eResources: www.routledge.com/9781138293168

Printed in the United Kingdom
by Henry Ling Limited

CONTENTS

FIGURES

TABLES

MINI-CASES

THEORY BOXES

INTRODUCTION

Experience is a concept that is unavoidable in contemporary marketing strategies to the point that almost all products and services are now sold as "experience." The experiential approach of consumption first appeared in the marketing and consumer behavior field in 1982 following the publication of the seminal work of the two pioneer authors Holbrook and Hirschman who opened the path to other outstanding marketing scholars, such as Bernd Schmitt, who introduced experiential marketing in 1999, and to marketing professionals, such as Pine and Gilmore, who described the paradigm of the experience economy in our contemporary societies. Since then, customer experience has become a central pillar of the foundation of the economy in the current context. Other articles and books followed, first in North America and then in Europe.

The various definitions of customer experience emphasize the importance of intangible dimensions (e.g., subjectivity, emotion, symbolism, ideology, socialization) of customer experiences and behaviors. In diverse marketplaces and sectors (retail, restaurant, hotel, tourism, luxury, digital, publishing, healthcare, insurance, banks, etc.), companies are turning to customer experience offers to retain actual customers, attract potential buyers, and increase sales in design environments in which the experience will merge from physical place to virtual space (e.g., website, social media). This change can be enhanced by shifting the focus from the use of traditional marketing mix logic (7Ps) to a new experiential marketing mix technique (7Es), a set of manageable components that the company can use to design and offer the ultimate customer experience that is suitable, enjoyable, and profitable.

This book is based on one of the fundamental ideas related to the definition of a strategic framework of the new "experiential marketing mix." This framework highlights controllable components of the mix companies can use to implement effective experiential marketing and communication actions in order to create and

Experiential marketing mix	Marketing mix
☐	☐
☐ Experience	☐ Product
☐ Exchange	☐ Price
☐ Extension	☐ Place
☐ Emphasis	☐ Promotion
☐ Empathy capital	☐ People
☐ Emotional touchpoints	☐ Physical
☐ Emic/etic process	☐ Process

Experiential marketing mix vs. marketing mix

share value with their customers. The controllable components of the experiential marketing mix refer to the 7Es (Experience, Exchange, Extension, Emphasis, Empathy capital, Emotional touchpoints, and Emic/etic process).

Therefore, marketing managers should concentrate on seven key decision domains related to the 7Es that constitute the experiential marketing mix while designing the customer experience offers and planning their marketing plans. The 7Es all-together are connected with each other and related to decision-making, which means that a decision in one domain can affect strategic or marketing decisions in others. Each company should build up such a composition of 7Es, which can help it meet its organizational and strategic objectives and guarantee a strong and sustainable competitive advantage generated by value creation and sharing, highest level of customer satisfaction and loyalty, and positive image offline and online.

This book focuses on the idea of the new experiential marketing mix and how its 7Es could be a strategic framework and a tool to help companies design and implement successful customer experience strategies. The book lists various examples and mini-case studies that will help the reader understand how the experiential marketing mix comes to life through the conceptualization and provision of customer experiences. New technologies have provided useful tools to enhance the experience, but other aspects and challenges pertaining to experience delivery and design are also elements that contribute to magnifying the customer experience. In this book, I review the experiential literature and the recent evolutions in the field of marketing and consumer behavior. I also build on my prior works related to the experience in luxury, digital customer experience, food experience, and tourist experience to present a framework that allows companies to implement the experiential marketing mix. This book offers critical analysis, applied cases, and new tools that I introduce through three main parts: the illustration of the origins and the rise of customer experience in marketing, the new experiential marketing mix and its 7Es, and the future challenges in experiential marketing and the customer experience design fields.

The first part of this book includes three main chapters. In Chapter 1, I examine the key changes in consumer behavior that lead companies to consider an experiential logic within their strategies to respond to today's consumers who are expecting their brand experiences to be efficient, personalized, and emotional. In this chapter, I focus on four major transformations in consumer behavior: digital, empowerment, emotion, and postmodernism. These new trends can affect in a positive or a negative way customer experiences, and thus customer satisfaction and loyalty. In the second chapter, I analyze theories underpinning customer experience marketing by providing a cross-sectional analysis of diverse studies in human sciences and business disciplines that tackle the concept of "customer experience." Prior to explaining what customer experience is in the marketing field, I attempt to clarify the meanings and origins of "experience," the customer journey, and the touchpoints that bring customer experience to life. Chapter 3 will introduce a new framework that offers an integral conceptualization of customer experience marketing. This new framework defines customer experience as a process that distinguishes between experience markers, drivers, and its outcomes. Using the experiential marketing mix framework, I will attempt to contribute to prior works in marketing by proposing an iterative comprehensive framework for conceptualizing customer experience marketing.

In the second part of this book, I present the experiential marketing mix and its 7Es that are introduced, explained, and illustrated by examples and mini-cases throughout seven chapters starting with Chapter 4, which focuses on the "E" of "Experience," its stages, territories or Experience Territory Matrix (ETM), and its measurement tool EXQUAL to improve the quality of customer experiences. In Chapter 5, I examine the component of "Exchange" in the experiential marketing mix, which emphasizes the idea of value exchange beyond the price logic in the marketing mix. This component will be analyzed by exploring two main topics that generate consumer value: the co-creation process and collaborative marketing. Then, Chapter 6 will focus on the "Extension" as a variable of the experiential marketing mix that replaces "Place/distribution" in the traditional marketing mix. Extension refers to a more dynamic and evolving process of value distribution based on the logic of continuum, rather than a static settlement. In this chapter, I introduce the logic behind the experience continuum and the importance for companies to integrate both intra- and extra-domestic consumption experience focusing on the buyer behavior and the consumption and/or usage practices. Chapter 7 introduces "Emphasis" as an experiential component in replacement of "Promotion" in marketing mix. I define the emphasis approach through two key communication strategies: the creation of a brand culture and the brand storytelling, two factors that companies should take into consideration in their communication campaigns to create a meaningful experience, and thus share values with their actual and potential customers within their experiences with the brand. In Chapter 8, I talk about "Empathy capital" as a component of the experiential marketing mix that replaces the variable of "People." I will introduce the concept of empathy, the formation of empathy capital of employees, and the empathy experience that can help companies to retain their customers and improve the quality of their experience by focusing on their needs from their own perspective. Chapter 9 addresses the experiential component related to "Emotional touchpoints," which refers to the logic of shifting the focus on consumer experience touchpoints to the identification of the emotional impact of touchpoints. I also introduce in this chapter the emotional touchpoints toolkit that companies can use to create positive experiences. Chapter 10, the last chapter in Part II of this book, introduces the "Emic/etic process" to design successful consumer experiences as well as the idea of the construction of a sociocultural customer journey.

The third part of this book, which relates to the future challenges facing experiential marketing and customer experience design, includes three main chapters. In Chapter 11, I introduce the first challenge related to the rise of a phygital customer experience, which is a result of the digital revolution and the transformation of the many activities and functions of "real life" into corresponding digital entities. In terms of experiential marketing strategy, phygital suggests the multiplication of bridges thrown between two worlds, physical and digital, to give consumers a more fluid and richer experience. Chapter 12 focuses on a second challenge linked to customer experience design by implementing storyliving strategies and tools. Finally, in Chapter 13, I will conclude by addressing the challenge of using alternative research methods to study and understand consumer experience online and offline. I will focus on two key market research tools: experiential research methods and E-experiential research techniques.

In this book, I have combined my professional expertise and my research, as well as my prior works on the customer experience topic in different fields to introduce a new framework for designing and managing customer experience and a new marketing mix for companies, brand managers, and marketing professionals who can implement the experiential marketing mix by using 7Es to design suitable, successful, and profitable customer experiences that guarantee a sustainable competitive advantage. This book provides both an extensive review of existing knowledge in this field and examples, tools, and mini-cases that I hope will help readers, researchers, students, marketing professionals, and scholars, gain a better appreciation of how customer experience can be defined, conceptualized, implemented, and measured in different consumption fields. Enjoy your reading experience!

PART I

Customer experience marketing

Back to origins

1

FOUR KEY CHANGES IN CONSUMER BEHAVIOR

Digital, empowerment, emotion, and postmodernism

Purpose and context

Today's consumers are becoming familiar with instant accessibility and will expect their brand experiences to be personalized and emotional. Thus, brands need to better understand their customers and the emerging social trends to deliver experiences customers really want, through meaningful messages that echo through different marketplaces and touchpoints. Understanding consumer experiences is an essential mission for marketers and scholars and cannot be examined without considering the key changes in consumer behavior that will impact marketing most in the future, such as the transition from a modern to a postmodern consumer society or the common use of technology and digital devices. This chapter seeks to explore four major key changes in consumer behavior: digital, empowerment, emotion, and postmodernism. These new trends can affect customer experience and help companies design suitable experiences by taking into account both tangible (e.g., functional) and intangible (e.g., symbolic, social, emotional) needs.

Learning outcomes

At the end of this chapter you will learn more about the macro, meso, and the micro factors that can positively or negatively affect consumer behaviors and the whole customer experience. This chapter will bring a comprehensive framework that includes tangible and intangible elements you should consider to design a suitable and satisfying customer experience.

Digital transformation and its impact on consumption

This section will introduce the main drivers of the digital transformation in today's societies. I will examine the way the drivers of the digital transformation can affect consumption activities, and the main emerging challenges and opportunities for brands and companies.

Drivers of digital transformation

So far, I have identified three key drivers of the digital transformation: technological, demographic, and socioeconomic (Figure 1.1).

- **Technological drivers.** The report of the World Economic Forum published in 2016 identifies four major technological drivers that led to today's digital transformation: mobile and Internet penetration, connected devices, big data and the cloud, and user interfaces. Table 1.1 summarizes the characteristics of each trend and its implications in terms of social changes and consumption practices. The combination of these technological consumption trends has contributed to the development of new consumer behaviors and expectations, as well as business innovation, meaning that companies have to rethink their offers to make them fit with the emerging profile of digitized consumers.
- **Demographic drivers.** There are two demographic drivers of digital transformation: urbanization and accessibility. Urbanization has contributed to the development of new ways of delivery and supply approaches to match consumer wants and expectations. The United Nations (2014) predicts that almost 60% of the world's population will settle in urban zones by 2050. Furthermore, the World Economic Forum[1] says: "a large part of this emerging demographic is based in developing markets where improving standards of living and income are driving increased access to digital technology and connectivity" (2016: 7). Mobile phones and Internet access are available even in the most disadvantaged consumption cultures in the world. Making technology accessible for everyone has contributed to enhancing the development of new digital-driver consumption modes. For digital pure players, making technology accessible to everyone, including vulnerable people (e.g., individuals with disabilities) is a vital

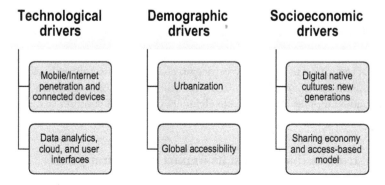

FIGURE 1.1   Key drivers of digital transformation

TABLE 1.1 Characteristics of the digital transformation

Technology	Characteristic
Mobile and Internet penetration	The World Economic Forum report (2016) states mobile phone penetration has increased from 1% of the population in 1995 to 73% in 2014 and Internet penetration has almost doubled over seven years. The number of smartphone subscriptions is also predicted to reach 4 billion by 2025 mostly in emerging markets
Connected devices	The number of connected devices in the world is estimated to continue to rise allowing the translation of information from environments and behaviors into smart data that provides real-time customization
Data analytics and the cloud	The intensification of data collection through emails, connected objects, mobile apps, social and e-commerce platforms, and the need for automated advanced analytics will continue to grow and will need more virtual space or cloud for storage
User interfaces	User interfaces allowing humans to interact with machines are becoming more common, enabling tasks to be carried out more quickly and efficiently. In the future, physical user interfaces can be replaced by control and interaction through Artificial Intelligence

element in their strategies. Grach (2015) states that Microsoft,[2] for example, has a long tradition and a strong positioning in terms of allowing and facilitating accessibility. For more than 25 years, Microsoft has concentrated its efforts on developing technologies that facilitate the use of devices by individuals, empower them, and provide them with the appropriate tools and training to use technology that meets their functional, social, economic, educational demands, and other expectations.

MINI-CASE 1.1   HOW APPLE IS MAKING TECHNOLOGY ACCESSIBLE DURING GLOBAL ACCESSIBILITY AWARENESS DAY (GAAD)

The idea of a Global Accessibility Awareness Day (GAAD) started in 2012 with a blog post written by a web developer, Joe Devon. The objective of GAAD is to raise awareness about making technological experiences, including web, mobile, social media, and other digital devices accessible and usable to people with different disabilities. In 2017, Apple highlighted GAAD with a "designed for everyone" video series. Apple has a long history of working to make technology accessible through developing hardware products and software platforms. To display all the digital tools developed to increase accessibility, Apple posted in the GAAD a series of seven videos to YouTube

(continued)

(continued)

showing how true and reliable individuals can develop several usages of Mac, iOS, and Apple Watch accessibility qualities ranging from Switch Control to the use of Siri and VoiceOver. Each video tells the story of specific individuals with disabilities and shows how Apple is making digital experiences accessible, easy to use, and convenient:

- Video 1: *"Designed for Carlos"* displays Carlos, the singer and drummer of a metal band using VoiceOver on his iPhone to call transportation, take photos, and post updates online;
- Video 2: *"Designed for Andrea D"* shows Andrea, a nursing student, using her Apple Watch to track wheelchair-based workouts and sharing her activity with friends to encourage the disabled community;
- Video 3: *"Designed for Meera P"* displays Meera, a teenager, who loves soccer and expresses herself using TouchChat on an iPad;
- Video 4: *"Designed for Patrick L"* displays Patrick, radio DJ and music producer cooking for his family by using iOS app TapTapSee to identify ingredients through his iPhone camera;
- Video 5: *"Designed for Shane R"* displays Shane, a choir director, using made for iPhone hearing aids, Live Listen, and iPad app Essential Elements in her music teaching with middle school band students;
- Video 6: *"Designed for Ian M"* shows Ian, a Pacific Northwest lover, using Siri to start FaceTime calls or capturing photos using Switch Control;
- Video 7: *"Designed for Todd S"* shows Todd who runs a technology consulting company using Siri, Switch Control, and HomeKit to manage his lights, sound, security system, doors, and locks.

- **Socioeconomic drivers.** So far, I have identified two main socioeconomic factors that drive digital transformation in today's societies: the rise of digital native consumption cultures and the alternative sharing economy model:

  o *The rise of digital native cultures*: millennials and post-millennials are part of an emerging digital native culture that is a global phenomenon. In these global youth cultures, young people born between 1980 to the present are viewed as digital natives (Tapscott, 2009) and a distinctive generation with consumption practices that make them different from their prior generations. Millennials and post-millennials are the dominant largest current generation within the marketplace (Sweeney, 2005). They are also viewed as empowered and digital experts who can use their new knowledge to improve their consumption experiences and their social life. Furthermore, young people have developed multitasking behaviors, as well as collaborative and interactive modes of consumption enabled by social media. While these millennials and post-millennials belong to a dominant living generation of consumers, which has a great economic potential, brand managers and marketing professionals should develop a deeper understanding of their consumption cultures where social and mobile technologies and the Internet allow them to embrace new consumption practices, such as online sharing and collaborative behaviors.

MINI-CASE 1.2   COLLABORATIVE TOURISM EXPERIENCES AMONGST MILLENNIAL AND POST-MILLENNIAL TOURISTS IN THE SHARING ECONOMY

Considering millennial and post-millennial tourists as co-producers or co-creators of value has changed the marketing way of thinking from top-down to bottom-up. Millennial and post-millennial are considered as a "collaboration generation," since they are active producers of user-generated content who can contribute to the co-creation of value by activating their digital skills and knowledge to shape the company's offers. Thus, millennial and post-millennial tourists became more powerful and influential and are commonly considered as a valuable and authentic foundation of innovation and information for industries and consumers. Batat and Hammedi (2017) analyzed three popular

TABLE 1.2 Collaborative consumption and sharing tourism website usages amongst millennial and post-millennial tourists

Sharing tourism websites	Airbnb	Couchsurfing	Wwoofing
Collaborative dimensions	Market-mediation Anonymity Temporality (short stay)	Consumer involvement Temporality (short stay)	Market-mediation Temporality (short stay)
Motivations	Functional needs Economical benefit Travel optimization	Social needs Shared experiences Authenticity Socialization	Values Engagement and ethics Pro-environmental behaviors
Typology of sharing practices	Access-based model	Collaborative consumption Sharing economy	Access-based model Collaborative consumption Sharing ideologies and workforce

Source: Adapted from Batat and Hammedi (2017)

(continued)

(continued)

collaborative consumption initiatives amongst millennial and post-millennial tourists: *Airbnb, Couchsurfing,* and *Wwoofing* to explore the meanings of collaborative consumption and the dimensions of engagement, sharing, expertise, and efficacy in millennial and post-millennial collaborative consumption in tourism. The conclusions of their study show that 1) Airbnb.com is a functional tool for collaborative consumption amongst millennials and post-millennials, 2) Couchsurfing.com is used by millennials and post-millennials for tourism social experiences, and 3) Wwoofing.com is a form of responsible and engaged collaborative consumption. The main differences are summarized in Table 1.2.

○   *The new sharing economy*: shifting from a traditional ownership model to a shared consumption refers to the idea that while in the past decades consumers were interested in owning products and services to confirm, extend, or even modify their self-identification throughout their purchase, today's consumers prefer sharing everything to which access is allowed by assembling resources, products, or services. According to Batat and Hammedi (2017), the sharing economic model and its underlying processes, governance modes, and consumer motives are driven by multiple macroeconomic factors. One key factor is the decreasing consumer faith in the business sphere as an outcome of the recent economic crisis. Further, while, the rates of joblessness have increased and the buying power of consumers has crashed, consumers need to develop new modes and behaviors to make or save money, which is the reason why consumers are now more sensitive to alternative business models, such as peer-to-peer, that focus on consumers as possible providers and shoppers.

Also, the necessary technology for introducing a connected peer-to-peer marketplace has, in recent years, become accessible at a more balanced rate. There is similarly an environmental issue that motivated today's consumers to embrace the new sharing economy, which is supposed to be a more eco-friendly driven initiative. For consumers, the "sharing economy" has multiple advantages: it guarantees equal and high satisfaction, promotes sustainable behaviors amongst communities, and empowers them through shifting the power from producers to consumers.

For companies, the potential of the sharing economy is significant. PricewaterhouseCoopers estimated that by 2025, the five main areas of the sharing economy with peer-to-peer lending, online recruitment, peer-to-peer housing, car sharing, and music and video streaming will generate $335 billion (Hawksworth and Vaughan, 2014). The speed of growth with which sharing systems have spread would also suggest that this new trend might represent an important threat to established industries, and thus needs regulation.

MINI-CASE 1.3   SURF AIR: THE SHARING ECONOMY FOR BUSINESS TRAVEL

Surf Air is an innovative Californian-based airline company that utilizes the principles of the sharing economy (e.g., Uber and Airbnb) to offer convenient, customized, and exclusive business air travel experiences.

Surf Air is transforming the flying experience of frequent business travelers by offering unlimited flight services for five to eight fellow passengers in the US and in Europe for a fixed monthly fee starting from $2,000 plus a $1,000 membership fee (all-you-can-fly). The company uses a private jet and offers services that allow travelers to avoid queues, travel simply and quickly, and in a comfortable modern aircraft by using private and small terminals.

The concept is simple, according to Talling-Smith chief executive officer of the independent aviation upstart Surf Air (Europe): "Frequent travelers can pay one single monthly membership fee and fly on our routes, subject to capacity, as frequently as they like on a private jet, with no extra charges other than that one monthly payment."

Digital transformation challenges and opportunities for brands?

Today's companies are experiencing immediate indicators of the important shift towards a digital reality characterized by multiple transitions: from product to experience, from owing to sharing behaviors, and from brand power to the power of persuasion. These digital trends can be considered as challenges or opportunities for brand managers and marketing professionals.

- **From products to digital experiences:** Pine and Gilmore (1998, 1999) state that consumers increasingly buy experiences rather than products or services. Consequently, designing valuable consumer experiences has become a top priority for marketers today. Gartner says that 89% of businesses anticipate competing principally on the basis of customer experience (Sorofman, 2014). As digital technologies become pervasive, marketing professionals are particularly interested in understanding the influence of digital technology on customer experience. Digital contexts build distinct and unique experiences due to their socio–material characteristics (see Chapter 11).

  Digital contexts also allow high levels of interactivity, so that consumers can play a proactive role in designing valuable experiences. As a result, different consumer cultures specific to the digital environment have emerged giving birth to experiences specific to that environment. While digital technologies become pervasive, brand managers and marketing profession-als should be particularly interested in understanding the formation of the new emerging values that consumers assign to their products and services in digitalized contexts. Thus, companies are encouraged to go beyond the traditional good-centric logic by generating an "online value proposition" to design consumption experiences tailored to the digital context (Chaffey and Ellis-Chadwick, 2012: 232).

Marketing authors such as Punj (2012) and Rodgers and Sheldon (2002) have previously investigated digital experiences, looking at the particular gratifications that consumers gain from using digital technologies. Overall, their works focused on the outcomes of digital consumption that have been found to:

o   Promote positive utilitarian experiences;
o   Enhance socialization and relational experiences;
o   Simulate entertainment, hedonic, and playful activities;
o   Focus on aesthetic experiences.

Yet, it is not clear in these works how digital experiences differ from their physical counterparts. With regards to utility, Ratchford, Talukdar, and Lee (2007) indicate that consumers search for products and services and buy them online because it is more convenient. Thus, going online is:

o   More time effective;
o   Cognitively and physically less demanding than offline;
o   More convenient and allows consumers to make better decisions.

Consumers feel that they are able to find the product or service which fits their needs or desires best because they have much more information available and access to wider choices. They also feel that they can obtain the best price for a product thanks to price-comparison tools. Using Holbrook's (1999) ter-minology of consumer values, we can state that digital technologies enhance experiences of efficiency (convenience) and excellence (better decisions).

THEORY BOX 1.1   HOLBROOK'S CONSUMER VALUE TYPOLOGIES

Holbrook defines eight typologies of consumer values: efficiency, excellence, status, esteem, play, aesthetics, ethics, and spirituality. These eight values can give us a framework to analyze consumption experiences in both the physical place and the virtual sphere. The eight different types of value presented in Holbrook's typology are explained below.

1) *Efficiency*: measured by specific proportion of productions to efforts. Frequently using time unit as a denominator;
2) *Excellence*: related to consumer satisfaction and product or experience quality. It includes the evaluation of some objects for their ability to achieve a particular objective or purpose. It might also be valued without the focus on the outcome accomplishment;
3) *Status*: consumption is focused on how it affects an individual's image as perceived by other people within a particular sociocultural context;
4) *Esteem*: consumption is related to a responsive evaluation of one's own consumption practices and how they may potentially impact one's public image in a positive or a negative way;
5) *Play*: it involves having fun within the consumption context;
6) *Aesthetics*: beauty is one of the aesthetic dimensions related to experience;
7) *Ethics*: reflects how consumption will affect others or how they will react to it;
8) *Spirituality*: refers to the idea of losing one's self by producing a sense of adoration or mystic experience.

The shift from products to digital experiences also underlines the emergence of playful and aesthetic consumption experiences. Playful experiences are common because the interactive nature of digital technologies promotes the emergence of flow when searching for information (e.g., web surfing) and using a product (e.g., playing video games) (Hoffman and Novak, 2009). For example, Mathwick, Malhotra, and Rigdon (2002) state that rich media also allows users to build aesthetically pleasing and attractive images and sounds and to develop elaborated stories transporting consumers in imaginary worlds where they can escape reality and revel in their dreams, producing aesthetic consumption experiences.

Furthermore, social media is an important component of digital experiences. Mathwick, Wiertz, and de Ruyter (2008) indicate that social media produce feelings of "we-ness," that is, feelings of fellowship and togetherness in a group and allow the development of strong social relationships, providing consumers with pleasurable experiences of social integration. When consumers become core members of a community they can:

o   Gain a social status in the group;
o   Receive approval and admiration by their peers in the community;
o   Achieve pleasurable experiences of social enhancement.

As indicated by Kozinets (2010), communications on social media are digitally mediated; consumers can bond with like-minded individuals whom they could not have reached otherwise because of geographical and time constraints.

Altogether, digital technologies, therefore, facilitate the emergence of relational value in digital consumption experiences. Therefore, past research indicates that digital technologies produce experiences of enhanced efficiency (convenience) and excellence (best fit), facilitate the emergence of play (flow), aesthetic experiences (narrative transportation), and allow the development of relationships that would have been otherwise impossible to build (linking value). Such characterizations of digital consumption experiences are very similar to that of offline physical consumption experiences where these different types of value cohabitate. It provides a picture of digital experiences as being quantitatively different from their offline physical counterparts (stronger or weaker experiential value, more positive or negative experience) rather than qualitatively different (a different thing). Sparse research has started to characterize how digital experiences are qualitatively different from their physical counterparts. Digital experiences have been characterized as:

o   Virtual and imbued with transience (e.g., Denegri-Knott and Molesworth, 2010);
o   Unstable (e.g., Watkins, 2015);
o   Fragmented and with a sense of augmented reality (e.g., Kedzior, 2015);
o   Networked and polyvocal (e.g., Kozinets et al., 2010);
o   Wavering between private and public conversations.

However, these results are preliminary and fragmented calling for further research on the conceptualization of digital customer experiences used to build an integrated framework.
- **From owning to sharing and collaborating:** in the digital era, a shift from possession to accessibility might be detected throughout an extensive assortment of marketplaces. While in the traditional context consumers would purchase goods and become the owners, in digital environments that are based on the idea of the "accessibility-based system," consumers pay for "temporary access-rights" to a product. Several initiatives based on "access-business" models have emerged and introduced this business model as an alternative economy to the property economy enabled by the use of technologies and social media.

The digitized consumers can then have other options to satisfy their needs by sharing, collaborating, renting, swapping, and so forth, rather than buying and possessing. Furthermore, the new consumer believes that the more he/she shares consumption items and services the fewer earth resources will be consumed, is another motivation to the rise of the sharing economy, which also allows more efficient and sustainable modes of consumption. According to Batat and Hammedi (2017), three main concepts in relation to the shift from traditional to new sharing economy have been examined in the marketing field (Table 1.3): sharing, collaborative, and access-based models (or Internet-facilitated sharing).

TABLE 1.3 Sharing, collaborative consumption, and access-based models

Sharing economy concepts	Authors	Definitions
Sharing	Belk, 2007 Benkler, 2004 Schor and Fitzmaurice, 2015	Sharing includes the action and procedure of delivering; what is ours to others for their usage and/or the act and activity of getting or winning something from others for our usage Some authors even define sharing as "nonreciprocal pro-social" behavior Sharing is more likely to occur in family, close relatives, and friends than amongst strangers, which might also be referred to as "sharing in" When sharing refers to an exchange between strangers, it is then called "sharing out" Sharing could be tightly linked to joint lifestyles, where individuals with same expectations or interests get together to share and swap physical to less-tangible resources (e.g., time, space, skills, and money)
Collaborative consumption	Felson and Speath, 1978 Belk, 2014	This concept was originally defined as moments in which one or more individuals consume financial items in the procedure of entering into collective actions with a single person or multiple others Despite its focus on the joint-activity, the definition remains broad since it does not focus enough on the gaining and delivery of any resource(s) Collaborative consumption emphasizes the coordination of consumption at a certain period and context, but the consumption act could be subject to a transactional/market exchange. The presence of compensation (either monetary or non-monetary) makes collaborative consumption different from sharing (e.g., bartering, trading, and swapping could also be considered as collaborative consumption activities)
Access-based models	Chen, 2009	Also called Internet-facilitated sharing is similar to sharing but does not require a transfer of ownership. Yet, access could vary from sharing, in that access is not essentially selfless or prosocial, as sharing requires the presence of either economic exchange or reciprocity. The shift to more access-based regimes is defined by short-term restricted usages of resources coordinated and controlled by groups of providers Access-based models have also existed in other forms of sharing mainly in non-profit or public sectors (e.g., borrowing books or consuming art by museum visitors) and are originated by conventional rental methods in the market, like car or flat rentals

The shift from old business models to collaborative and creative ways of ownership through participation and collaboration, calls for rethinking the way brand managers and marketing professionals are targeting today's digitized generations who will always consider new and creative ways to obtain products and services for free. Further, these generations are also considered to be engaged, responsible, ethical, and in search of brands, products, and services that are suitable to their values.

Following the actual digital context, we can say that social and mobile technologies radically disrupted consumer behaviors and, therefore, require changes in marketing and communication strategies. Indeed, digital tools are increasingly empowering consumers who become expert, skilled, and active users of different digital platforms, not only to share their activities and opinions, but also their own products and services. It has been emphasized that the increasingly powerful crowd is expected to facilitate peer-to-peer transactions by allowing a monetization of consumers' assets and purchases from each other directly at lower costs and sometimes in more convenient ways. The flexibility and cost-reduction of these alternative models will compete with the existing offers and may be viewed as prejudiced and unfair. Furthermore, in some European countries, sharing initiatives facilitated by technologies are considered illegal. For example, in the transportation sector, Uber, a ride-sharing service has been banned in France, Netherlands, and Spain since it represents an unfair competition to traditional taxi drivers.

- **From the power of the brand to the power of persuasion:** while the brand encompasses three main components: functional (e.g., product, design); relational (e.g., relationship with customers, personal); and symbolic (e.g., values, DNA, logo, personality) that are powerful elements of brand differentiation, positioning, and competitive advantage creation, the power of persuasion requires the ability to change not just action but attitude towards the brand. For example, a luxury brand that creates brand new products with accessible prices (e.g., masstige and co-branding H&M and Karl Lagerfeld) may gain new customers, but it hasn't necessarily changed how it is perceived. Brands can also use influencer marketing as a powerful tool of persuasion. While marketers have long recognized the importance of using celebrities and celebrity products as a source of value influence, in the digital context consumers can also become influencers and brand endorsers who may have billions of followers. Thus, there is a multitude of factors (e.g., psychological, sociological, economic) explaining the "why" of the power of persuasion of online ordinary individuals. Individuals who may become icons in their own right, who may be endorsed by popular brands in implicit or explicit ways, and even more who may create their own brand and recommend it to their followers. Pitkin (2011) suggests three main ways in which online influencers can make other consumers like, share, buy, or even hate brands: influencer connectivity, influencer product adoption, and influencer authority (Figure 1.2).

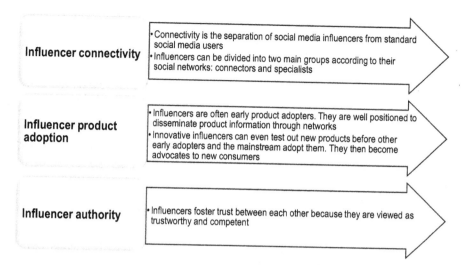

FIGURE 1.2   Strategies influencers use to affect consumers' spending patterns

The making of the empowered consumer

Stating that the increasing use of social and mobile technologies is shifting market power from suppliers to consumers, and thus creating a new profile of consumer: the empowered consumer is part of today's digital and experiential consumption context. Implications for brands and marketing professionals are significant in terms of defining new strategies to survive and take benefit from this consumer trend. This section presents the idea of consumer empowerment, its pillars, and the main opportunities and challenges for brand managers and marketing professionals.

What is consumer empowerment?

Hunter and Garnefeld (2008) note that consumer empowerment can be defined in two ways: as the fact of giving consumers power through resources – and as a personal and subjective situation produced by perceptions of collective control. Hunter and Garnefeld define consumer empowerment as "a consumer's subjective experience that they have greater ability than before to intentionally produce desired outcomes and prevent undesired ones and that they are benefiting from the increased ability" (2008: 2). In other words, for consumers, the empowerment experience is two-fold: they request the company to provide them with adequate and transparent information – and a controlled process, which is relative.

The discussion on the concept of "consumer empowerment" has been promptly growing throughout the previous years. It refers to skills, competencies, rights, and abilities individuals develop through their consumption experiences that allow them to make better choices. The European Commission

(European Union Commission, 2011: 11) defines consumer empowerment as "a multifaceted compound measure" that refers to collecting information on consumer abilities, awareness of his/her rights, and his/her commitment. In the digital era, and in order to become empowered, consumers are expected to develop adequate knowledge and skills to help them understand and select the offers that are suitable to them.

Furthermore, marketing scholars state that empowered consumers have a strategic role for brands. They are more likely to drive innovation, productivity, and create a competitive advantage by means of access to relevant information and share them with other consumers. Denegri-Knott, Zwick, and Schroeder (2006) introduced a categorization of the works that have been conducted on consumer empowerment in marketing. They proposed three leading approaches: consumer sovereignty, cultural power, and discursive power.

- **Consumer sovereignty** refers to the idea that the consumer is empowered when he/she is able to behave as a reasonable and self-centered agent. As Denegri-Knott and colleagues wrote: "consumers combine resources and skills to make producers do what they would not do otherwise . . ." (2006: 963). In this case, consumers' choices are thus an added value that encourages companies to make well-organized production, better and good-deal goods, and social growth.
- **Cultural power** considers the marketplace as a home of struggle between buyers and sellers. While sellers attempt to control and manipulate consumers' selections and choices, consumer empowerment reveals a planned behavior, strategies to respond to customers' behaviors and incentives by resisting and distinguishing themselves from markets (Kozinets, 2002: 23).
- **Discursive power** focuses on social, economic and cultural differences, and acquaintance diversity as makers of empowerment or disempowerment. The idea of discursive power acknowledges a positive function of the interaction between consumers and brands, who are viewed as partners. Consumer empowerment is thus the "ability to construct discourse as a system [. . .] determine(s) what is true or false [. . .] the ability of the consumer to mobilize discursive strategies to determine what can be known and what actions can be undertaken . . ." (Denegri-Knott, Zwick, and Schroeder, 2006: 956).

What are the pillars of consumer empowerment?

As mostly documented by marketing scholars, consumer empowerment is a multidimensional concept that encompasses multiple cognitive, personal, and social elements. So far, I have identified four pillars to consumer empowerment as they are shown in Figure 1.3.

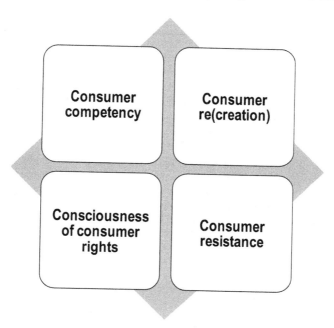

FIGURE 1.3   Four pillars of consumer empowerment

- **Consumer competency:** it is essential to differentiate between consumer competence as an "outcome," in which a combination of a set of significant and appropriate assets to deal with a particular context, and consumer competence as a "process" of using diverse incomes (Bonnemaizon and Batat, 2010). Consumer competence categorization encompasses three key dimensions: cognitive, functional, and social (Table 1.4).

Beyond this categorization, Batat (2014) states that consumer competence is a social construction as it results from social interactions within the marketplace. Akrich (1992) shows that a big part of the product conception process is grounded on the awareness that consumers are competent market actors. Companies can create a competitive advantage through the transformation of consumer skills into innovation. As suggested by Vargo and Lusch (2006), the competent consumer is able to participate in the construction stage of value by initiating "operant assets," which are "the fundamental source of competitive advantage" (Vargo and Lusch, 2008: 6). Operant assets refer to tools used by companies to empower, involve, and allow consumers to develop competencies that create values.

Hunt (2004) stated that operant resources encompass a variety of elements: material (e.g., raw materials), person (e.g., abilities and acquaintance of workers), structural (e.g., controls, processes, and cultures), cognitive (e.g., information about

TABLE 1.4 Three categories of consumer competency

Typology	Characteristics
Cognitive competence	It refers to the ability of consumers to interpret the speeches and the promotion communications of the businesses It also reflects the intellectual efforts developing in the buying activity: • Knowledge-seeking process; • Creation of meanings; • Awareness of customer rights and duties.
Instrumental competence	It refers to the customer's capacity to manipulate the physical consumption items before, during, and after the purchase process Tangible goods create an essential segment of the consumer context, such as computers or digital devices, social media (e.g., YouTube), or the technologies offered by firms, such as collaborative platforms and Internet websites that let the consumer produce his/her own product
Usage competence	It allows the consumer to express him/herself and provides his/her comment and response on the platform, the product, and the service delivered by the firm Usage competence is also related to the initiation of the creative competencies: • Creation of new representations; • Developing new knowledge; • Finding empirical answers to everyday real inquiries on consumption; • Deviations/creations of new meanings.

marketplace sectors, challenges, and technology), and social (e.g., relationships with competitors, sellers, and clients). Following this idea, I can acknowledge that the identity of the knowledgeable and competent consumer shapes itself in the connection that brands develop and preserve with their customers who view themselves as skilled, only if the firm identifies them as such.

• **Consumer re(creation):** refers to the capability of consumers to use the actual brand or company product and/or service to create new items by using two approaches: transgression and re-appropriation.

   o *Re-appropriation* is the process by which consumers combine and incorporate various resources through their multiple experiences to create their own identities and a shared consumption culture. Further, re-appropriation refers to the skills and the potential of today's digital consumers to create knowledge and new forms of consumption. To account for such creativity and consumption, Lévi-Strauss (1962) stated that consumers develop their creative potential through the use of strategies such as deviation – when consumers develop a divergent usage of consumption items and deviate them from their "former usage" to create a new meaning. This will generate a variation between the actual brand positioning and reality that refers to the observed behavior in different consumption cultures – and/or bricolage, which reflects the accumulation of multiple consumption references. Re-appropriation through deviation and/or bricolage allows consumers to develop meaningful consumption experiences, experiment new practices, and develop social competencies. It is then through the re-appropriation of consumption items and experiences that consumer competence will emerge and evolve throughout the individual's lifetime.

o *Consumer transgression* refers to the tendency of consumers to break rules and transgress. It is a hallmark of the today's consumption experiences, as well as an important phase in the construction of consumer identity. Consumer transgression and system of values go together and cannot be conceived one without the other. When consumers transgress, it is always against an established system of values. Batat (2014) states that the ability to transgress is an integral part of consumer empowerment as it underlines his/her ability to (re)create new products and services. For example, certain online practices, such as illegal downloading, are considered a matter of rules' transgression but are viewed by consumers as consumption skills that they are expected to acquire and develop throughout their consumption experiences to be fully competent market actors.

MINI-CASE 1.4   RE-APPROPRIATION OF BRANDS AND PRODUCTS AMONGST ADOLESCENT CONSUMERS

Batat (2014) states that adolescents between 11 and 15 have the ability to produce their own product and customize it through a re-appropriation process, which requires particular skills. According to Batat, for these adolescents, consumption doesn't end with the product's acquisition and everyday usage. It goes beyond this practical facet offered by the producer.

Adolescents are keenly pursuing the quest to create their identity and, as a consequence, search the diverse alternatives of consumption items that make up their youth culture. They attempt to appropriate the object or service by customizing it to reply to their requirement for self-affirmation and to help in building their individuality. The product is, therefore, considered as an item that is an extension of their identity and reproduces a personal identity and their aptitudes to create something with significance built into the adolescent subculture.

In the culture of hyper-consumption in which manifestation of one's identity is followed through acquisition of goods, adolescents use products to grow social acquaintances and to harvest their personalities. This is broadly experienced by adolescents between 11 and 15 years of age and demonstrates the competencies and capacities of these young people to *bricole* their identity and to use goods in modes other than those they were originally planned for, and thus conveying them symbolic, hedonistic, and social dimensions.

MINI-CASE 1.5 VIRGIN RADIO "LOUDER IS BETTER": TRANSGRESSION AND INSOLENCE AS YOUTH VALUES

French radio station Virgin launched an advertising campaign in 2011 called "Louder is Better" that highlights the rebellion and the rejection of parental rules, often at the center of conflict relations between parents and children in the adolescence phase. The television spot features a French mother unconsciously lip-synchronizing along with the Black Eyed Peas. The spot shows a teenager going to see his friends. As soon as he gets into the car, his mother comes out to yell at him. Not wanting to hear her, the child defies the authority of his mother and increases the sound of the music on Virgin radio to cover the sound of his mother that gives the impression that the mother sings in playback on the Black Eyed Peas.

To differentiate itself in a very competitive 15–35-year-old market, the French radio station Virgin has launched this advertising campaign whose motto is youth "transgression" (which is highly valued amongst teenagers) in its extreme extravagance and humor.

- **Consciousness of consumer rights:** awareness of consumer rights may encompass three main consumption knowledge domains:

    o Consumers' capabilities to understand prices and develop knowledge about marketplace, brands, symbols, and logos;
    o Consumers' knowledge of their rights (consciousness of prejudicial contractual terms, biased offline and online business practices, warranty rights, etc.), of public and private organizations defending them, and of diverse information about consumer affairs and public policies;
    o Consumers' capabilities regarding complaints when they experience fraudulent situations.

MINI-CASE 1.6 A PARTNERSHIP BETWEEN BANK OF AMERICA AND KHAN ACADEMY TO HELP PEOPLE DEVELOPING BETTER MONEY HABITS

Bank of America partnered with Khan Academy, an online basis of free tutoring for parents and teachers, to create "Better Money Habits." The "Better Money Habits" website (BetterMoneyHabits.com) provides free instruments and kits with a self-directed layout that offers consumers a suitable mode to develop financial knowledge in their own personal way, assess themes as desirable, and employ the information to their own situation. At BetterMoneyHabits.com, one can use informative videos and infographics for matters, such as credit, saving and budgeting, debt, home buying and renting, taxes, car buying, personal banking and security, etc. As stated by Andrew Plepler, Bank of America's Environmental, Social, and Governance Executive, "The positive role we play in society is something we have demonstrated every day. Our purpose is to make financial lives better – the beauty of this partnership for us is that it brings that purpose to life by empowering consumers to take small steps that can make a big difference."

- **Consumer resistance:** today's consumers who are digital savvy and overexposed to commercial discourses tend to be more knowledgeable in terms of decoding advertisement messages. They also develop different strategies, such as accumulating information, before shopping to resist salespeople pressure, get a bargain, and avoid purchasing items that they would not be interested in. The ability of today's consumers to resist marketplace solicitations and pressure from salespeople can be enhanced by collecting information via different formal and informal online and offline sources.

  The ability to develop this competence, and thus become empowered consumers should be discussed since not all consumers can feel comfortable in dealing with salespeople (psychological and social factors). In fact, consumers with low self-esteem and low self-confidence may face vulnerable situations within the marketplace. Nevertheless, experiencing vulnerable situations can also be a source of competence, construction, and resistance since consumers may develop coping mechanisms and learn from their previous experiences to resist better.

How is the empowered consumer driving new brand opportunities?

Today's consumers are living in the digital age that empowered them through using the Internet, social and mobile technologies, cloud, and so forth to access information about brands, products, and services. These empowered consumers have access to more information, more choices, and more occasions to globally share and disseminate their opinions and thoughts about brands they value or they hate. Consequently, there has been a radical change in the balance of power between companies and their customers. This has led marketing professionals and brand managers to rethink the way they interact and view the empowered customer in order to remain competitive and take benefit of the changing landscape by moving beyond a simplistic one-way relationship that places the consumer at the end of the process. While the rise of the empowered customer undoubtedly signifies a threat to companies who are reluctant to rethink their customer orientation strategies, it also offers a unique opportunity to engage empowered customers and use their creative potential and skills to help them build innovative products and provide the ultimate customer experience. Consumer empowerment can then drive brand success and new opportunities. Indeed, brand success does not only depend on a "good idea of products and services" or a "good marketing strategy," but it also needs a "good connection" with the customer. This means that brand loyalty requires respecting the customer and recognizing his/her skills and power, which should not be underestimated. Therefore, empowered consumers need to be stimulated, nurtured, informed, respected, and valued.

MINI-CASE 1.7 HOW EMPOWERED CONSUMERS ARE DRIVING NEW BRAND OPPORTUNITIES

Co-creation is one of the processes that companies use to involve their customers, empower them, deliver outstanding customer experience, and innovate. Co-creation allows brands and empowered customers to work together to create new products, concepts, services, and ideas and drive new opportunities for companies. Amongst the examples illustrating how the empowered consumer is driving new brand opportunities and innovation, I can cite the following brands:

- **LEGO** has created a platform to collect ideas and develop new products based on the submission of feedback and fans' votes. If an idea generates 10,000 votes, LEGO examines the project and identifies a winner for an official LEGO Idea set to be manufactured and universally distributed. The inventor provides last product agreement, obtains a percentage of the sales, and is recognized by the brand as the inventor and acknowledged on all packaging and marketing. This co-creation empowers customers and uses their creative potential and their entrepreneurial ability to drive innovation that values loyal customers and rewards them.
- **PepsiCo**: in 2007, PepsiCo launched its first "DEWmocracy" campaign by creating an online interactive role-playing game that involved fans in the design of a new Mountain Dew drink and in the final vote for a favorite flavor amongst three finalists. The game was designed as an immersive journey where players can participate in several meaningful experiences that allow them to collect tools to develop the attributes of the new product (e.g., flavor's taste, color, logo, graphics, etc.). The flavor "Voltage" was the winner and went into production as a new line of Mountain Dew. As a result, the Voltage flavor was one of the most successful products created by customer launches in PepsiCo beverage history.
- **DHL**: as the world's leading mail and logistics services company, DHL knows very well that improving and optimizing supply chains and logistics rely on innovations that are based on the co-creation with customers.

For example, DHL organizes hands-on workshops with customers in different countries (e.g., Germany, Singapore, etc.) to co-create solutions that advance the delivery experience. As a result, one of the most important innovations created during a workshop in Germany was Parcelcopter, a test drone delivery that takes only eight minutes rather than the usual mail-delivery by vehicles that takes half an hour.

The key role of emotion in the consumer brand experience

While authors admit some personal and individual effects on decision-makers, the conventional framework of consumer behavior is mainly cerebral in nature. The new emerging consumption trends have contributed to the shift in marketing paradigm. Kotler, Kartajaya, and Setiawan (2010) stated that marketing has moved beyond the age of "messaging" to affecting customers' emotions. Kotler and colleagues emphasized the key role of emotion in studying consumer decision-making: "the essential difference between emotion and reason is that emotion leads to actions while reason leads to conclusions" (2010: 170).

As society has evolved into digital and experiential consumption, marketing scholars started to examine the impact of emotions on consumer decision-making. The reason is that the "decision to buy and be loyal to a brand is greatly influenced by emotions" (Kotler et al., 2010: 170). Furthermore, emotions are a powerful resource for capturing experience-driven consumer affection with brands and consequently incorporating brands into the consumer's everyday habits and his/her identity project.

Thus, creating emotional connections during the shopping process or the brand consumption experience has a strong impact on the decision-making process and consumer satisfaction. Indeed, consumer emotional involvement increases brand loyalty and sales by improving brand image and positioning. While emotion is often at the heart of consumer brand experience and behavior, emotional marketing and branding are, therefore, necessary to capture and create positive emotions that make the offline and online customer experience more enjoyable.

This section will first define the notion of emotion, its categorization, and the key role of consumer emotion in the decision-making process. Second, the role of employees as emotional motivators and emotional branding strategies through the consumer experience will be presented and illustrated through examples.

Defining the notion of "consumer emotion" and its typologies

There are several definitions of the notion of "emotion." In 1981, Paul and Anne Kleinginna identified more than 90 definitions of "emotion" that can be found in different disciplines. Following a multidisciplinary and chronological analysis, the two authors proposed a new definition that is more universal and concrete enough to be translated into managerial, marketing, and operational actions: emotions are the result of the interaction between subjective factors and objective ones attained by neural systems . . . this induces experiences, such as feelings of awakening, pleasure, or displeasure . . . that can lead to the creation of adaptive behaviors . . . This definition highlights three main characteristics of the notion of "consumer emotion": physiological, behavioral, and dyad emotion/ rationality. The interactions between these three dimensions have a direct impact on the decision-making process in the buying experience.

Whether positive or negative, consumer emotion is composed of a mixture of feelings that emerge within consumption experiences and can be primary or secondary. Furthermore, consumer emotion is not static, but evolving through experiences and includes both positive and negative peaks that occur when a consumer is in contact with social actors and other components of his/her immediate environment (e.g., salespeople, brands, services, institutions, other consumers, etc.). In cognitive psychology, emotions are split into two groups: elementary (primary) and elaborated (secondary) emotions.

Elementary emotions are universal and express visible emotions through facial expressions that each individual is capable of recognizing and decoding in different cultures. There are six elementary emotions essential to individual and collective survival: joy, sadness, disgust, anger, fear, and surprise.

- **Joy** is produced by the desire for discovery and triggers consumer willing for closeness. It also occurs when the expectations and needs of consumers are met;
- **Sadness** is often associated with loss or lack. It causes isolation, self-enclosure, and the acceptance of loss;
- **Disgust** is induced by harmful attitudes and leads to rejection. It is also important in protecting individuals from unsafe behaviors and risky situations;
- **Anger** is a defensive reaction that prepares for attack when the individual faces a danger or an obstacle in the pursuit of his/her goals;
- **Fear** is triggered through a state of alert when there is a threat;
- **Surprise** can take two aspects: positive or negative. It creates either a reflex of withdrawal or closeness that is driven by curiosity.

The elaborated or secondary emotions are derived from elementary emotions (joy, sadness, disgust, anger, fear, and surprise) and are influenced by consumer personal background, his/her childhood, consumption experiences and his/her external environment. They often encompass two or a mixture of primary emotions (e.g., contempt is a mixture of two emotions: fear and anger) or from an emotion, such as fear, that creates anxiety. Each type of secondary emotion expresses a complex mixture of feelings caused by consumers' interactions with the brand and overall with the immediate external environment (Table 1.5).

As shown in Table 1.5, these emotions, whether primary or secondary, are constructed during childhood and culminate in adulthood. Throughout the brand experience, consumers express both positive and negative emotions, which differ and fluctuate according to periods of time and sociocultural interactions with the environment. Figure 1.4 shows the different emotions expressed by the customer during his/her purchase experience.

TABLE 1.5 Classification of emotions and feelings

Feelings	Types of emotions
Related to joy	Serenity, enchantment, ecstasy, and enthusiasm
Related to anticipation	Vigilance, curiosity, interest, expectation, and attention
Related to fear	Terror, panic, fear, consternation, apprehension, and shyness
Related to surprise	Amazement, fun, uncertainty, and distraction
Related to sadness	Grief, pain, depression, and melancholy
Related to disgust	Aversion, repugnance, and boredom
Related to anger	Rage, hostility, and fury
Related to trust	Admiration, tolerance, and acceptance

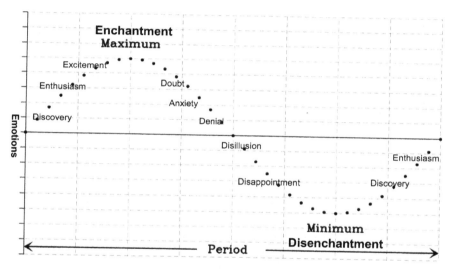

FIGURE 1.4 The evolution of emotions during customer experience

Figure 1.4 shows that consumer experience is an evolving and ongoing process that creates a multitude of negative and positive emotions due to customer' interactions with, for example, restaurant employees, the welcoming protocol, other customers, decoration, service, food, etc. In this case, the customer will go through several stages expressing positive and negative emotions throughout his/her restaurant experience.

Consumer emotion is, therefore, a key component that has a strong impact on consumer decision-making and his/her satisfaction. Thus, the most attractive and competitive brands are those that succeed in touching their clients before making them think. Brands can use emotional marketing strategies (e.g., customer-oriented service) as well as communication tools (e.g., storytelling) to target consumers on the basis of their emotions whether they are positive or negative as well as primary (fear, joy, anger, etc.) or secondary (guilt, admiration, pride, exclusivity, etc.). For example, amongst the most used emotions in luxury where sentiment is at the heart of the consumer purchase decision-making process, I can cite the following: love, happiness, and admiration.

**MINI-CASE 1.8 ARIEL INDIA, PROCTER &
GAMBLE, DELIVERING A MOVING
INTERGENERATIONAL MESSAGE ABOUT
GENDER INEQUALITY**

The partnership between Ariel India (Procter & Gamble) and the creative agency BBDO Worldwide was marked by the launch of the new commercial part of the #ShareTheLoad campaign, which conveys a powerful and touching international communication about origins and gender imbalance. The video portrays several responsibilities and tasks a working young mother assumes over the sequence of one evening: preparing dinner, helping her son with his schoolwork, checking travel for her father visiting from out of the city, working after-hours, and fulfilling home-based responsibilities (e.g., doing the family's washing).

The woman's father who watches her as she rushes around the house while her husband sits drinking tea in front of the TV feels remorseful for not sharing the load with her mother when she was a kid, and for not supporting her when she played house as a little girl. "I never told you that it's not your job alone, but your husband's, too," he thinks to himself. At the end of the commercial, Ariel India's #ShareTheLoad commercial asks an important question – Is laundry only a woman's job? – and answers it boldly: nope.

The role of employees as emotional motivators

Transforming employees into brand ambassadors is a key challenge in the experiential and digital era. Indeed, engaged employees build strong brands and durable emotional connections with customers. Employees are real emotional stimuli and play a vital role in enhancing customer positive experiences and attitudes towards the brand. It is important for companies to focus on the "emotional capital" of their employees who are in contact with customers.

Emotional capital refers to the predisposition of employees to show empathy, which is an important component of the customer experience. Emotional capital of employees has a significant impact on improving the quality of the experience and enhancing the immersion of customers in a pleasurable context in which they feel good as well as "understood." Companies can engage in the emotional work with their employees as emotional motivators to help them become strong brand ambassadors by focusing on three main aspects and encouraging each employee to:

- Develop positive attitudes towards his/her work (e.g., enthusiasm, involvement);
- Foster spontaneity and kindness towards customers;
- Recognize the rights of the clients.

Although these principles are obvious, they are complicated to follow, especially when the physical fatigue and stress of the employees are high due to lack of sleep or physical toll of standing for hours. Furthermore, transforming employees into brand ambassadors depends on the organization of work, which is in correlation with factors, such as gender. For example, in the hospitality industry, hotels assign tasks to certain employees in contact with customers according to two factors:

- Gender: female employees are often in charge of the front desk and males are assigned to concierge or valet tasks;
- The position held: technical staff and maids are rarely in direct contact with customers.

Emotional branding through the consumer experience

Magids, Zorfas, and Leemon (2015) state that when companies connect with customers' emotions through launching products to maximize emotional benefit, the payoff can be huge. The importance of building strong emotional brands to create a durable competitive advantage has been highlighted in the brand management domain by Morrison and Crane (2007) who introduced the concept of "emotional branding," which is defined as the commitment of consumers in a profound, long-term, intimately emotional connection with the brand that is beyond the advantage based on satisfaction. Brands can then create strong bonds with their customers by developing a holistic framework that immerses customers in emotional experiences. Emotional branding has been studied through different approaches. So far, for example, I have identified eight distinct perspectives:

- Emotional content in advertising;
- Emotions in building brand bonds;
- Emotions in brand attitude formation;
- Emotions in service brands;
- Emotions in B2B branding;
- Emotions in brand value and purchase intention;
- The role of emotions in brand attachments;
- Emotions in customer loyalty.

Postmodernism and the transition to experiential consumption

In the past two decades, there has been a major shift in consumer values and experiences in terms of drivers for consumers to purchase and recommend products and services. Firat and Venkatesh (1995) who imported postmodernism – introduced by French philosophers and sociologists – from humanities to marketing and consumer behavior studies, suggest a change of societal paradigm by shifting the focus from a modern to a postmodern consumer society.

As a consequence of globalization, technology, and sociocultural mutations, change in the twenty-first century is discontinuous, occurs faster than ever, and in a disrupted manner. Therefore, new schemes of production and consumption (e.g., collaborative consumption, sharing, low-cost, just-in-time, DIY, online shopping, and so forth) have progressively emerged over the past decade and are substituting the modern approach of mass production of standardized goods (products and services).

This new context is also transforming the consumption activities, as well as the forms of workforce and marketing strategies required to respond to the postmodern consumer trends in the digital era. These transformations are evidence of the inherent and ultimate change the consumer society is facing by entering a new era of "postmodernism." In order to benefit from these changes, brands and marketing professionals should conduct fundamental transformations in their thinking process as well as their consumer approaches, offline and online marketing and communication strategies, loyalty programs, customer services, and so forth to offer the ultimate customer experience.

This section provides a cultural questioning of modernism and introduces the key characteristics and values of today's postmodern consumers living within a digital era. The implications for brands and marketing professionals, notably in terms of changes that are required to meet postmodern consumer expectations, are highlighted at the end of this part.

From modernism to postmodernism

The definition specified to modernity and postmodernity is distinctive from that assumed to modernism and postmodernism. According to Venkatesh and colleagues (1993), while modernity and postmodernity indicate a period of time in history, modernism and postmodernism refer to a set of thoughts. As Venkatesh and colleagues (1993: 220) write: "while modernity refers to the period in Western history starting from the late sixteenth century, modernism refers to the social-cultural economic idea systems and institutions." Or, as pointed out by Firat and Venkatesh (1995: 240): "while postmodernity refers to the current period in world history signifying the change of course of modernity if not its end . . . postmodernism is a cultural condition and philosophical position associated with postmodernity that questions the fundamental assumptions of modernism."

The shift from modernism to postmodernism can be explained by two key factors: economic context and cultural norms. While the economic aspect of modernity refers to massive production, standardization, and industrialization, the cultural dimension in the modern era highlights the influence of traditions and customs embedded within a particular cultural context in terms of consumer values, beliefs, behaviors, and attitudes towards brands. Frochot and Batat (2013) state that the modern consumer society is uniform, hierarchical, and based on the idea of an objective universal reality. Thus, there are several characteristics of the modern consumer society:

- Product first, consumer second;
- Distinction of production from consumption;
- Industrial progress, capitalism, and productivity improvement;
- Consumer rationality and cognitive process;
- Develop objective science by testing reality through experiments;
- Science, institutions, and politics are the truth;
- Universal morality and law;
- Life is organized according to dichotomies: consumer/producer, rational/irrational, cognitive/emotional, etc.

Thus, modernism has been framed in the eighteenth century in Western history during which many thoughts have been developed as a project that contributes to the prosperity of humankind and his enlightenment (Habermas, 1984). Overall, modernism is related to the idea of rationalism that is considered as the core component to be incorporated into all kinds of thoughts and views. Venkatesh suggests that "modernity is related to the rule of reason and the establishment of rational order" (1992: 202).

Therefore, if the main features of modernism were the ideals of progress, human rationality, and its usage to accomplish sovereignty, postmodernism questions all these elements together with the emergence of experiential consumption as well as the ecological and social justice issues. Cembalo, Migliore, and Schifani argue that "there are no certain dates to indicate the origin of the postmodern age: many people state that this period started from the end of the 20th century, especially in association

Modernism ⟫ Postmodernism

- Modernity refers to the rationality of the consumer behavior because of his/her capacity to identify, understand, and satisfy his/her needs

- Knowledge is a universal project, society is homogeneous and structured by hierarchies based on both objective reality and reason

- The society is organized by distinctions of the opposites: we cannot be that and this at the same time

- The subject is fragmented: the influence of sociocultural structures vs. the rational individual

- The truth does not exist: critic of science and the idea of univocal progress

- The distinctions disappear: juxtaposition of apposite values and the combination of image and reality

FIGURE 1.5 The shift from modernism to postmodernism

with the spread of mass media and global communication" (2012: 42). Though, Firat and Venkatesh (1995) state that postmodernism did not suddenly appear but existed during modernity without a conceptual framework until recently.

Postmodernism is characterized by suspicion towards modern totalitarian thoughts, established rules, standardized knowledge, and the absence of diversity resulting in social chaos and the loss of reference points. Individuals should then redefine their identities and values to achieve their own emancipation, affirm their differences, and thus liberate themselves from modern dominant representations. Thus, postmodernism rejects the idea of a universal reality by underlining its fragmentation, plurality, and diversity, even beyond human understanding. Furthermore, postmodernism offers marketing scholars and brand managers a thought-provoking framework to examine or re-examine consumption practices and experiences by shifting the focus from product to consumer. Figure 1.5 illustrates the shift from modernism to postmodernism and the principals on which it is based.

As shown in Figure 1.5, the rise of postmodernism is related to the questioning of the key modern era foundations. So far, for example, I have identified six major foundations of the consumer society that have been discussed in marketing by postmodernist scholars, such as Firat and Venkatesh (1995) or Addis and Podestà (2005):

- **Foundation 1:** in the modern era, forces such as science, rationalism, and technology are considered as the core factors that contribute to shaping modern society. This assumption excludes the influence of the macro forces as well as the sociocultural and historical context in which individuals live, act, and interact with other market actors. According to Vattimo (1992), modernism deals with superficial realities and offers simple solutions that do not consider the complexity of social interactions and the paradoxes in human behaviors. The postmodern logic is then based on the idea that the society is a social and historical construction, which means that reality and its truth is not objective since it is not only the result of the combination of science and technology, but also includes elements such as aesthetics, language, discourses, customs, ideology, narratives, meanings, irrationality, and other factors that should be examined by marketing scholars to provide brand managers with relevant insights on consumer expectations and needs in terms of their consumption experiences.
- **Foundation 2:** while modernism has a narrow and simplistic view of consumer behaviors and does not allow a deeper understanding of consumption experiences since it views the consumer as merely a cognitive and rational actor, postmodernism considers culture and symbolism as an integral part of consumer experiences.
- **Foundation 3:** according to Rosenau (1992), modernism has failed because the material progress promised has turned out to be illusive, deceptive, and has had negative consequences, such as poverty, inequality, social injustice,

human misery, and violence. Furthermore, the modern society does not allow a balance between growth and the quest for ethics, social justice, and sustainability. In the postmodern era, environmental and social issues are part of the postmodern ecosystem which, as stated by Habermas (1984), takes into account 'lifeworld' in which the individual can find self-expression and acts following his/her own value system through more engaging forms of action, participation, and consumption practices.

- **Foundation 4:** while in the modern society, consumers are considered as rational and unemotional market actors since they belong to a Western economic system that allows no emotions, symbolism, or spiritual behaviors, in the postmodern era, consumers have been liberated from the rational scheme and thus can express their paradoxical behaviors.
- **Foundation 5:** the modern society is based on a system of thinking that structures and categorizes individuals and their behaviors by dichotomies, such as emotional/cognitive, tangible/intangible, object/subject, western/eastern, right/wrong, male/female, professional/personal, private/public, producer/consumer, etc. The postmodern society questions this categorization that is considered as a naïve and unsuccessful approach to examine consumer behaviors and attitudes.
- **Foundation 6:** the modern society views the consumer as destroyer, in opposition to the producer who creates. Consumption in the modern era is then secondary to production and cannot be placed as equal to production since it does not create anything of significance for humanity or society. While in the modern era, production is about creating products that add value to human everyday life, and thus is viewed as a sacred activity, postmodernism defines the act of consumption as equal to production since it is a value-added activity. Postmodern consumers are not only destroyers but also creators of value.

The rise of the postmodern consumer society

The consumption field was obviously transformed with the shift from a modern to a postmodern society. Throughout the former, consumption was influenced by the utility value of products and/or services. Consumption was comprehensible and part of a relatively unchanging context in which consumers were susceptible to choose conventional commodities. Further, individualism was insignificant in a modernist consumption culture and thus diversification of commodities beyond the functional options was limited.

The rise of a postmodern consumer society has contributed to the development of a new body of knowledge that views consumption as a "sociocultural meaningful experience." Another interesting characteristic of postmodern consumption is hedonism, which refers to the idea that consumption may also be a desire for something different in terms of new and/or pleasurable experiences. Thus, hedonism goes together with functional motivations that drive consumer behaviors and attitudes towards brand adoption and/or rejection. Emotional and experiential motives of consumption underline the shift in value systems of post-modern consumers that brands and marketing professionals must take into account to adapt their offers with the appropriate packages combining both experiential and functional elements that are adapted to the suitable target.

Furthermore, while modern consumer society places the consumer at the end of the process and views him/her as rational, postmodern consumption goes beyond a purely economic vision of the marketplace by focusing on both the emotional and cognitive dimensions of consumer experiences and the meanings the latter gives to his/her consumption practices that involve brands, products, services, environment, and social interactions with salespeople, multiple stakeholders, and other consumers. Firat and Venkatesh (1995) bring clarity to explain the rise of the postmodern consumer society through the identification of five main transformations:

- The separation of the private and the public spheres;
- The building of the consumer society through diverse public discourses, practices, and media initiatives;
- The task of men to the field of production and of women to the private sphere;
- The conversion of women into consumers;
- The conversion of consumers into shoppers by the use of marketing techniques.

The paradigm of a postmodern consumer society is not new. In former studies, marketing and consumer scholars introduced the idea of the culture of consumption as a framework in which consumer behaviors and purchase habits can be examined. Based on the works of postmodernist scholars who enormously contributed to marketing and consumer behavior fields (e.g., Lyotard, 1984; Firat and Venkatesh, 1995), I have identified seven key characteristics of today's postmodern consumer society: fragmentation, juxtaposition, media culture, tolerance, hyper-reality, anachronism, and pastiche. Table 1.6 continues the development of these seven postmodern dimensions.

The framework developed in Table 1.6 will provide brand managers and marketing professionals with relevant insights on consumer experiences within both the marketplace and the private sphere that is unreachable by brands, such as hosting friends and family for dinner or attending a private concert/exhibition. Furthermore, although brands are able to get access to the consumer private sphere and collect data by conducting surveys, it is difficult to understand the meanings consumers assign to brands and their paradoxical consumption habits according to a modern perspective, which is based on the idea of consumer rationality. This, in turn, suggests the need for a new postmodern consumption framework capable of interpreting the dynamism and the paradoxes in consumer attitudes towards brands.

TABLE 1.6 The seven postmodern characteristics

Characteristic	Definition	Example
Fragmentation	It can be defined at two levels: individual and social. The fragmentation of the individuals due to the weakening of their identity lead them to no longer project themselves into traditional models and aspire to a greater flexibility of identity	The explosion of the traditional patriarchal model The plurality of femininity The rise of new family structures (disrupted, single-parent, homosexual, etc.)
Juxtaposition	It emphasizes the erasing of hierarchies established (elitist culture/popular culture, masculine values/feminine values, etc.). It also reflects the coexistence of opposing elements	The juxtaposition of information and entertainment "infotainment" or "edutainment"
Media culture	It is the consequence of the intensive exposure to media content resulting in the creation of strong media knowledge and shared media cultures	Reality shows such as The Voice, Top Chef, etc.
Tolerance	It stems from fragmentation and juxtaposition and refers to the multiplication of consumer values	The representation of minorities and ethnic groups in advertisements
Hyperreality	It is the representation of the image in communication. The image stands out from its referents and becomes a strategic component in marketing discourses	The strong image of Lara Croft, the character of the video game Tomb Raider
Anachronism	It refers to the explosion of temporal references through the mixture of styles where old representations and icons are updated and mixed with new references	Vintage fashion Iconic cars updated such as Mini Cooper and New Beetle
Pastiche	It refers to the era of recycling media references and content. Creation is none other than copying and pasting of what does already exist. We do not invent anything, we do recycle	The concept of the city of Las Vegas is based on the idea of recycling other existing cities such as Paris, Venice, etc.

According to Douglas and Isherwood (1979), in several consumption fields (e.g., food, clothing, tourism, and leisure), activities become extremely symbolic acts charged with meanings that consumers share within the same consumption culture. Therefore, the goods that are consumed to satisfy functional needs cannot be detached from their symbolic dimensions and the meanings consumers associate with these goods in their day-to-day consumption experiences. Thus, in the postmodern consumer society, production is neither a meaningful activity, nor a domain of value creation.

- The reason for this is, as Mourrain (1989) points out, that postmodernism has displaced the focus from production to consumption, which is viewed as a domain that celebrates consumer liberation and his/her re-enchantment.
- Another reason is that postmodernism focuses on the loss of references and the liquidity of individual identity that is constructed and shaped in the consumption arena.

This makes understanding consumer motivations very complex, as it creates paradoxes in behaviors and attitudes, such as purchasing eco-friendly and sustainable items, but also unsustainable goods. This unpredictability of consumption preferences in the postmodern society effectively emphasizes an absence of a "one-dimensional direction" that is reflected in the postmodern consumers' attitudes towards brands in their daily consumption experience.

THEORY BOX 1.2   SOLID VERSUS LIQUID CONSUMER IDENTITY

By drawing on the works of Bauman's (2000) theorization of liquid modernity, which reflects how everyday life has shifted from being stable and protected to being more ambiguous and fast-changing, Bardhi and Eckhardt (2017) introduced the concept of liquid consumption in the marketing field to explain why and how consumers sometimes do not own consumption items or may not create connections with brands and other consumers who use the same brands. Furthermore, Bardhi and Eckhardt (2017) established a distinction between solid consumption that refers to an enduring consumption based on ownership and materiality – and liquid consumption, which refers to ephemeral, access-based, and dematerialized consumption practices. The distinction between solid and liquid consumption can be defined according to two main levels: product and consumption practices. For each level, different components have been identified: consumer value, type of connection, benefits, level of ownership, significance, stability, and temporality.

According to Thomas (1997), the postmodern consumer lives in a society filled with "doubt, ambiguity, and uncertainty" and it is in this situation that brands and marketing professionals need to understand by identifying the macro sociocultural forces influencing consumer behaviors, attitudes, and motivations in order to satisfy the needs and expectations of the consumer in terms of brand experiences if they wish to subsist in the postmodern marketplace.

In quest of clarity on some of the postmodern consumer society challenges faced by brands and marketing professionals, the next section is directed more precisely at two key questions: Who is the postmodern consumer and what are his/her needs and expectations? What are the implications of the rise of a postmodern consumer

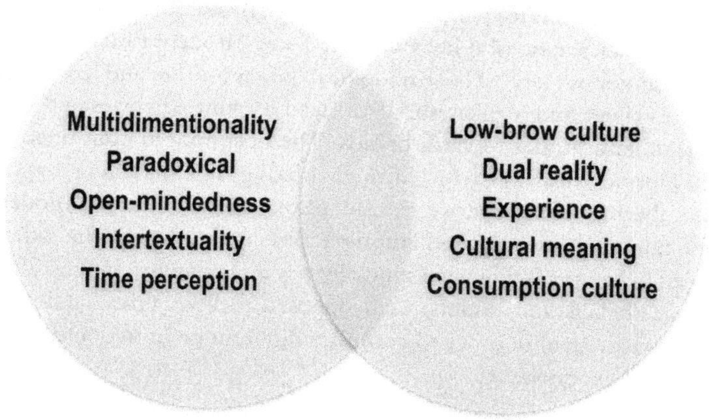

FIGURE 1.6   Ten characteristics of the postmodern consumer

society for brands and marketing professionals? So far, I have identified ten characteristics of postmodern consumer behavior (Figure 1.6), specifically in terms of the objectives and changes brands and marketing professionals must achieve in their strategies offline and online in order to offer a satisfying and ultimate customer experience, which represents a critical competitive advantage.

These ten categories introduce the differences in behaviors and attitudes associated with postmodern consumers that could have far-reaching implications for brands.

- **Multidimensionality:** the multidimensional postmodern consumer refers to the fragmentation of society, behaviors, individuals and their identities that result from the proliferation and diversification of offers, brands, images, products, discourses, and so forth. Consumption experiences become fragmented by replacing single attitude/behavior by multiple realities, which make sense to consumers according to their own perception. Multidimensional behaviors and the fragmentation of consumer experiences contribute to the rise of emerging representations and behaviors that are more or less accepted depending on the cultural context. Multidimensionality allows the postmodern consumer to choose different roles, behaviors, and identities at the same time (e.g., being a wife–consumer and mother–consumer or student–consumer and worker–consumer). The multidimensional aspect of consumer experiences often requires a fragmentation of the self in order to deeply experience each consumption setting in which consumers may express multiple behaviors and attitudes towards the same brand, product, and service. Firat, Sherry, and Venkatesh (1994) refer to this situation as "multiphrenic selves," which means that the postmodern consumer changes his/her image frequently by including all consumption practices and can introduce his/her multiple consumer identities rather than conforming to a single one (e.g., purchasing a luxury watch, renting it, buying a second-hand one, and getting a countrified luxury watch).

- **Paradoxical behavior:** almost all postmodernist authors agree on the idea that consumer paradoxical behaviors are a key characteristic of the postmodern consumer society. The paradoxical juxtaposition and combination of opposites (Firat and Venkatesh, 1993) lead to contradictions and confusions in consumer attitudes towards brands. The postmodern consumer expresses his/her paradoxical behavior through mixing and matching opposites, or by combining contradictory consumption styles. The postmodern consumer can juxtapose opposed emotions (loving and hating the same brand), opposed behaviors (buying authentic luxury and counterfeit luxury), opposed thoughts (beliefs and doubts), and opposed feelings (great and bad hotel/service experience) in order to cumulate different cognitive, pleasurable, and meaningful experiences.

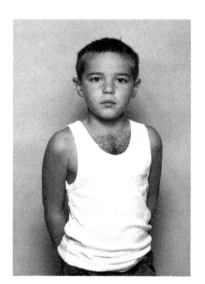
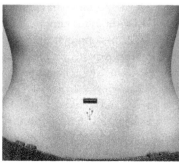
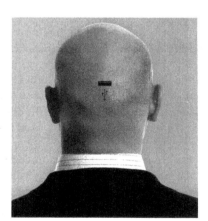
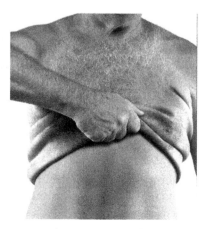

PHOTO 1.1   The expression of juxtapositions

FIGURE 1.7   The fabric of tolerance in the postmodern society

- **Open-mindedness:** the idea of open-mindedness and tolerance stems directly from the two above mentioned factors, namely consumer multidimensionality and the paradoxical juxtaposition of opposites (Figure 1.7). The multiplication of values due to these two factors and the decline in social hierarchies allow individuals to exist as such without being judged since any alternative structure is viewed as legitimate (e.g., the representation of minorities and ethnic groups in advertising).

  In order to foster tolerance in a multicultural postmodern society, consumers need to develop multicultural capabilities that allow them to understand, successfully interact, and communicate with individuals from various consumption cultures. Brands and marketing professionals can also help consumers develop their multicultural competence, and thus become more open-minded by:

  o   Valuing diversity in their offers (products and services) and their advertising to educate consumers about diversity;
  o   Displaying an attitude of respect for diversity in their communication;
  o   Constantly seek to expose consumers to diversity and alternatives beyond the mainstream and immediate reality (e.g., gender, sexuality, age, culture, class, race, or ethnicity);
  o   Embracing and celebrating differences by creating unique brand experiences in different cultural contexts, traditions, etc.

- **Intertextuality:** it refers to the idea that in the postmodern era, creation is a result of a pastiche, which is nothing but a copy of what already exists, in that "we invent nothing, we recycle." Pastiche is a popular technique used in postmodern texts in domains, such as music, pop culture, architecture, art, literature, advertising, etc. as a mechanism of intertextuality and refers to an imitation of the existing styles mixed with a variety of eclectic ingredients. For example, Quentin Tarantino movies are a good example of pastiche in the postmodern society. His films imitate a variety of genres that inspired him when he was a child (e.g., western movies). Though, pastiche is as different from collage as it is about creating something new by mimicking as many types as possible.

MINI-CASE 1.9   LAS VEGAS: A POSTMODERN EXPERIENCE OF THE CITY

Las Vegas is a city that has reinvented itself from the land of desert. It emerged in 1931 after the state legislature allowed gambling. From 1941 onward, it became the city of casinos and the accelerated build-up of the city has proliferated until recent years. In those series of landscape rebuilding endeavors, Las Vegas moved from being a small street city with many casinos to a highly qualified entertainment complex of corporate-owned enterprises offering tourists the ability to cut-free from their routine daily life and invest in the probability to win large amounts of money from the gambling tables. The themed resorts of Las Vegas have imitated world famous places, landmarks, or monuments, such as the Eiffel tower, canals of Venice, Statue of liberty, Egyptian pyramids and so on.

Eiffel Tower

- Real: it was built in 1889 by Gustave Eiffel for Universal exhibition. At 1063 feet tall, it offers a beautiful view of Paris and includes two restaurants. It is the best symbol of the city of Paris.
- Vegas version: the project began in May 1997 and was completed in April 1999. At 540 feet tall, it offers a French gourmet restaurant and observation deck on the top.

Coliseum

- Real: it is considered the biggest amphitheater in the Roman Empire. Built between 70 AD to 80 AD with 50,000 seats. It was used for gladiator fights, animal hunts, and other public shows.
- Vegas version: built in 2003. It has room for 4,300 people. The theatre was built for Celine Dion. It is a technological wonder that has a half-acre stage and high tech equipment.

Statue of Liberty

- Real: it was given to the US from the people of France in 1886. At 305 feet tall, it represents the symbol of liberty. It is made of copper on steel and the flame on the hand is made of gold. Artist Frederic-Auguste Bartholdi sculpted the statue.
- Vegas version: it is located in front of New York–New York Hotel & Casino. Opened in January 1997. The hotel aims to replicate architectures that reflect real New York City skylines.

The Las Vegasians address their replicas as – *you don't have to tour around the world to see some of the famous places.* They are fake structures, but it seems hard to notice the definite differences for some features and for some tourists. Of course, these items are not the main symbol of the city. But visitors who come to Las Vegas have the satisfaction of seeing them and experiencing them. Furthermore, Las Vegas allows visitors to behave freely as they really are. That is why the slogan of Las Vegas is – *What happens here, stays here.* In other words, it is believed that Las Vegas is the place where people can do things that they cannot or will not do in any other place. Therefore, Las Vegas is not simply an unreal destination or an inauthentic experience with imitated structures, it is an alternative-reality that offers visitors the possibility to escape from a rational everyday life structured by rules and routines.

- **Time perception:** refers to consumer relationship with time that can be perceived in two ways: linear and experiential. While the former reflects the measurable time unit, the latter focuses on the subjective experience of time and meanings consumers assign to the transformation of time into action, event, or activity.
- **Low-brow culture:** it is due to intensive exposure of the postmodern consumer to media content who becomes knowledgeable in terms of media references. Thus, media culture becomes the new foundation of collective imagination by creating a shared global low-brow culture, a form of popular culture with mass appeal and a weak intellectual dimension. In the postmodern consumer society, low-brow culture becomes a legitimate culture that exists by itself with high-brow and traditional culture.
- **Dual reality:** refers to hyperreality and is one of the key characteristics of today's postmodern consumer societies. Hyperreality merges two realities: real and virtual, both are constructed and shared by members of the same consumption culture. Postmodernist authors state that there is no distinction between reality and fantasy. Postmodern consumers can then identify with fictional individuals (e.g., Batman, a fictive marvel comic reflects human values, such as justice and courage) or experience dual reality in thematic urban and suburban shopping malls (e.g., West Edmonton Mall) or attraction parks (e.g., Walt Disney World).
- **Experiential consumption:** postmodern consumers search emotional memories, sensations, and symbols to construct holistic and immersive individual experiences that stimulate their minds, touch their emotions, and engage them personally (Schmitt, 1999), while indulging in fantasies, feelings, and fun (Holbrook and Hirschman, 1982). These consumer experiences are private, discovered over a period, and naturally, include many feelings. Furthermore, customer experiences happen throughout two series: customer involvement (fluctuating from

inactive to active) and connection or external associations (going from absorption to immersion). Pine and Gilmore (1998) described four realms related to consumer experiences: 1) entertainment (passive, absorption), 2) educational (active, absorption), 3) escapist (active, immersion), and 4) aesthetic (passive, immersion). The richest experiences encompass aspects of all four realms.

- **Cultural meanings:** postmodern consumers do not purchase brands for the sake of brands but rather for the cultural meanings they assign to them. Therefore, marketing professionals need to consider cultural meanings in consumption as well as the symbolic associations and the ways consumers interpret the cultural, environmental, and functional aspects of the brands they are consuming.

MINI-CASE 1.10   THE CULTURAL MEANING OF HOMEMADE FOOD CONSUMPTION

Homemade food preparation and consumption is known to originate from a sense of kinship in that it evokes images of mothers, grandmothers, or other family members. Consumers' perceptions of what makes food "homemade" is synonymous with family togetherness, tradition, and uniqueness. Homemade food retains the identity of the producer and is made for sharing with others. Overall, people connote "homemade" as having different, more flavorful tastes, and better smells that are unique and intrinsically linked with kin.

Younger consumers describe homemade products as being intrinsically linked with the closeness of family, something that represents the antithesis of impersonal commercialization of mass-produced food.

While middle-age consumers may describe homemade as not only involving the labor of kin but also involving foods that need to be made from scratch, seniors see a different connotation of homemade. They describe "homemade" as the opposite of how young people cook food. For seniors, homemade must involve authentic ingredients and must follow a historic script – that the production of food is something akin to a moral obligation – something grandparents and parents do to keep traditions alive.

- **Consumption cultures:** marketing scholars, such as Arnould and Thompson (2005), placed the "experience" at the heart of the Consumer Culture Theory (CCT), which challenges utilitarian, modern dominant logic in the consumption field. The CCT paradigm enriches traditional marketing by going beyond a simplistic view of consumer behavior and taking into account social representations and the cultural context in which consumption meanings are embedded. In this sense, CCT conceptualizes consumer experience as a personal event in a building and the change of the individual with a focus on the emotions and sensitivity of the consumer.

Summary

This chapter has examined the four key changes in consumer behavior that affect customer experience: those related to the digital context, the empowerment of consumers, the rise of the emotional consumer, and the shift from modern to a postmodern consumer society. It has explained how brands can rethink customer experience by focusing more on the changes emerging and how they can benefit from them by designing experiences that match customer expectations, thereby potentially increasing customer satisfaction, loyalty, and advocacy.

Notes

1 World Economic Forum White Paper (2016), Digital Transformation of Industries: Digital Consumption http://reports.weforum.org/digital-transformation/wp-content/blogs.dir/94/mp/files/pages/files/digital-enterprise-narrative-final-january-2016.pdf, retrieved February 7, 2018.
2 Shelley Stern Grash (2015), Making Technology Accessible for Everyone https://blogs.microsoft.com/chicago/2015/04/23/making-technology-accessible-for-everyone/, retrieved March 17, 2017.

2

THEORETICAL UNDERPINNINGS FOR CUSTOMER EXPERIENCE MARKETING

Origins, customer journey, and experience touchpoints

Purpose and context

The notion of customer experience responds to two major challenges: the changing behavior of customers and the advent of a "new consumer" who has emotional expectations and symbolic needs that go beyond the simple functional benefit. In this chapter, I provide a cross-sectional analysis of diverse studies in human sciences and business disciplines that tackle the concept of "customer experience" to answer two questions: 1) What do we mean by customer experience, meaning, what do we know about what happens in the customer experience throughout the consumption and the purchase process? 2) Does the customer experience allow companies to differentiate their offers and retain their customers? Prior to explaining what customer experience is in the marketing field, I attempt to clarify the meanings and origins of "experience," what are its characteristics, components, and typologies, and how customer experience can contribute to the rise of a new marketing of the experience. I will conclude the first part of this chapter with the proposition of a new definition of the concept of customer experience. Next, I will introduce two key concepts: the "costumer journey" and the touchpoints that bring customer experience to life.

Learning outcomes

At the end of this chapter you will be able to understand the origins of the concept of "experience" and its foundations before its advent in the marketing field. This chapter will also provide you with the analysis of different works and empirical examples that will help you to determine appropriate strategies and critically evaluate different approaches of the customer experience from the perspective of the consumer as well as from the perspective of the company in order to begin the process of planning and designing the ultimate customer experience.

Customer experience: from philosophy to marketing

Customer experience has become an inevitable subject in the media, the business world, and several economic sectors, such as tourism and hospitality, luxury, retail, banking, etc. Though, the concept is often confused with that of "customer relationship management," or sensory marketing, and relational marketing. For this reason, I propose to return to the origins of the concept of "experience" by highlighting its journey from humanities to marketing. Then, I explain how "customer experience" can lead brand managers and companies to a new era of experiential marketing.

The concept of "experience": what am I talking about?

Experience can be defined as the acquisition, whether deliberate or not, of the understanding of human beings and things through their practices in the real world, and thus its contribution to the development of knowledge. For example, companies dream to recruit "young people" who have a diversity of experiences. In this case, the emphasis is on the "knowledge" developed through the experiences accumulated by the young person. For brands, it is about going beyond the knowledge developed; in this scenario, brands would aspire to offer their customers a positive, memorable, emotionally charged, and unforgettable experiences.

The experience is, therefore, important to develop a strong emotional connection between the brand and its customers, which can enhance their loyalty, and consequently lead to the dissemination of a positive image of the brand via word-of-mouth offline and online.

Therefore, a cross-sectional analysis of the different disciplines that have approached the notion of "experience" recommends going beyond the narrow definition of "customer experience" often given by media and marketers.

A broad review of the works showed that the "experience" concept is not obviously related to one specific field or discipline. Works on experience are part of an extensive variety of scientific disciplines, including philosophy (e.g., Reed, 1996; Dewey, 1964), sociology (e.g., Bourdieu, 1979), marketing management (e.g., Pine and Gilmore, 1999), consumer research (e.g., Schmitt, 1999; Holbrook and Hirschman, 1982), and design sciences (e.g., Sleeswijk-Visser, 2009). These different disciplines attribute diverse definitions and conceptualizations to the concept of experience, and thus the definition of customer experience in marketing and consumer research may well benefit from valuable input from other disciplines. In so doing, three main theoretical perspectives were considered: philosophical, sociological, and anthropological (Figure 2.1). The connection with marketing will naturally be established thereafter.

The multidisciplinary analysis, far from being a recent phenomenon specific to marketing in the contemporary consumer society, shows that the notion of "experience" made its first appearance in 1265 in the writings of philosophers under the Latin term *"Experientia,"* which means "attempt, trial, test." This raises the question, when was experience first associated with consumption and marketing?

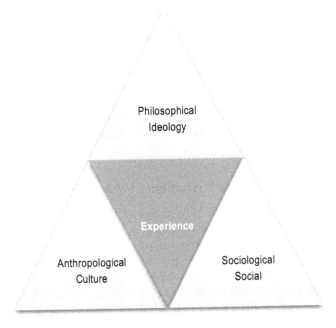

FIGURE 2.1 Three perspectives on the concept of experience

The objective here is not to enter into a deep historical analysis of the human and social disciplines that have dealt with the genesis of experience, much less to discuss the theories and perspectives of the authors in various disciplines. That said, the objective is to summarize the outcomes of each disciple in order to understand the importance of this issue and how it applies to defining and understanding the customer experience in the marketing field. The results of my cross-sectional analysis show that there are five major forms of experience: ideological, sociocultural, symbolic, consumer experience, and customer experience.

- **Ideological experience:** phenomenologist philosophers and psychologists argue that experiences are private events that happen in reply to certain stimuli (e.g., Husserl, 1931; Brentano, 1973). They are often not self-produced but also induced. In philosophy, experience is seen as an ambivalent ideological notion. It represents the connection of individuals with material reality and the formation of knowledge and know-how. But at the same time, it

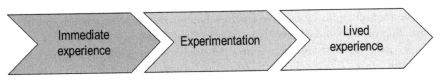

FIGURE 2.2 Three forms of experience in philosophy

is irrational, random, emotional, intangible, and unrelated to the material world. Philosophers define the experience as the domain of unpredictable mutations that distinguish three forms of experience (Figure 2.2).

o *Immediate experience*: it is a misleading experience that can be regarded as a source of error because it gives a distorted picture of reality. Plato in "Allegory of the Cave" explains how prisoners attached to the bottom of a cave perceived the shadows cast at the cave as elements of reality. Consequently, knowledge does not come from experience, but rather from thought, as Aristotle or Descartes show. Other philosophers like Kant consider that immediate experience can teach individuals things and provide them with new knowledge.

o *Experimentation*: it is necessary for the validation of our hypotheses in a given field (e.g., making the assumption that Walt Disney World offers a fairytale experience and then visiting the park to test the "hypothesis"). The knowledge generated in this case is not directly linked to the experience, but rather to the hypotheses that the individual seeks to test and to solve empirically (by experiencing) by validating, or not, the consistency of the hypotheses within the fieldwork, as Popper shows.

o *Lived experience:* it is the practical experience lived and constructed by individuals. It is the fundamental basis for the formation of knowledge and learning. For example, in-depth theoretical knowledge in a given consumption domain (luxury, gastronomy, technology, tourism, etc.) allows a practical application of its knowledge in reality. For instance, a consumer who learns about gastronomy or wine tasting, will be led to live the experience in a gourmet restaurant, and thus enjoy this new experience thanks to the accumulation of theoretical knowledge in this field. As Francis Bacon shows, the lived experience results from the sum of our theoretical knowledge, the accumulation of experience, and the conversion of knowledge accumulated into practice.

• **Sociocultural experience:** the transition from philosophy to sociology was marked by the publication of the book *Sociology of the Experience*, more than 20 years ago by the French sociologist François Dubet in 1994. In his book, Dubet develops the principles of a sociology that takes as its fundamental objective "the experience of the social actors." For Dubet, the experience can be multiple and complex. It does not refer to a pre-constructed role in which the individual chooses his/her way of acting.

The notion of experience has also been highlighted in sociological studies through the analysis of the "place of lived experience" (discussed earlier in philosophy). The lived experience is anchored in a specific sociocultural context and linked to a process of formation of social representations. In sociology, authors focus on the "sociocultural experience," which is associated with the lived dimension in a social and cultural context where individuals have relationships with other social actors, institutions, marketplaces, family members, other stakeholders, and elements of their immediate environment (Figure 2.3).

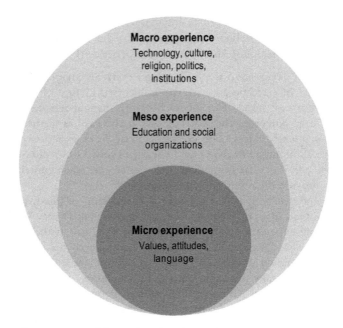

FIGURE 2.3 Components of the sociocultural experience

- **Symbolic experience:** in anthropology, a discipline inspired by philosophical and sociological theories, experience has been approached from the angle of "experimentalism," a term introduced by John Dewey in 1964 who states that the control of ideas is made by experiments, by the development of a successful experimental plan, and by testing hypotheses through conducting empirical fieldwork. Therefore, Dewey contributed to the definition of experience by highlighting its individual, symbolic, and cultural dimensions. Producing an experience refers, then, to acting on the real conditions of one's life, and engaging in a process of self-fulfillment. Experience is, therefore, seen as a source of individualization that conditions and transforms individuals by acting in making them unique and different since they have experienced multiple experiences that contribute to their individualization process.

The contribution of anthropology to the definition of experience underlines the important role of meanings and symbolism that are anchored in the culture to which individuals belong. Thus, culture is seen as a symbolic system in action within an environment in which individuals share cultural elements.

According to the anthropologist Clifford Geertz (1973), understanding the symbolic experience of individuals requires a profound analysis of symbolic forms, particularly tacit values that will produce meaning. These symbolic forms bring together objects, acts, relationships, and events that help to define an experience "that makes sense" for individuals according to their own perspective. For example, the symbolic form of a calendar will serve to organize a society by determining time, rituals, activities between work and holidays, etc. While the month of August in northern hemisphere countries has the connotation of summer holidays characterized by hotness, sunny days, rest, relaxation, pleasure, etc., in southern hemisphere countries, such as New Zealand, the same month has a different meaning and is often related to winter, coldness, and work.

THEORY BOX 2.1   EXPERIENCE AS A SET OF CULTURAL ELEMENTS

The anthropologist Clifford Geertz defines culture as a framework of meanings embodied by representations and symbols that are conveyed throughout history, a scheme of innate conceptions that express themselves through symbols, and by means of which individuals interact and communicate, perpetuate, and construct their awareness of life, their feelings, and their attitudes towards it. For Geertz, culture is more than a set of customs and institutions; it encompasses interpretations that individuals in a society give to their own experiences of meaning that they constructed through the episodes they live. It is not just about understanding how people behave, but how they see things that will structure the lived experience of individuals.

What is customer experience?

In the last decade, customer experience has taken over relational marketing and its concept of customer relationship management (CRM), which was widely used by companies in the 1990s. The interest of marketing scholars and businesses in the new "customer experience" concept can be explained by the limitations imposed by the use of a CRM approach that has significant shortcomings, such as the idea that CRM and relationship marketing do not adequately address the intangible and symbolic needs and expectations of consumers. CRM and relationship marketing are then criticized for being mainly focused on the following aspects:

*   The product and its tangible characteristics;
*   Quality improvement;
*   Sales increase through promotional strategies;
*   Rewarding customer loyalty.

Being product-oriented and sales-oriented is, therefore, completely opposed to the idea of a consumer-centric approach used in customer experience, which requires taking into account both the consumer's functional and emotional benefits.

- **From the buyer's journey to experiential journey:** the concept of customer experience developed in marketing studies addresses the relationship with the customer in terms of the consumer's lived experience that changes and evolves throughout his/her purchase and/or consumption journey (before, during, and after). The idea of experience journey goes beyond the need to understand the buyer's journey, as the customer experience design encompasses sociocultural and other macro, meso, and micro factors that are directly or indirectly related to the way consumers live and evolve through their experiences. These factors can affect the whole customer experience and the connection with the brand, either in a positive or in a negative way, and thus have an impact on sales increase, customer satisfaction and loyalty, brand reputation and images, and so forth. The two journeys (purchasing and experiential) are different, but remain very complementary and important to design a successful customer experience. Table 2.1 continues the development of the differences between the buyer's journey and experiential journey.

Although the fashion effect of customer experience as a hot topic may encourage brand managers and marketing professionals to use the experiential journey in a very narrow way without really considering the complexity and multidimensionality of the concept of customer experience – and without deeply understanding the

TABLE 2.1 Buyer's journey vs. experiential journey

Elements of differentiation	Buyer's journey	Experiential journey
Objective	Focuses on the price as well as the tangible and technical attributes of the product	The focus is on customer loyalty
Strategy	Narrow customer service, which focuses on the use of promotional strategies	Emphasizes customer – a high customer service through personalization and customization
Customer	Low commitment of customers Limited and/or unqualified personnel	Permanent contact with customers Qualified staff and enhanced presence
Relationship	Moderate contact and exchange with customers	Quality is based on the product, especially on the service delivery and the relationship with customers
Competitive advantage	Product quality and price are the top priority	Developing a durable connection, loyalty, and positive word-of-mouth are at the top of the company's priorities
Offering	Focuses on functional aspects	Focuses on functional, emotional, and relational aspects
Tools	Traditional market research (quantitative and qualitative)	Experiential and e-experiential market research

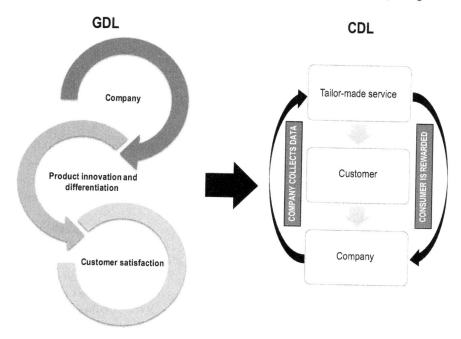

FIGURE 2.4 Good-dominant logic (GDL) vs. customer-dominant logic (CDL)

paradoxes of consumer behaviors – the majority of companies view this approach as a relevant strategy that creates a durable competitive advantage and enhances customer connection with the brand. Thus, companies need to learn more about their customers and their experiential expectations in terms of their well-being together with their functional needs. In so doing, aspects, such as service quality, personal training, immersive consumer surveys, and new marketing tools should be considered to design the ultimate customer experience. Companies with a consumer-centric approach that know their customers well can then assist them and help them to evolve throughout their "experiential journey," beyond their "shopping journey," which is usually at the center of marketing strategies. Figure 2.4 explains the two approaches: consumer-centric based on an experiential logic and product-centric that reflects a good-dominant logic.

As shown in Figure 2.4, the success of an experiential approach should have end-customer focus through a customer-dominant logic (CDL) instead of a good-dominant logic (GDL) approach.

- **From good-dominant logic (GDL) to customer-dominant logic (CDL):** the CDL approach suggests taking "end-user/customer" as a starting point that will replace the "product" in the traditional Porter value chain (2008) that is widespread in companies. The predominant logic in Porter's value chain is based on the idea that the company transforms "raw materials" into "final or in-service products," and then delivers them to the end-customer with after-sales service. In doing so, the company focuses primarily and exclusively on the creation of a "good product" or a "good service." A good offer (product or service) will necessarily satisfy the final consumer and transform the prospect into a current customer. Thinking in this way is easier and manageable for the company because it can place the customer at the end of the offer creation process (Figure 2.5).

Figure 2.5 shows that the departments involved in the creation process are all focused on the tangible and technical attributes of the product, which is viewed as solid added value enabling the company to differentiate itself from its competitors in the marketplace. This path clearly refers to Porter's value chain, which follows a traditional GDL approach.

However, shifting from a GDL logic focused on the tangible characteristics of the product to a CDL approach that places the client at the core of the firm's strategy and offer will lead to the involvement of all organizational actors. This encourages different departments to work together and collaborate at all phases of the growth process, including the allocation of budgets, which can be more or less homogeneous. Involving multiple departments (e.g., R&D, marketing, finance, sales, etc.) enables all employees in the company, regardless of their department (e.g., marketing, finance, commerce, HR, etc.), to better understand the functional and experiential expectations of their customers, and thus optimize offer creation, manufacturing, and manage creativity and innovation in a very efficient way by merging their knowledge in a collaborative work focused on the creation of the ultimate "experiential offer."

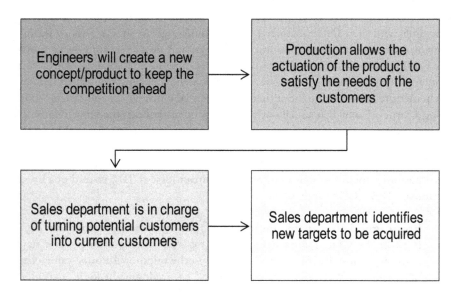

FIGURE 2.5 Value chain logic

The implementation of a CDL approach focused on the consumer requires innovative marketing studies that consulting firms and companies should set up to analyze the behaviors of their customers while concurrently examining all the relevant dimensions, both functional and emotional factors related to customer experience. Indeed, innovative market research companies are able to fully understand the characteristics of the consumer experience, as well as the real motivations to purchase for their customers. Although the implementation of this approach is costly for the company, it can enable it to achieve significant returns on investment, create a strong competitive advantage, and help brand managers and marketing professionals to be more efficient by better mastering the "experiential journey" that includes functional, emotional, and subjective aspects. Thus, marketing studies should rethink their consumer insights and market research tools by using what I call "**experiential and immersive market research**" tools to be closer to their customers who experience consumption and purchase both offline and online.

MINI-CASE 2.1 B&C CONSULTING GROUP: EXPERIENTIAL AND E-EXPERIENTIAL MARKET RESEARCH TOOLS

B&C Consulting Group is an innovative market research and consumer insights consultancy group that focuses on developing new tools to study customer experience offline and online by applying immersive and experiential techniques that help companies to understand the tacit meanings consumers assign to their consumption practices.

B&C Consulting Group also develops innovative online co-creation techniques that rely on the use of apps such as "EthnoMobile" to involve customers in the study of their own behaviors by becoming co-investigators or co-researchers. The EthnoMobile offers a cross-glanced interviewer/interviewee on customer experience in a private setting often inaccessible to businesses. Consumers are invited to download the "MobExperience" app that allows them to express their opinions and emotions through a digital interactive diary. Consumer-generated databases include videos, images, texts, questionnaires, and geolocation data.

- **The rise of customer experience in marketing:** the transition from a product-centric logic to an experiential logic underlines the determining role of customer experience and its legitimacy in both academia and business. Indeed, for marketing scholars and companies, a customer experience framework is holistic by nature and is likely to link a set of variables (e.g., functional, emotional, environmental, cultural, etc.) whose analysis is most often conducted separately. The notion of "customer experience" first emerged in marketing in 1982 following the publication of a seminal article "The experiential aspects of consumption:

consumer fantasies, feelings, and fun" published by two pioneering marketing scholars, Holbrook and Hirschman, in a top-tier American journal: *Journal of Consumer Research*. Since this publication, the concept of experience has been integrated into the field of economics in the book *The Experience Economy* published by Pine and Gilmore in 1999 whose contributions become a central pillar of the foundation of the economy in the current context. Later, other scientific articles and books followed, first in the United States and in Northern Europe, and then in Southern Europe in the late 1990s and early 2000s. According to Lemon and Verhoef (2016), the origins of customer experience can be traced back to the 1960s, when the first influential theories on marketing and consumer behavior were established and disseminated, particularly, the work of Philip Kotler (1986) and John Howard and Jagdish Sheth (1969).

The different definitions of customer experience emphasize the importance of aspects such as "subjectivity," "intangibility," and "symbolism," which are viewed as an integral part of the purchasing and consumption processes. Thus, I can state that the transition from "conventional/traditional marketing" to "experiential marketing" supports the fundamental role of these dimensions for companies since it creates a durable competitive advantage based on effect, emotion, and empathy connecting the brand with its targets. Consumption is thus no longer limited to functional benefits customers may be looking for, but it is also an "experience" in which the consumer can be involved and immersed. Companies need to rethink their strategies by evolving their traditional marketing tools to better understand the whole customer experience in all business sectors. Table 2.2 continues the development of the major changes related to the transition from traditional marketing to experiential marketing.

As shown in Table 2.2, the experiential logic suggests that, in comparison with traditional marketing models, the components must be reexamined in the light of the concept of customer experience. Therefore, companies should not only focus on functional stimuli, but also on emotional stimuli. The main difference between traditional and experiential marketing is the "goal of consumption." The perceived consumption purpose, as each consumer would define it according to his/her own

TABLE 2.2 Traditional marketing vs. experiential marketing

Elements	Traditional marketing	Experiential marketing
Emphasis	Focus on functional aspects and benefits	Focus on customer experiences
Offerings	Product type and rivalry are attentively outlined	Consumption is a holistic experience grounded within a particular culture
Clients	Consumers are perceived as rational decision makers	Consumers are both rational and emotional market actors
Approaches	Methods and tools are analytical, quantitative, and verbal	Methods and tools are heterogeneous and varied

perspective, goes beyond the "maximization of the utility value" related to goods in search of the "maximization of lived experience," which incorporates not only functional criteria (e.g., quality, price, etc.) but also symbolic, emotional, relational, and aesthetic criteria (e.g., brand is perceived as an extension of one's identify, well-being, social capital, etc.).

Consumers will then seek to maximize their emotional benefits and evaluate their customer experience from the "pleasure" they will derive from it. In this perspective, companies should no longer measure customer experience through customer satisfaction, but more through the intensity of both the memory and pleasure customer brand experience will generate. It is, therefore, important for companies to set up a new strategy that relies on experiential marketing tools to create and stimulate customer experience.

- **The principles of experiential marketing:** in experiential marketing, it is assumed that companies have evolved from a status of producer of goods and then of services, to a new role of "producer of experiences." Experience, is thus seen as an undeniable competitive advantage that allows companies to differentiate their offers and to establish a strong relationship with their customers. In this perspective, the memorability of the consumption experience is a key element of success that is linked to consumer loyalty and positive word-of-mouth. For marketers, experiential marketing contributes to an understanding of certain consumption and purchasing behaviors, particularly in the field of cultural products, such as music, leisure activities (e.g., movies), tourism, luxury goods, and so forth. Experiential marketing also highlights the determining role of emotions in assessing or valuing the experience of consumers for whom it is no longer simply a question of consuming a product but of experiencing consumption in interaction with the brand and other market actors in a social context, and most often by appealing to all the senses of the individual.

MINI-CASE 2.2 ABERCROMBIE & FITCH: A MARKETING APPROACH FOCUSED ON THE CONSUMER EXPERIENCE

Abercrombie & Fitch (A&F) is an American company created in 1892 by David Abercrombie and Ezra Fitch. The two founders launched this brand of clothing for men practicing outdoor sports activities. In its early years, the brand was the symbol of high-profile Americans and was worn by politicians and professionals. In wanting to increase market share and enlarge the offer to the general public, the brand went through a failure followed by a bankruptcy in the 1970s. The brand's revival in the 1980s, thanks to its acquisition by Limited

(continued)

(continued)

Brand Company, initiated a new marketing policy that has opened the market to teenagers by offering them a diverse and varied range of sports and urban products and by introducing experiential and sensory concept stores. In every store in the United States and Europe, the experiential concept is uniformly designed and includes sensory elements to engage the consumer in a unique and enjoyable experience. The main objective of the experiential strategy of A&F around the world is to focus on the five senses (excluding taste) for a deep immersion in the brand universe:

- The visual appearance at A&F is reflected in an atmosphere of dim lighting, bringing serenity, a warm welcome to customers, and highlighting the colorful clothes;
- The tactile aspect is very important and is reflected in the touch and fitting of the items without the need of help from sellers;
- Hearing is also reflected through the ambient music like in a "nightclub" to meet the expectations of trendy and festive young people;
- For the smell, sellers have instructions that they must spray the brand perfume on clothing every hour.

In addition, the brand welcomes its customers with a photo-taking ritual with mannequins: men and women sports, natural beauty, and half naked. All of these elements, the lived experience as well as the interactions with the sellers, constitute a pleasant and memorable experiential offer for the customers. By engaging its customer in a sensory universe, A&F offers a global and immersive customer experience that leads to:

- Creating a tangible memory mix (a souvenir photo with the models) and intangible through the concept store;
- Eliminating negative signs (the concept store is a world of celebration and carefreeness);
- Being in tune with the emotions and impressions of customers (vendors are assigned by sector and are available to meet customer needs);
- Creating a thematic environment: the trendy nightclub.

Therefore, experiential marketing allows A&F to create a connection and a privileged relationship with its customers, especially teenagers who are often described as unfaithful to brands.

Today's customers are, therefore, increasingly seeking immersion in diverse and varied experiences in order to seek out multiple new meanings to give to their life. For companies, this change is accompanied by the implementation of new management tools. It is, therefore, no longer managing the relationship with the customer, but rather managing the customer experience. The major purpose of experience management tools is to involve the customer in a pleasurable experience designed by the company that offers him/her the possibility of living it in "full or semi-integral immersion" in interaction (in the marketplace) or not with the company (at home).

THEORY BOX 2.2 EXPERIENTIAL MARKETING AND CUSTOMER EXPERIENCE FOUNDATIONS

What is the foundation of experiential marketing and customer experience? The experiential perspective is based on the idea of the experience economy initiated by Pine and Gilmore in 1999 who attempt to respond to the desires expressed by consumers who are perceived as emotional social actors in search of sensitive and emotionally charged consumption experiences. Thus, experiential marketing goes beyond the idea of satisfying functional and tangible needs and focuses more on the growing quest of consumers for immersive and diverse experiences to investigate new meanings and escape their daily lives. In the experiential logic, the consumer is not a passive market actor who reacts to simulations, such as advertising or promotions, but rather a producer of his/her own consumption experiences including hyper-real experiences.

When did the evolution of experiential marketing begin? Since the 1960s, consumption has progressively detached from an essentially functional conception built on the value of use. First, Baudrillard in 1970 stated that consumption has become, since the 1970s, an activity of production of meanings and an area of symbolic interactions: consumers do not consume products, but they consume the meaning of these products and the image they convey. It is in this logic that the concept of "consumer experience" was theorized in marketing by scholars, such as Holbrook and Hirschman in 1982, as a personal and subjective experience that is often emotionally charged and whose evaluation is translated into pleasures and memories.

How can companies lead and design the customer experience? Customer experience is considered as a fourth category of offering that adds to goods, products, and services. It represents a common value shared between the producer and the consumer. Companies must seek to help their customers in the production and accomplishment of their experiences. Reintegrating the idea of immersion, experiential marketing proposes to transform consumption into a series of extraordinary immersions for the consumer, which can be translated through several elements, ranging from communication to the atmosphere of the sales environment.

TABLE 2.3 Designed and expected customer experience

Type	Designed experience	Expected experience
Characteristics	It is the operational conversion of the desired experience through the use of stimuli, theming, and perceptions to generate emotions	It refers to consumer anticipation of the experience generated by marketing, communication, and commercial actions. The consumer can also live the vicarious experience through stories of other customers
Example	The experience of an idealized holiday village or thematic attraction park where everyone is supposed to be enchanted, happy, and in a good mood	We can find expected experiences in highly experiential areas, such as tourism, hotels, restaurants as well as cultural activities (film, concert, etc.) where anticipation is forged by word-of-mouth and commercials

By taking an experiential marketing perspective, companies place the customer at the center of their strategy and the creation process. This placement reduces the gaps that may exist between the different experiences. For instance, the experience expected by the consumer should not be too far from the experience designed by the company (Table 2.3). The company must also be able to intervene on the elements that constitute the consumer experience in order to adjust its offer to both symbolic and emotional needs, as expressed by consumers.

Furthermore, businesses should help and assist their clients in creating their own experiences. To do so, Pine and Gilmore (1998) propose five main factors of experiential marketing that companies have to take into account in the conception of the "experiential offer." These factors are presented in Figure 2.6.

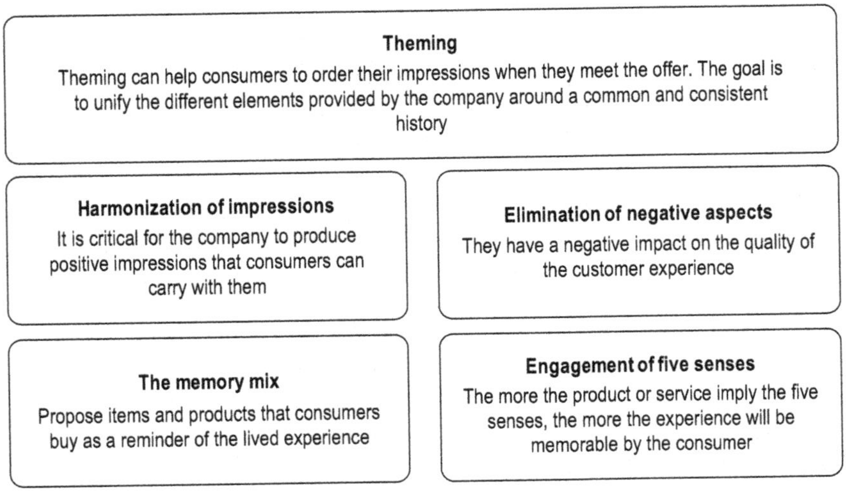

Theming
Theming can help consumers to order their impressions when they meet the offer. The goal is to unify the different elements provided by the company around a common and consistent history

Harmonization of impressions
It is critical for the company to produce positive impressions that consumers can carry with them

Elimination of negative aspects
They have a negative impact on the quality of the customer experience

The memory mix
Propose items and products that consumers buy as a reminder of the lived experience

Engagement of five senses
The more the product or service imply the five senses, the more the experience will be memorable by the consumer

FIGURE 2.6 Five factors of experiential marketing

MINI-CASE 2.3   NESPRESSO, THE IMMERSIVE EXPERIENCE OF COFFEE

Nestlé Nespresso SA is a growing Nestlé Group company. In 1986, Nestlé Nespresso launched high-end portions of coffee in the Swiss and Italian markets. Its objective was to offer the end-user or business the experience and quality of the espressos served in the best Italian cafes. Over the past eight years, Nestlé Nespresso has shown growth rates between 35 and 40%. Thus, Nespresso used the differentiation strategy based on the experience and the valuation of the customer to distinguish its product from that of its competitors.

Nespresso's unique business model has enabled it to build relationships based on proximity and long-term customer loyalty. Consumers have the opportunity to communicate directly with the brand and learn about new offline and online products by selecting the channel of their choice: e-commerce platform, call center, and an international network of stores offering rewarding consumer experiences that include the following elements:

- The concept store. The concept store of Nespresso includes a multitude of shops worldwide. These shops offer immersive experiences that combine both a sensory and olfactory approach to centralize the consumer by offering coffee tastings.
- The product. It includes three main aspects: a variety of great coffee crus, elegant coffee makers, and personalized customer service. Since 2003, the company has been sourcing coffee from a sustainable agriculture program. 20% of the coffee bought by Nespresso comes from Rainforest Alliance, the main NGO working in sustainable agriculture. This commitment creates a lasting bond based on sharing common values with the consumer.
- The club. Nespresso has never positioned itself as a simple coffee retailer. To develop brand awareness, Nespresso has implemented the concept of "club" to develop and retain customers: a club of buyers and "tasters" of coffee. It is a customer service that raises each buyer to the rank of insider within a Nespresso club, accessible in 13 languages, 24 hours a day, and with more than two million members. Nespresso's strategy to value customers and provide them with unique experiences has enabled the brand to build a strong and exceptional relationship with its customers. The club is open, but the members are always treated as if they were part of a closed circle (e.g., magazine of exclusive offers, limited series).
- E-commerce. Developing new products and opening up to new communication techniques through social media (e.g., Facebook or Twitter) are also priorities for Nespresso.

(continued)

(continued)

- Communication. The objective of Nespresso is to develop its image amongst the overall expert and non-expert coffee drinkers through advertising campaigns with George Clooney, who became the Nespresso icon. His image and style fit perfectly with the brand and allow customers to feel valued. In addition, his slogan "What else?" has become the symbol of the brand that makes everyone accept a simple invitation to drink a cup of coffee.

More than drinking a coffee, what Nespresso offers is an "Ultimate Coffee Experience." More than a product, Nespresso wants to establish an experiential relationship with its customers, by focusing on customer valuation, ultra-selective and exclusive distribution of its products, smart coffee machines with elegant design, and improving customer service that elevates each buyer to the rank of insider within a Nespresso club.

- **Why do companies need to focus on customer experience?** Competing in today's global context is becoming very challenging. As customers often view products and services as similar, companies attempt to distinguish themselves from rivals by leaning their offers towards generating unforgettable customer experiences, a strategy in which many functional and emotional stimuli can be activated by the company through multiple actions and functions.

  Service excellence and product quality are no longer sufficient to attract and retain consumers in the current context. Companies must offer, in addition to exceptional know-how and their reputation, a "unique" and "rewarding" customer experience. There are still brands that have a very average or negative customer experience because they rely only on the quality of their product, their history, and their position as a leader in the marketplace. However, a negative customer experience when buying leading brands could be considered as a marketing disaster. All companies have not yet succeeded and need to focus more on how to value and consider their customers in order to retain them. Indeed, new competitors and digital pure players have arrived and started to attract disappointed consumers, especially in the service industry (e.g., Airbnb replacing hotels, Apple iTunes replacing the music industry, Netflix replacing the movie industry, Amazon replacing retail, etc.). This tendency shows that companies do not know how to design the ultimate customer experience that makes sense to their customers. Indeed, designing suitable customer experiences is difficult because it stems from very emotional, subjective, and symbolic characteristics that highlight the paradoxical behaviors of today's consumers. This makes designing a satisfying customer experience very challenging for companies who do not have a deeper understanding of the tacit and explicit needs of their customers.

Theoretical underpinnings for customer experience

The analysis of the marketing literature shows that a variety of terms have been used by authors when examining consumption experiences in the marketplace. While certain studies for instance discuss "customer/client experience" and "consumer/consumption experience," others focus on concepts such as "brand experience," "market experience," "shopping experience," "Internet experience," and other concepts as indicated in Figure 2.7, which presents the key concepts used to study the concept of "experience" in marketing and consumer behavior studies.

Following a historical analysis, Lemon and Verhoef (2016: 71) identified seven important subsequent inputs to customer experience: 1) customer buying behavior process models from 1960s to 1970s; 2) customer satisfaction and loyalty in 1970s; 3) service quality in 1980s; 4) relationship marketing in 1990s; 5) customer relationship management (CRM) in 2000s; 6) customer centricity and customer focus from 2000s to 2010s; and 7) customer engagement in 2010s. A review of the literature (Table 2.4) shows that the definition of "customer experience" as a construct in marketing is related to a variety of characteristics that are inseparably related to the concept of experience.

However, as shown in Table 2.4, there is no overall consensus on the definition of customer experience as a construct, and even more authors use the term of user (experience) that does not provide a comprehensive picture of the complexity and

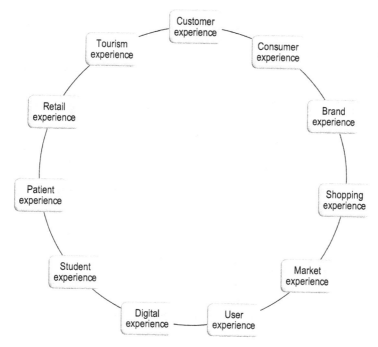

FIGURE 2.7 Concepts related to experience

TABLE 2.4 Customer experience definitions

Perspective	Aspect	Literature
Consumer	What individuals actually wish for are not products but fulfilling and enjoyable consumption experiences	Abbott (1955); Alderson (1957)
Consumer	A wider understanding of consumer behavior, especially acknowledging the importance of emotions in decision making	Hirschman and Holbrook (1982)
Company	Experiences are distinct from goods and services	Pine and Gilmore (1998); Schmitt (2003; 2010)
Consumer and company	Every service exchange generates a customer experience, regardless of its nature and form. Customer experience is holistic and includes the customer's cognitive, emotional, sensory, social, and spiritual answers to all exchanges and communications with a company	Schmitt, Brakus, and Zarantonello (2015)
Consumer and company	Customer experience is the quality of customer care as well as advertising, packaging, product, and service characteristics, ease of use, and reliability. It is the inner and personal response customers have to any direct or indirect contact with a company	Meyer and Schwager 2007
Consumer and company	Customer experience is a multidimensional construct that includes the customer's cognitive, affective, emotional, social, and physical responses to the retailer. Customer experiences can be classified along with the elements of the retail mix (e.g., price experience, promotion experience)	Verhoef et al. (2009) Grewal, Levy, and Kumar (2009)
Consumer and company	Brand experience is subjective and contains four distinct, but connected, elements: sensory, affective, intellectual, and behavioral	Brakus, Schmitt, and Zarantonello (2009)
Consumer, company, and environment	Customer experience is a combination of the cognitive, emotional, physical, sensorial, spiritual, and social elements that affect the customer's direct or indirect exchange with (an)other market actor(s)	De Keyser et al. (2015)
Technology	Technology as an experience encompasses four dimensions of experience: sensual, emotional, compositional, and spatio-temporal	McCarthy and Wright (2004)

dynamics of the concept. Overall, as stated by Lemon and Verhoef (2016), Verhoef et al. (2009), and Schmitt (1999), scholars and businesses have to consider that customer experience is a multidimensional concept that includes cognitive, behavioral, emotional, sensorial, symbolic, and social components that the company has to include within its offers to fully satisfy its customers. Following this logic, I offer hereby an integral and updated definition of customer experience.

CUSTOMER EXPERIENCE: DEFINITION

Customer experience is connected with the "lived" dimension of the experience, which is embedded within the sociocultural context in which consumers interact with each other and with other social agents, institutions, market actors, family, etc. that constitute their immediate environment. Thus, customer experience is multidimensional, composite, and an evolving construct. It is a combination of a harmonious blend of several factors and actors that have a direct or indirect impact on designing successful experiences in connection with the marketplace or not. Further, customer experience can be defined from two main perspectives: consumer and company. Unlike the traditional marketing approach, which focuses on goods (products and services), experiential marketing offers a transformative experience where the consumer engages in a process of self-fulfillment. The impact of the lived experience is global and generates a continuum in the hyper-real world by way of digital means.

As my definition shows, the notion of "experience" has been studied by considering two main perspectives: marketing management perspective and consumer perspective.

- **Experience from a consumer perspective: Holbrook and Hirschman's contributions**: one of the first thought-provoking academic articles that examined and conceptualized the notion of "experience" from a consumer perspective in marketing was Holbrook and Hirschman's (1982). In their article "The experiential aspects of consumption: Consumer fantasies, feelings, and fun," Holbrook and Hirschman provide a deep analysis underlying the limitations of the traditional information processing model. Further, they identified a new approach emphasizing the key role of "hedonic" components in consumption experiences. Holbrook and Hirschman define hedonic consumption as designating "those facets of consumer behavior that relate to the multi-sensory, fantasy, and emotive aspects of one's experience with products" (1982: 92). As stated by Babin and colleagues (1994), hedonism is, therefore, seen as an important part in an individual's evaluation of consumption experiences. In the consumer perspective, the utilitarian functions of products, symbolic meanings, and emotions are thus reinforced as important dimensions of product evaluation.

Holbrook and Hirschman suggested a comprehensive and holistic framework that relates to the analysis of intangible, subjective, and emotional dimensions within consumer experiences. As stated by Schmitt:

> By positioning their article against the hegemony of the information processing perspective in consumer research, Holbrook and Hirschman felt that information processing neglected important consumption phenomena that involve fantasies, feelings, and fun — including playful leisure activities, sensory pleasures, daydreams, aesthetic enjoyment, and emotional responses.
>
> *(2010: 62)*

For Holbrook and Hirschman, the information processing theory portrays consumers as "rational thinkers" who aim at maximizing their utility value. This perspective is limited since it does not allow the explanation of several consumption phenomena (e.g., emotional response, sensory pleasures, playful leisure activities, and so forth). Therefore, thinking of experience from a consumer perspective is relevant as this vision suggests that consumers do not always behave as rational thinkers with thoughtful judgmental evaluations, and they often display rational activities viewed as "primary processes," where their thinking is based on "pleasure values" rather than on "rational assessments." Thus, the experiential view from a consumer standpoint, as stated by Holbrook and Hirschman is considered as "phenomenological in spirit and regards consumption as a primary subjective state of consciousness with a variety of symbolic meanings, hedonic responses, and aesthetic criteria," (1982: 132). Figure 2.8 summarizes the key foundations of Holbrook and Hirschman's conceptualization of consumer experience and the elements that distinguish it from the traditional logic of information processing theory.

Consumer experience is phenomenological in spirit and regards consumption as a subjective state of consciousness	Consumer experience emphasizes the symbolic meaning, subconscious processes, and nonverbal cues resulting from consumption	Affect plays a key role, and not just as an influence on attitude and arousal, but in terms of the full range of possible consumer emotions (e.g., love, fear, etc.)

Going beyond the focus on the consumer as information processor, which can limit understanding of consumer behavior	Consumption experiences also occur when consumers consume and use products and they can be direct or indirect

FIGURE 2.8 Key foundations of Holbrook and Hirschman's conceptualization of consumer experience

However, research on experience from a consumer perspective did not entirely reject the information processing theory, but rather advocates that emotional and symbolic components of the consumption experiences also needed to be addressed: "patronage decisions regarding hedonically consumed products are based primarily on the symbolic elements of the product rather than their tangible features" (Holbrook and Hirschman, 1982: 97).

The Holbrook and Hirschman's conceptualization of the consumer experience as a subjective and personal experience influenced later works in consumer research, which show a strong focus on consumer feelings and emotions that arise from his/her consumption experiences. It is, thus, no longer only "buying" but "experiencing," and mostly experiences are "embedded" since they are related to every sense of the individual (e.g., Addis and Holbrook, 2001).

Furthermore, if leisure and non-ordinary activities, which are by definition emotional and memorable, have been privileged topics in the experience consumption field, it seems that the explosion of subjectivity and emotional attitudes are widespread in today's consumer societies. Therefore, there is, as argued by Firat and Dholakia (1998), an extension of the domain of experience to all consumption activities in which consumers tend to immerse themselves and explore a multiplicity of new meanings of their life. It is this full and deep immersion in consumption experiences, ordinary or extraordinary, that offers an exclusive and memorable pleasure to consumers.

While the experience from a consumer perspective was widely applauded by academics, Holbrook and Hirschman's seminal article and contributions to understanding the concept of "consumer experience" were somehow so revolutionary that it took a long time for researchers to digest them and develop this theory further in marketing and other fields, such as services, tourism, retail, and so forth. Indeed, it is only in the late 1990s that a series of books and articles were published on "experience management" and since then, experience has become a major research topic amongst marketing and management scholars, and marketing professionals alike.

- **Experience from a marketing management perspective**: several academic, professional books, and textbooks have been published on the topic of experience in marketing management that cannot be fully reviewed here, but the book *Experiential Marketing* published by Bernd Schmitt (1999) and *The Experience Economy* published by Joseph Pine II and James Gilmore (1999) are amongst the main contributions that allowed the dissemination of the concept of consumer experience from a marketing management perspective in both academia and business. Experience in the marketing management field in the late 1990s and 2000s principally shadowed Holbrook and Hirshman's vision.

The marketing management perspective underlines the idea of a new experiential marketing that was first introduced in the article "Welcome to the experience economy," published in *Harvard Business Review* by Pine and Gilmore in 1998, as part of their work on the experience economy from a marketing management perspective. Pine and Gilmore presented in their book, subsequent to the publication of their article, their definition of experiential marketing referring to it as "when a person buys a service, he or she purchases a set of intangible activities carried out on his/her behalf. However, when he/she buys an experience, he/she pays to spend time enjoying a series of memorable events that a company stages to engage him/her in a personal way" (1999: 2). Experiential marketing is thus about injecting meanings within the core of the company offer. Therefore, experiential marketing mainly identifies marketing plans and actions that provide consumers with profound consumption experiences to make a purchase decision.

O'Sullivan and Spangler (1998), for example, suggest that the key concepts of the experiential marketing approach can be categorized as:

o   Customer involvement (physical, mental, emotional, social, and spiritual);
o   Customer's co-participation in the product's offer;
o   Importance of the product's or service's symbolic values;
o   Product's or service's multifunctionality;
o   Centrality of experience in consumption.

Pine and Gilmore suggest that companies should reflect on experiences throughout two ideas: customer participation and connection to design suitable customer experiences. By following the logic of experience from a marketing management perspective, the consumer becomes an active economic actor within his/her consumption experiences. Furthermore, the role of companies is to understand what constitutes an experience for their customers, how to design suitable experiences, and how to manage them to enhance customer loyalty and satisfaction. Yet, translating a consumer-centric perspective into practice that has economic benefits is challenging, but companies have to shift to this new economic model.

As stated by Pine and Gilmore, economies have evolved from companies making goods, then services, and finally now having to produce experiences to sell their products. In order to achieve a competitive advantage towards their competitors, companies should produce experiences, a new category of offer that can be marketed to consumers.

The vision of Pine and Gilmore, as it pertains to experience, highlights the idea that "an experience occurs when a company intentionally uses services as the stage and goods as props, to engage individual customers in a way that creates a memorable event" (1998: 98). Thus, the key focus is on how companies can create and enhance customer experience memorability through products and services. Yet, experience memorability has been recognized as a key factor to a successful experience as well as a forecaster of future purchase and positive word-of-mouth; however, its evaluation remains complex.

MINI-CASE 2.4   B&B ACCOMMODATION TO ENHANCE MEMORABILITY BY EXPERIENCING LOCAL CULTURES

Memorable tourism experiences are related to experiencing local cultures where tourists can interact with locals through new accommodation models, such as Bed & Breakfast. In recent years, B&B operators have augmented considerably in numbers around the world. This is somewhat a result of current economic decline and the fact that this kind of lodging is attracting too many young people traveling with small budgets. B&Bs are characterized by their multiplicity, while some B&Bs can provide an experience equally similar to a hotel accommodation, others can be more of a 'mom and pop' accommodation experience, and while they certainly may be more attractive to a tourist because of the low prices, others are positioned as luxury housing experiences. Numerous categories of B&B can be found on the market:

- B&B "home-stay," which offers up to four guest rooms. This type of B&B is regularly in the host's own house to make an additional source of revenue.
- B&B, or small lodge, has up to 12 guest rooms. Most of these B&Bs, or small lodges, are the owner's main or substantial source of income.
- B&B comprising a principal or shared house where the host usually stays and offers guests the use of the bathroom and living and dining parts, whilst guests sleep in smaller one-room cabins.

The main elements of a B&B activity are accommodation, hospitality, breakfast, and other facilities. In each of these areas, there are particular needs from the customers that B&B owners will encounter. Regarding lodging, B&B must be comfortable and the host should be welcoming and friendly to the guests. The host should have a kind demeanor and present the guests with the facilities offered. Several visitors select a B&B for the personal welcome and hospitality that they wish to experience. Falling short of these expectations can affect the experience and result in the loss of return customers and negative image. Breakfast is an ordinary service that is included in the price of the room: it can be a simple continental breakfast (coffee, milk, an assortment of bagels or muffins or yogurt) or a full cooked breakfast (such as British B&Bs offer). There are other services that can be considered, for example B&Bs can sell their own products (jams, products from their agricultural activities, etc.) along with various recommendations and advice about local attractions.

Schmitt suggests a conflict between two opposite but complementary views: 1) traditional marketing's product-orientation that focuses on functional characteristics and benefits, and 2) experience marketing's customer-oriented focus on experiences

(2010: 62). As stated by Schmitt "rather than focusing on narrowly defined product categories (e.g., shampoo, shaving cream, blow dryer, and perfume) and their features, experience marketers focus on consumption situations, such as "grooming in the bathroom," and ask how products and brands can enhance the consumption experience" (2010: 63). Consequently, experience in a marketing management perspective should be based on the idea that experiences may be evoked by feelings that may happen as an outcome of online or offline consumption activities defined by elements, such as atmosphere, storytelling, concept-store, products, packaging, communications, interactions, sales relationships, public relations, and the like.

Experience touchpoints through customer journey

Exploring customer experience through customer journey over time is important for practitioners who are willing to design a satisfying experience path that evolves through consumer journey and his/her interaction with multiple channels and actors, both offline and online. The changes that occur during the journey may affect the quality of customer experience. In order to guarantee the same quality of experience, companies have then to include multiple functions and departments as well as marketing and communication actions in designing and delivering suitable experiences throughout the customer journey. Thus, it is important for companies to advance a better and more robust comprehension of what the characteristics of customer journey are, its stages, and its impact on the whole customer experience. From the experiential viewpoint, consumption experience is neither seen as being limited to prepurchase activities, nor to post-purchase ones, but it comprises a succession of other actions, which affect consumers' decisions and future activities. Arnould and Price (1993) have identified four major stages consumers follow within the consumption experience:

- Pre-consumption experience: includes searching for, planning, day-dreaming, foreseeing, or imagining the experience;
- Purchase experience: originates from choice, payment, packaging, interaction with salespeople, service, and environment;
- Core experience: includes sensation, satiety, satisfaction/dissatisfaction, irritation or flow, and transformation;
- Remembered experience: refers to the nostalgia experience activated by photographs to re-live a past experience.

Lemon and Verhoef (2016) conceptualize customer experience as "an iterative and dynamic 'customer's journey' with an entity over time during the purchase cycle across multiple touchpoints" (2016: 74). Lemon and Verhoef suggest that the customer experience process shifts from prepurchase to purchase to postpurchase, which is, as stated by these authors, reliable with previous research (e.g., Howard and Sheth, 1969). According to Lemon and Verhoef, customer journey includes past purchase and consumption experiences, external factors, and touchpoints that are related to each stage in the consumer journey and that can change and evolve from one stage to another. Although the process model for customer journey and experience proposed by Lemon and Verhoef (2016: 77) is a successful conceptualization of experience touchpoints through customer journey, and the three phases make the process somewhat more manageable (Lemon and Verhoef, 2016; Schmitt, 2003), the framework provides a narrow view in fully examining customer experience, since it does not integrate perception levels, the distinction between digital and physical touchpoints, and the elements, which the firm can control and those which it cannot control.

Therefore, the customer journey process and experience touchpoints can be defined as a continuum that includes personal and individual responses that customers have to any interaction with brands, products, services, salespeople, other customers, and elements of the immediate environment at three main levels: micro, meso, and macro, including both physical and digital experience touchpoints. This definition shows that customer experiences, as a dynamic journey, are influenced by aspects and touchpoints that a company can control as well as by elements that are outside of the company's control. Consequently, brand managers and marketing professionals can never fully control the customer journey and the consumer experience touchpoints, they can only try to anticipate the needs of their customers by developing a deeper understanding of their functional, symbolic, and emotional needs, and thus create and manage their experiences within the context and the stage.

Summary

This chapter has examined three main topics: the origins and the rise of customer experience, its relationship with customer journey, and experience touchpoints. The concept of the customer experience is dynamic, multidisciplinary, and addresses the relationship with the customer from his/her own point-of-view that changes according to the stages of its consumption process (before, during, and after the experience). The customer experience is closely linked to the quality of services, the concept of well-being, learning, training, and marketing tools that accompany the customer in his/her consumption and purchase experiences. The idea is that the customer evolves throughout his/her "experiential journey," which goes beyond the "shopping journey" usually at the center of marketing strategies. Companies should be able to anticipate and design ultimate customer experiences by identifying touchpoints and generating emotions (negative or positive) that can affect the lived experiences, the memorability, and word-of-mouth transmission of information. This chapter has demonstrated how the analysis of all the dimensions related to customer experience and its stages and touchpoints can be used by companies to better understand consumer needs (tangible, symbolic, emotional, relational, etc.), retain customers, and attract new ones.

3

A FRAMEWORK FOR CONCEPTUALIZING CUSTOMER EXPERIENCE MARKETING

Drivers, markers, and outcomes

Purpose and context

In Chapter 3, I will introduce the customer experience marketing framework, which looks at customer experience design as a process that distinguishes between experience markers, drivers, and outcomes. I contribute to the existing works in marketing and consumer research by offering an integral iterative comprehensive framework for conceptualizing customer experience marketing. Understanding customer experience marketing is a critical issue and needs to be addressed by scholars and practitioners to build experiences that create strong connections with customers. The framework (Figure 3.1) explains how customer experience functions and what marketing and communication tools and strategies companies should consider implementing in order to create valuable, memorable, and profitable customer experiences. This chapter provides an analytical and strategic framework along with implementation tools and illustrative examples from different sectors.

Learning outcomes

After reading this chapter, you will be able to define customer experience marketing, its markers, drivers, and outcomes. You will be able to explain the objective of the customer experience marketing framework and describe the way brand managers and marketers can develop implementation tools and strategies based on this framework. You can also appreciate the role of emotions in creating memorable customer experiences, understand how it can be managed to generate a worthy experience, explore the various senses and what might trigger them, and identify the major customer experience components.

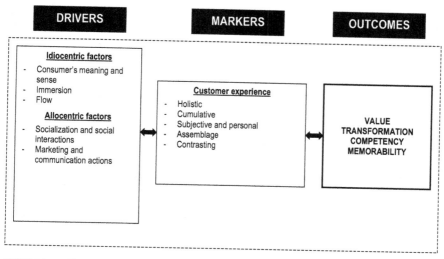

FIGURE 3.1   Customer experience marketing framework

Drivers of customer experience marketing

By framing customer experience marketing as a process, I have identified two main categories of drivers: idiocentric (self-oriented) and allocentric (others/environment-orientated). These two categories encompass a number of factors that will be detailed and illustrated through examples in the next section.

Idiocentric drivers of customer experience

Idiocentric drivers are composed of three components: meaning and sense, immersion, and engagement. These drivers are consumer-oriented and are generated by consumer subjectivity within his/her own consumption and purchase experiences.

- **Consumer's meaning and sense:** although experiences, as stated by Holt (1995), can have a shared and collective dimension, consumption experiences are fundamentally personal and their meanings belong to individuals who have experience them. Experience responses through dimensions, such as cognitive and emotional, depends on an individual's reaction to the same lived experience. Consumers make sense of their consumption experiences according to the symbolic aspects they assign to them and the way experience will lead to the construction of their own personal and social identity.

  Symbolic consumption as a construct has been examined since the 1980s in marketing and consumer research following two core perspectives: identity and meaning construction (e.g., Levy, 1959; McCracken, 1986). Table 3.1 summarizes some definitions, perspectives, and characteristics of the symbolic consumption as a concept in marketing.

TABLE 3.1 Definitions, perspectives, and characteristics of symbolic consumption

Perspective	Definition	Characteristic
The meaning of products in society	Acquisition of products is based on the ability of products and brands to transfer and communicate cultural meanings	Consumers perceive the meaning of the products based on other people's opinions
The consumer's identity	The use of the symbolic content of brands to express one's identity Consumer's perception of products and brands in order to acquire, create, preserve, and present his/her identity	Consumers add meaning to the products they purchase Consumption takes part as a process of identity creation

Marketing scholars state that, companies should go beyond the thinking that focuses on the tangible aspects of their products and consider more the symbolic facets of their goods. Levy underlines that "managers must attend to more than the relatively superficial facts with which they usually concern themselves when they do not think of their goods as having symbolic significance" (1959: 117). For example, a wedding ring is not only a tangible object defined by its shape, design, the color of gold, brand, composition, carat, and so forth, but it also symbolizes love, commitment, devotion, and faithfulness that two individuals will share. It is then only by giving a meaning to consumption experience that consumers can memorize it, and thus recall and repeat it if they were satisfied.

MINI-CASE 3.1 KFC AS A SYMBOL OF CHRISTMAS CELEBRATION IN JAPAN

How has KFC become a Christmas tradition in Japan? KFC has become the symbol of Christmas thanks to Takeshi Okawara, who managed the first KFC restaurant in Japan. For 3,336 yen (about 37 US dollars), KFC offers a Christmas chicken dinner with cake and champagne included that should be ordered months in advance to avoid waiting in huge queues that last more than two hours. Although Christmas is not a national holiday in Japan (only 1% of the population is Christian), the Christmas Chicken box has become an iconic meal since 1974. It started with a simple advertising campaign that had a significant impact on sales of fried chicken at Christmas time, which made KFC a big influencing market actor in establishing the Christmas tradition in Japan and thus boosting business. Following KFC's successful campaign that managed to give a Christmas meaning to fried chicken, Wendy's fast food adopted this concept for its stores in Asia in 2011 and is now offering alternatives to chicken for Christmas celebrations, such as burgers with truffles for only 1,280 yen (about 17 US dollars), which is much cheaper than KFC.

Thus, companies should not only satisfy customers' needs by offering a good quality of products and services, they should also incorporate meanings and emotions within their offers by connecting symbolic consumption with meaningful experiences that consumers may perceive as relevant to their own perception. Indeed, certain groups of consumers may perceive the symbolism of consumption objects in ways that differ from other groups' perceptions. This can be explained by cultural differences or inner variables that can affect consumer's perceptions of consumption symbolism and the meanings generated by the latter.

According to Elliott and Wattanasuwan (1998), consumers can also use advertising to create meanings based on symbols, icons, texts, and other elements. The use of symbols is related to the creation of associations between a "signifier" and a "signified." For example, when creating an advertisement for eco-friendly products, art directors may choose green colors, supposing that it will generate a feeling of nature, color of life, renewal, energy, growth, safety, freshness, environment, harmony, and so forth. The color green is a signifier as it is used to induce certain feelings in the consumer experience of the advertisement. All the meanings related to it are referred to as (signified). Figure 3.2 shows the Starbucks associations between a "signifier" and a "signified."

Though, the creation of meanings is not only related to the exposure phase; it also generates and evolves through social interactions and interpersonal communication amongst consumers who are capable of creating and sharing a collective meaning. For companies, it is then important to develop a better understanding of the experience,

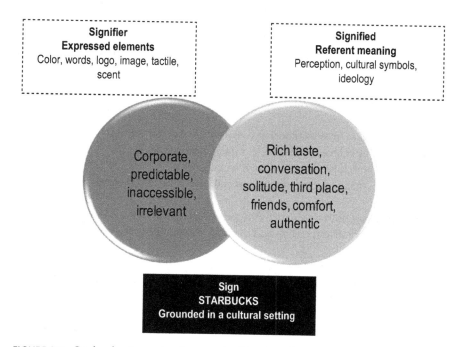

FIGURE 3.2 Starbucks sign as it relates to signifier/signified

the sensemaking process, and the symbolic dimension of consumption. Anderson and Meyer (1988) state that sensemaking is a continuing process in which a multiplicity of significances are generated as consequences of the consumer's own interest-focus, culturally located influence of marketing and advertisement understanding, brand interpretation, product buying, and consumption experience.

As brand managers and marketing professionals seek to increase and enhance their knowledge in terms of consumption experiences and consumer emotional and symbolic expectations, the use of semiotics, which refers to the study of signs and meanings embedded within their cultural context, is recommended. Indeed, by using semiotics, companies can decode symbols, identify future trends, and innovate.

THEORY BOX 3.1   THE IMPORTANCE OF SEMIOTICS IN BRANDING, MARKETING, AND MARKET RESEARCH

Semiotics is a discipline with a philosophical linguistic foundation that has practical implications for branding, marketing, design, cultural studies, and market research. It can be used as a methodology, as a framework, or as a theory. Semiotics refers to the relationship between a sign, an object, and a meaning. We can define semiotics as the science of examining all the signs and symbols of a brand, a communication, a packaging, a service, or a product within a particular cultural setting. Semiotics can help marketers and brand managers create brand associations based on lived experiences of consumers that make sense for them, and which allow brand differentiation and innovations. Signs that can be discursive/verbal (e.g., involving meaning and language-based thought) or non-discursive/nonverbal (e.g., involving emotion, art, music, dance, etc.) refer to the object in the mind of an interpreter. The foundations of semiotics include the following ideas:

- The fundamental relationship between symbol, object, and individual;
- Symbols become significant and meaningful in discourse;
- Every symbol has one or more meanings;
- Symbol meanings are socially and culturally embedded within a particular setting;
- Signs have both denotative (the precise meaning or the literal definition) and connotative (positive and negative associations) meanings.

Semiotics has proved its importance in marketing and market research as a powerful technic that creates the distinctive value of products, services, and brands and as a sophisticated analytical tool that allows the identification of meanings of consumption, objects, and consumer behaviors that otherwise would be difficult to reveal. Therefore, semiotics is about the discovery and the management of *meaning,* which combines multiples *memes* (units of meaning) that are products of *cultural creatives* and must be passed on. Indeed, whereas in conventional market research we ask consumers for their ideas, opinions, and behaviors, semiotics narrowly studies consumption culture to reveal the fundamental and the tacit cultural motivations for consumer answers. Thus, semiotics provides marketers and brand managers with relevant insights that produce strong and creative results that can be used for different strategic activities, from brand development to strategic planning.

MINI-CASE 3.2 NINTENDO WII, THE SEMIOTICS OF GAMING CULTURE

Nintendo Wii is a good example of the power of semiotics in creating a more sophisticated mode of interactions in the gaming culture. The Wii shows that the focus on interaction with the user is more important than sophisticated graphics and sells better than when focusing solely on graphics. The key success of Wii comes from the use of semiotics in understanding how users will perceive and use the product in their gaming culture. The elaboration of the Wii was a creative consequence that not only impacts the gaming culture but also changed the way we play video games. Previous to the introduction of the Wii, gaming was related to masculinity, geek culture, and youth cultures. The meaning of gaming was then associated with isolation, obesity, introvert, and other negative images that symbolize lazy and inactive people incapable of developing social relationships.

By launching the Wii, and thanks to the use of semiotics tools, Nintendo created a new meaning of gaming by leveraging the culture and changing its negative image. Whilst conventional research would have asked gamers to express their needs, the use of semiotics allows Nintendo to step outside to observe, analyze, and decode the meanings and the cultural triggers of the gaming culture. As a result, the semiotics analysis emphasized the importance of interaction, immersion, and socialization in the gaming culture regarding gaming as more than an isolated activity, but instead as something that can bring the family together by redefining the norms of gaming and making it more social. The Wii was a successful solution (even though it has a lower video resolution quality) because it offers an enjoyable social gaming experience.

- **Immersion in consumer experiences:** immersion originates when a consumer interacts with a firm's experiential atmosphere. We can define immersion as a mode of access to a pleasurable consumption experience.

Thus, immersion suggests an activity wherein customers will get involved in an experiential setting (usually themed) to be transported by way of an experience sufficiently different from their daily habits to create an ultimate setting in which they will experience intense and unforgettable emotions. Bitner (1992) refers to immersive environments as a servicescape to underline the effect of the physical setting in which service is delivered. The servicescape can have a positive or a negative impact on the quality of customer experience, as well as on consumer's behaviors and on the interpersonal employee relationships and interactions amongst consumers. The servicescape model includes facilitator, functional, and sensory elements, that can be classified into two main categories:

o   Exterior elements: parking, architecture, signage, landscape, etc.
o   Interior elements: décor, fragrance, sounds, layout, signals, ambient conditions, such as air quality, lighting, etc.

THEORY BOX 3.2   WHAT DOES SERVICESCAPE MEAN?

In 1992, Bitner introduced the concept of "servicescape," which recognized that the physical setting has a significant influence on both consumers' and employees' experiences. The servicescape comprises three dimensions: ambient conditions (temperature, music, noise, air quality, etc.), spatial layout and functionality (e.g., layout, furnishing), signs, symbols, and artifacts (e.g., signage, style, décor, etc.). In other words, the servicescape reflects a non-human component of the context in which service encounters happen. Bitner states that the servicescape does not comprise: processes (e.g., methods of payment, billing, cooking, cleaning); external promotions (e.g., advertising, PR, social media, websites) or back-of-house (kitchen, cellars, store-rooms, housekeeping, staff change rooms, spaces) where customers do not normally visit. Originally, the notion of servicescape referred to the constructed setting (as opposite to the usual or social setting) and the reply amongst external stimuli and individual behaviors that are articulated through emotions that generate either *avoidance* or *approach* to the setting. Approach means that consumers appreciate the servicescape, stay longer, and explore further. Avoidance implies that consumers will leave the premises or will reduce the duration of their experience. In this line of thought, various atmospheric elements have been tested. For instance, some items are associated with avoidance, such as clutter or crowding. Other factors have been associated with higher satisfaction levels and purchase behaviors (e.g., color, music, layout, design, and lighting).

By changing these different elements, companies can create whole "experience worlds," which become new tools for promoting brands and products differently. While servicescape will seem evident to the design of the theme park experience, other service premises have heavily invested in their service-scape in order to create an experience that leads consumers to a different world during the time of the service delivery. This approach has always existed to some extent in service delivery, but it is even more prominent in the twenty-first century, especially in the food and beverage context as well as in retailing and hotels (e.g., boutique hotels have become design flagships in main capitals of the world).

Carù and Cova describe immersion as "a feeling of well-being, development, and satisfaction" (2003: 60). Thus, accessing a state of immersion is conditioned by consumers' ability to re-acquire the experience setting through which they change and customize the immediate setting to generate a sentiment of one's personal contexts. Carù and Cova state that the consumer can achieve the re-acquirement process through three major processes: nesting, exploration, and tagging (Figure 3.3).

Immersion in consumption experiences is a relevant approach since it is viewed both as a process that allows consumers to access and live intense experiences and as an outcome of a satisfying lived experience. This is particularly interesting for brand managers and marketing professionals since consumer immersion is the key factor to improving and enhancing consumer satisfaction and loyalty. Consumers who experience immersive consumption and purchase processes will be more eager to develop positive, pleasurable, and memorable feelings and thus re-experience the same feelings in future experiences. As stated by Carù and Cova (2003), what makes an experience pleasurable is the consumer's whole immersion in an original experience.

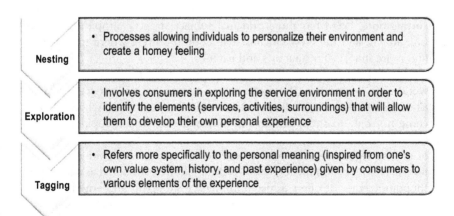

FIGURE 3.3 Consumer re-acquisition process

MINI-CASE 3.3   WEST EDMONTON MALL: AN IMMERSIVE SHOPPING EXPERIENCE

Shopping can be considered as an immersive and enjoyable customer experience. Malls have the potential to produce similarly enchanted and enjoyable experiences that are formally lived in parks, such as Disney World. Therefore, a satisfying and stimulating shopping experience is a fundamental dimension of customer satisfaction and loyalty. Shopping in malls and shopping centers in cities, such as Dubai, Hong Kong, Singapore, and New York, is still evolving as a significant component of an experiential economy. West Edmonton Mall (WEM) in Canada is an excellent case of the extensive customer-oriented shopping malls in North America – one that demonstrates the experiential and sociocultural aspects of buying experiences including, functional, emotional, sensory, and social aspects within immersive and entertaining settings. WEM was founded by the Ghermezians family in the late '70s in Edmonton, Alberta province, and is the third major shopping center in the world. The city of Edmonton attracts local people, tourists, and customer travelers from everywhere throughout the year.

WEM was constructed under the influence of traditional urban bazaars of Persia, which include both shopping and entertainment within one setting. The mall has been developed via two stages. The mall opened the first time in September 1981 with 220 stores and services. In September 1983, the family augmented the surface of the mall and added multiple attraction zones (e.g., Ice Palace Skating Rink, Playdium, Blue Thunder Bungee, Deep Sea Adventure, Xorbitor, Professor WEM's Adventure Golf, World Waterpark, Galaxyland Amusement park) and an additional 240 stores, boutiques, and services. Extra spots include an aviary with different exotic birds, bronze statues ordered specially for the mall, and a couple of aquariums. Furthermore, WEM has three principal subject streets, Europa Boulevard, Chinatown, and the New Orleans-style Bourbon Street where tourists can find more than 110 restaurants and eateries.

WEM attracts around 22 million visitors each year and is considered a world-class destination. The mall's stores, attractions, and services form an all-inclusive retail, hospitality, and entertainment complex, where people come not only to shop, but also to play and stay. The shopping malls in Edmonton are booming and offer uncountable zones, products, and services of diverse typologies, and all the activities are conceivable within one setting at WEM. Beyond the logic that WEM might be considered as a king-size shopping center, it offers a mixed immersive shopping and entertainment setting experiential enough to become the main place to visit. To respond to the growing demand for experiential and immersive shopping, WEM focuses on three vital elements:

- An ambient leisure model that suggests the creation of a pleasant and immersive shopping environment, which leads shoppers to extend their stay;
- A new generation mall model recommends that the property becomes a pleasurable place by providing fun and entertaining experiences as part of the tenant mix;
- The heritage-destination model refers to the focus on attractiveness for both shoppers and sightseers.

While today's consumers are seeking varied and captivating experiences, authors, such as Goulding (2000) and Ritzer (2004), argue that consumers will seek the consumption experience that allows them to escape their ordinary life by driving them in a pre-conceptualized, pre-established, safe, and themed sphere.

While certain authors argue that customers expect unusual consumption settings to produce strong, deep, and memorable experiences (e.g., Arnould and Price, 1993; Pine and Gilmore, 1999), others state that not all consumption experiences require an extraordinary dimension to attain immersion (e.g., Carù and Cova, 2003). Both "ordinary" and "extraordinary" consumption experiences can lead to a creation of intense immersion through special occasions (e.g., holidays and vacation are used by consumers who seek "*far niente*" or "to do nothing" to relax. They are not seeking leisure activities and extraordinary experiences, as they consider "*far niente*" as a non-extraordinary calm and relaxing experience that is highly immersive).

MINI-CASE 3.4 IMMERSION IN THE COCA-COLA PAVILION AT THE SHANGHAI WORLD EXPO

To create an immersive brand experience, Coca-Cola created an experiential pavilion celebrating the brand's culture during the Shanghai World Expo in 2010 in China. The Coca-Cola pavilion was one of the top 10 visited attractions generating more than millions of dollars of free media coverage. Inside the pavilion, Coca-Cola offered an immersive and holistic "Happiness Factory" experience to its visitors where every touchpoint in its pavilion was arranged to stimulate the senses: smell, sight, sound, taste, and touch to generate a highly emotional and community connection. To create an immersive themed environment, the Coca-Cola pavilion proposed a journey through the following steps:

(continued)

(continued)

- A "Happiness Factory Welcome" by the factory characters to amuse and welcome visitors to the pavilion;
- "Path to Happiness," which is a journey through the graphic properties of the Coca-Cola brand;
- "Bottle Through Time" refers to a journey through the historical evolution of the Coca-Cola bottle design through time;
- "Ice Story" is a collaboration with Jellymon Shanghai that brings to life five stories of ice cubes exploring their love for Coca-Cola;
- "Vintage Coca-Cola" is a journey through a collage of vintage Coca-Cola ads from around the world;
- "That Coke Feeling" is the spectacle of fizzing Coca-Cola bubbles transforming into people having a Coke moment;
- "Shanghai Skyline" is composed of animations meant to extend the experience of the Coca-Cola pavilion; it is used in their media plan to include the Shanghai Skyline and runs selected spots on the AURORA Tower for the six-month duration of the Shanghai Expo;
- "Open Happiness Karaoke" is a sing-a-long karaoke version of Coca-Cola's hit "Open Happiness."

Outside the massive pavilion, Coca-Cola bottle-shaped screens display the crowds of visitors and entertain them while they are waiting to get in.

Immersion in consumption experiences, whether they occur within ordinary or extraordinary settings, creates emotions and thus consumer satisfaction and loyalty. Though, as stated by Holt (1995), immersion and servicescape models focusing on emotional outcomes in consumption experiences tend to excessively evaluate the impact of sensorial factors as drivers of consumers' emotions. Holt suggests that there is a need for more multidimensional and holistic consumption frameworks dealing with and emphasizing the concept of immersion in the experience. Furthermore, Ritzer (2004) argues that we should examine consumer experience "re-enchantment" instead of only focusing on environmental and sensorial factors that may enhance consumer immersion to generate positive feeling and unforgettable consumption and/or purchase experiences.

THEORY BOX 3.3   WHAT DOES RE-ENCHANTMENT MEAN?

Taking a chronological perspective, this means consumers have experienced enchantment in the past and then, through imperfect present experiences, they were disenchanted before being re-enchanted in future consumption and shopping experiences.

Re-enchantment is a term used to describe practices aimed at improving the customer experience and buying experience in physical and cultural settings. The need for consumer re-enchantment in the postmodern consumer society was particularly apparent in response to the high competition in the marketplaces and the need to develop new experiences to attract customers to stores and build loyalty through the re-enchantment of consumers by designing thematic and immersive, pleasurable shopping experiences.

Offering a satisfying cognitive and emotional experience can be achieved by companies through the use of immersive digital tools and/or by focusing on immersive factors that can enable consumers to experience positive and unforgettable consumption settings, which have several advantages for firms and brands:

o   A positive influence of consumer behavior;
o   Reinforcing the memorization of brand and product information;
o   Helping consumers to be effectively involved within their experiences and social interactions with brands and salespeople;
o   Generating pleasure and stimulating consumer' senses;
o   Promoting exchanges and socialization within the marketplace.

Immersion is, therefore, necessary for the experience to be ideal, unique, and ultimate. Thus, five key immersive factors (Table 3.2) have to be considered by firms to help consumers be fully immersed: atmospheric, functional, human and social, cognitive, as well as symbolic and identity.

To make immersion optimal during a consumption or a purchase experience, the five key factors mentioned above (Table 3.2) are no longer sufficient

TABLE 3.2 Five key immersive factors

Factor	Characteristic
Atmospheric	Factors related to the external environment (temperature, smell, lighting, sounds, etc.)
Functional	Factors related to information needed to facilitate purchase (information on materials, delivery, price, functionality, etc.)
Human and social	Allow connections, establish links, and provide spaces for exchanges between customers, the brand, and its personnel
Cognitive	Related to the competence and the expertise of consumers regarding a consumption field. Consumers with superior knowledge and rich experiences will be more willing to easily immerse themselves in the universe of the brand, product or service and, therefore, enjoy their experiences
Symbolic and identity	Factors that refer to the individual's needs to define meaning in consumption practices. They can also be linked to the process of identity construction

to generate an intense customer experience in the marketplace. Companies need to take into account the "degree" of the "intensity" of the lived experience or what authors refer to as "consumer's flow experience."

- **Consumer's flow experience:** in 1968, Maslow acknowledged the idea of the *peak experience*, which is mainly relevant to the study of consumption experiences. Peak experiences are defined as instants of maximum contentment, happiness, pleasure, and fulfillment that can be attained through the experience of activities, such as art, aesthetics, nature, social experiences, and so forth. Thus, consumer's flow experience can be compared to a peak experience, in other words, an intense experience in which consumers will lose sense of chronological time and develop consciousness to be entirely in union and fused with the activity in which they engage.

    The concept of 'flow' first appeared in psychology, thanks to the works of the pioneering psychologist Mihaly Csikszentmihalyi (1990) who offered a deep analysis of the concept flow and its functioning. Csikszentmihalyi stated that the strength of the degree of immersion leads individuals to ignore their immediate setting (including the idea of time) and that the inherent recompense of the activity might lead them to search for experiences, even at high costs, for the simple purpose of doing it.

    Csikszentmihalyi defines the flow, or the optimal psychological state, as an ideal activation state in which the individual is fully immersed in the activity. In her later works, Csikszentmihalyi (1990) identifies multiple elements that are related to the onset and intensity of "flow" in an optimal experience (Figure 3.4).

    For Csikszentmihalyi, the flow experience refers to an "autotelic" dimension endowed with an intrinsic reward that is oriented towards oneself, and which finds its end in itself. In the works of Csikszentmihalyi, flow is related

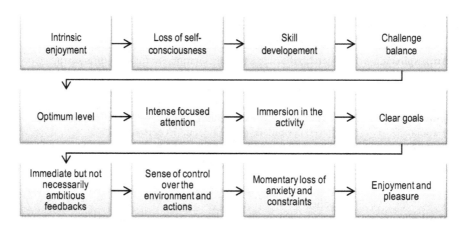

FIGURE 3.4 Flow process and steps

to the study of artists and their ability to get so profoundly immersed in painting and creating that they would ignore other areas of their life (e.g., eating,
sleeping, etc.). The activity is fully satisfying and goes well beyond the common
logic of "having fun." The idea of this experiential intensity is central since
flow is expected to arise when a setting exists that drives individuals beyond
their physical and intellectual limits without overwhelming them. The state of
intense immersion in the activity led Csikszentmihalyi (1991) to explore this
singularity, identify its roots, and the circumstances of its manifestation. The
definition of flow has two main characteristics:

○ Flow is viewed as a psychological state that grows as an individual is
  accomplishing a task and is fully involved in a sensation of attention that
  generates full immersion and enjoyment in the activity;
○ Flow is an all-inclusive, holistic feeling that individuals experience when
  they behave with full involvement.

Therefore, the consumer's flow takes place only during the experience.
Activities and behaviors attending a concert, watching a movie, practicing
tennis or swimming, viewing a captivating natural landscape, falling in love,
and so forth allow consumers to experience flow but only during a limited
amount of time, as they may disconnect if they are interacting with other social, sensorial, and environmental elements. As the flow experience generates
strong feelings, consumers could not experience it without cutouts or breaks.
For instance, consumers experience a set of successive immersions that can
lead, or not, to flow depending on the intensity of consumer immersion during a long encounter of the consumption or a purchase that is, otherwise, a
short-term experience in nature.

Amongst the conditions that lead to a state of flow within experiences is
the similarity between a consumer's activity, his/her level of competence, and
the perception of the challenge of the activity.

The challenges lived throughout an activity should also be high for flow to
happen (e.g., cleaning or doing the laundry will rarely create flow even though
it may require certain skills; however, activities such as writing a novel, painting,
or dancing will generate strong feelings of flow as long as it is applicable to the
individual's abilities). Therefore, companies should design suitable consumer
experiences that ease the access to an optimal experience, and thus lead to the
creation of flow. Marketing professionals and brand managers should heed the
following rules that lead to the creation of flow consumer experiences:

○ Experiences should suit the consumer's skills;
○ Create meaningful experiences for consumers;
○ Help consumers to set up their own goals;
○ Provide consumers with feedback;
○ Allow control and/or management of environmental elements that allow
  the immersion.

The implications of consumer experience flow can be divided into positive and negative outcomes. Csikszentmihalyi (1990) indicates that the increase of the time spent in flow may lead to:

o   Positive effects that enhance happiness, effectiveness, and feeling of well-being;
o   Negative outcomes since flow has been associated with addictions (e.g., immersive experience when playing video games) and risky behaviors (e.g., individuals who experience drugs or risky situations will need to repeat the experience, henceforth resulting in certain forms of addiction or at minimum recurrent behavior).

Drawing on the works of Csikszentmihalyi, consumer personality can also lead to the creation of flow that allows intense consumption and purchase experiences. For instance, certain traits and behaviors could be more motivated by the generation of flow than others (e.g., consumers who are curious, low self-centered, practice activities for essential motives only, have no need for extrinsic rewards and recognition).

For these consumers, the consumption experiences and actions recompense them only intrinsically, and they do not expect flow and intense immersion to fulfill their emotional, autotelic, and functional needs. Thus, the two notions of flow and immersion contribute greatly to the understanding of satisfaction in an experiential context. The difference between flow and immersion is highlighted in Table 3.3.

Both concepts can lead scholars and companies towards considering that satisfaction can be conceived as a state of being/feeling and as an outcome sought from the experience. These two concepts are essential to the analysis of the consumer/customer experience and allow for a better understanding of the extent to which some motivations translate into states of being that customers wish to achieve while shopping and/or consuming online and offline – and of the circumstances that need to be encountered for those states to occur.

TABLE 3.3 Flow vs. immersion

Element	Immersion	Flow
Characteristic	Process/state	State
Type of experience	Ordinary and extraordinary experience	Extraordinary experience (strong cognitive and emotional content and social interaction)
Duration	Short and discontinuous	Long and permanent
Emotion	Positive and/or negative	Positive
Condition	Engagement, involvement, control, and concentration	Control, temporal dissociation related to immersion, enjoyment, and curiosity

THEORY BOX 3.4 CSIKSZENTMIHALYI'S CONCEPT OF FLOW IN CONSUMPTION EXPERIENCES

Mihaly Csikszentmihalyi introduced the concept of flow, comparable to Maslow's concept of "peak experience," later. Csikszentmihalyi uses psychology to explain flow and its mechanisms. The first aim of Csikszentmihalyi's works was related to the study of artists and their level of involvement. Csikszentmihalyi defines flow in 1990 and 1991 by emphasizing

> How people describe the common characteristics of optimal experience: a sense that one's skills are adequate to cope with the challenges at hand, in a goal-directed, rule-bound action system that provides clear clues as to how well one is performing. Concentration is so intense that there is no attention left over to think about anything irrelevant, or to worry about problems. Self-consciousness disappears, and the sense of time becomes distorted. An activity that produces such experiences is so gratifying that people are ready to do it for its own sake, with little concern for what they will get out of it, even when it is difficult, or dangerous.
>
> *(1990: 142)*

One of the main fundamentals that form the existence of flow is the similarity between individual's activity, the level of abilities of the person, and the perception of the challenge of the activity. The challenges experienced during a certain activity should also be important for flow to occur. For example, culinary activities, such as cooking a meal, will hardly generate flow (even if it is possibly at the ability level of the domestic cooker), though surfing will create strong sensations of flow (as long as it is in accordance with the surfer's competencies). These consumption practices are perceived as a source that produces flow if they have been intended to ease the entry to an ultimate consumption experience: "they have rules that require the learning of skills, they set up goals, they provide feedback, they make control possible" (Csikszentmihalyi, 1991: 72).

In 1997, Csikszentmihalyi developed the tool of Experience Sampling Method (ESM) in order to examine the functioning system and process of flow. ESM includes an individual writing down on paper what he/she is doing, what he/she is thinking about, and his/her state of consciousness. Individuals are encouraged in an unsystematic way to write those parts. The findings of the ESM study indicate that individuals experience flow when practicing an activity but hardly when they are in an inactive state. For example, the study reveals that American teens experience 13% of flow when watching television, 34% when they engage in their hobbies, and 44% when they are immersed in sports and games. When examining the adult segment, work can signify a flow state

(continued)

(continued)

as well. Furthermore, the findings also showed that some characters could be more eager to generate flow than others. For example, a personality feature that represents curiosity, low self-centeredness, and the accomplishment of activities for basic reasons only, denotes an autotelic personality, which shows that the individual with this personality does not need extrinsic rewards and recognition, comfort, or power since the activities of this person engage him/her naturally and are something that people do for their own sake and not for their consequences (Csikszentmihalyi et al., 2005).

The implications of flow can be extensive and varied. Csikszentmihalyi recommends that the cumulative time spent in flow can generate positive outcomes, performance, and increases in pleasure and effectiveness. Negative facets of flow have been related to addictions (e.g., TV and video games) and risky behaviors.

Using the definition of Csikszentmihalyi, Hoffman and Novak, on the subject of online behaviors, proposed in 1996 a definition of flow applied to an online navigation experience (see Chapter 11).

MINI-CASE 3.5   RENAULT, AN ONLINE FLOW CAR EXPERIENCE

In 2008, Renault, a French car manufacturer group, launched its first experiential website. The Renault New Deal proposed the use of virtual reality and avatars to assist users and allow them to reach flow in their navigation experience. The website has many experiential components. The navigation is assisted by two virtual agents (to explain the offer of car financing), a visual space of (for) the user, and advertisement-free content. In order to allow flow, three atmospheric stimuli have been considered by Renault in designing the website: social, ambiance, and design factors.

- Social factors: virtual agents are human or unreal characters, usually embedded in the navigation experience. These agents animate the website and create social interactions during the visit, allowing users to live a full online experience and to not be disconnected since interfaces with a virtual agent are more engaging and provide more fun than those without. The presence of avatars reinforces the interaction between the user and the website, generates positive emotions, increases the perceived value of the brand, and leads to positive behavior. The agents of the Renault New Deal website are "Nicolas" and "Isabelle" and they have the ability to interact with users and answer their questions. The interaction is viewed as an interpersonal exchange, and this strong interaction gives the impression to the user that the website is personalized and adapted to his/her usages.

- Design factors refer to visual stimuli related to the organization and the structure of the website. The control bar, in particular, improves the navigability and the accessibility of the offer. The Renault New Deal website has an interactive video that combines text, images, and sounds. The component "control commands" (forward/backward, stop/resume, turn on/off, etc.) is the most frequently used design factor to get effective responses. During the browsing experience, the user engages on several levels that all together make the experience memorable.
- Ambiance factors and 3D décor. In online consumption experiences, environmental factors are important to facilitate flow by providing a sensory online environment. Three-dimensional online environments can compensate for the lack of physical contact and the reduction of the environment to the size of the screen. On the Renault New Deal website, 3D decoration is the most important environmental factor that allows immersion and flow. Audio and visual stimulations offer a hyper-real experience and are sufficient for some Internet users to immersive themselves in the real physical Renault store. The decor of the website looks very much like the Renault store in Champs Elysées avenue in Paris.

Allocentric drivers of customer experience

- **Socialization and social interactions:** socialization is one of the key drivers that contribute to the creation and the enhancement of customer experience. There are two perspectives according to which consumer socialization is studied in marketing and consumer research: (1) the stage perspective and (2) the procedural perspective.

  - In the stage perspective, consumer researchers' attention has been devoted to exploring psycho-cognitive stages and young consumers' social development. Early prominent research on consumer socialization (e.g., Ward, 1974; McNeal, 1987; Moschis and Mitchell, 1986) was based on Piaget's cognitive development theory (1975) because the theory represents the most commonly used theoretical foundation to study the learning process and the acquisition of knowledge amongst individuals within their consumption experiences.

    Essentially, Piaget proposed four periods of intellectual development (sensorimotor, preoperational, concrete operational, and formal operational) that define how an individual learns. During these stages, one assimilates information from his/her own experiences and the environment, alters or accommodates knowledge, and understands that which is already present in the mind. Piaget's four stages of intellectual development (Figure 3.5) describe both the way one thinks (e.g., concrete versus abstract) and one's interest (e.g., recognition of self versus others).

While the stage model represents a major advance in the understanding of a consumer's experience formation, critics have argued that it views consumer socialization as only a result and outcome of cognitive development and not as its principle foundation (Anderson-Cook, 2005). We can argue that such an approach assumes that consumers who receive direct influence from different social agents are considered to be passive actors, nonreactive, and unable to engage in interactive learning. Other scholars, inspired by such developments as Bandura's (1977) Cognitive Social Theory (CST), took a procedural approach to examine the main process of consumer experience formation.

o   The procedural approach of the socialization process as a driver of customer experience formation refers to a social learning process that incorporates different elements from an individual's social environment. In contrast to a cognitive approach based on stimuli and actions, Bandura's theory focuses on the reciprocity of interactions between the individual and the socialization agents involved in consumption learning. Bandura (1980) states that individuals do not only respond to stimuli, they do also interpret them. This bi-directional influence means that individuals are both producers and the product of their own environment.

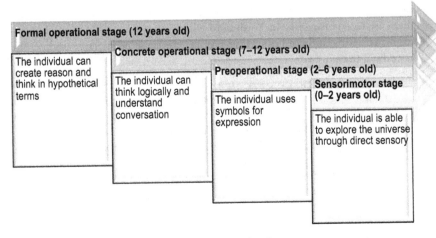

FIGURE 3.5 Piaget's four stages of intellectual development

THEORY BOX 3.5 BANDURA'S SOCIAL LEARNING THEORY: LEARNING BY OBSERVATION

Bandura's theory of social learning refers to three acquisition procedures that originate in the individual's environment: vicarious learning (results from imitation by the observation of a peer who executes the behavior to be acquired (trainer or member – leader – of the group); social facilitation refers to the improvement of the individual's performance as a result of the presence of one or more observers, which leads in many cases to group training; and cognitive anticipation – the integration of a reasoned response from similar situations, which will lead to the methods of cognitive educability – essentially implemented for adults.

According to Bandura, all the images of truth on which we found our activities, are, in fact, inspired by our experiences obtained through other individuals (vicarious experiences). We devote a lot of time in our lives to learning and acquiring knowledge through this kind of learning. Each individual constructs and develops a repertoire of other individuals he/she uses as reference points in various circumstances in his/her everyday life, such as our parents, our friends, our teachers, our co-workers, certain public figures who "inspire" us, etc. Almost without even noticing it, individuals replicate and repeat the behaviors they observe in others. However, these replicated behaviors are not automatic because people select the model and or reference, they observe it judiciously, they memorize it, and evaluate whether it is worth it to imitate these behaviors or not.

In vicarious learning, this assessment process is very critical. Indeed, it differentiates Bandura's way of seeing the learning process of other references and other schemes. Subsequently, this theory was renamed "cognitive-social learning." When people utilize their memory, they process mental images of what they have been observing in terms of behaviors performed by their models. They also use an inner discourse and they recall what they observed. From there, they make the decision to copy/imitate, or not, the behavior they observed. They can replicate it as it is or even modify it according to their objectives. The motivations of each person are different, as well as their interest in repeating the behavior. In the theory of social learning, Bandura distinguishes four main stages that change throughout the social learning process:

- Attention. It is absolutely critical that the learner's attention is concentrated on the model/reference and the behavior of the learner. Any distraction causes a disruption of the learning process.
- Retention. Memory plays a significant role in this stage. The individual who is assimilating a new behavior should stock it in his/her memory so that he/she can replicate it later on.

(continued)

(continued)

- Reproduction. In this stage, further than assimilating the behavior, the individual should be able to symbolically reproduce the behavior (e.g., one may watch for hours his/her favorite soccer player play soccer; this does not mean that he/she can replicate the movements of a professional soccer player since he/she should first develop the ability to perform the actions. Thus, there is a need to repeat actions many times in order to achieve the same results as his/her model). In addition, it requires a certain cognitive capacity in order to start all the mechanisms of symbolic recovery.
- Motivation. When we have an observed behavior in mind, we must want to imitate it. We can have different motivations for mimicking a behavior.

Following Bandura's social learning theory (1986), consumers' learning processes that will contribute to the formation and enhancement of their customer experiences can be understood according to three approaches:

- ○ Learning by imitating the behaviors of other people;
- ○ Reinforcement, which occurs in conjunction with modeling;
- ○ Social interactions through the influence of significant socialization agents.

Therefore, these two perspectives have contributed to the emergence of a number of consumer socialization models in marketing and consumer studies. Lasswell (1948) proposed the first socialization model where he established relations between five socialization agents. Therefore, I propose here a comprehensive consumer socialization model (Figure 3.6) that can help marketers

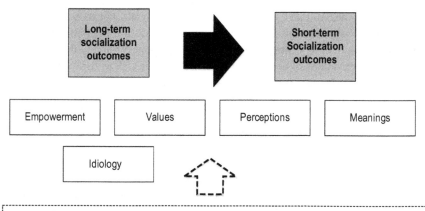

FIGURE 3.6 Consumer socialization model

and scholars to deeply examine how socialization agents contribute to and/or affect customer experiences.

As shown in Figure 3.6, socialization agents related to customer experience formation are formal or informal and may be further classified into four categories: family, peers, schools, and offline and online media. We can distinguish between two types of socialization outcomes: short-term outcomes related to consumption experience, perceptions, and meanings, and long-term outcomes that refer to the development of consumption values, ideology, and empowerment. These outcomes allow consumers to give a meaning to their consumption experiences and develop new practices and social skills according to the norms and the codes of their own consumption culture or subculture where the socialization process takes place.

- **Marketing and communication actions:** companies can undertake marketing and communication actions as allocentric drivers allowing the formation and the enhancement of customer experiences. Marketing and communication strategies aimed at the creation of experiences can be divided into four core approaches: consumer engagement, theming, storytelling, and sensory. This part continues the development of these four approaches by explaining the objectives and the components of each approach.

  o Consumer engagement: refers to the connection between the consumer and the organization (company and/or brand). This connection can be created and can evolve throughout the overall customer experience within the real place or the virtual space. Furthermore, customer engagement is about enhancing customers' interactions and exchanges within their experiences created and designed for them by the firm. When accomplished, a solid customer engagement approach will enhance brand image, positive word-of-mouth, and customer loyalty.

MINI-CASE 3.6   HOW AMERICAN EXPRESS CAPTURES THE LOYALTY OF CSP+ CUSTOMERS

To create CSP+ consumer engagement and loyalty, American Express applied an innovative and disruptive strategy that includes three main pillars:

- Creating engagement through customization by using LinkedIn data. Thanks to a partnership with LinkedIn, American Express was able to select a certain number of targeting criteria, such as school education, the number of years of experience, and the type of position and target prospect profiles to offer the most suitable map to profiles of people. This personalization was then staged through the "American Express Experience"

(continued)

(continued)

campaign. During a virtual week, each day the client was shown a key benefit of the card using a custom creative. The brand has designed experiments to educate and project prospects regarding promised benefits – access to lounges at airports, tables reserved in starred restaurants, etc.

- Disrupting the target. For the CSP+ customers being over-solicited, the goal was to surprise them. American Express proposed an application "Sleep for miles," which allowed customers to earn miles while they were sleeping. This application has been downloaded 30,000 times, received 350,000 visits, counted 100,000 registrants, and even reached the first place of the Appstore in the Entertainment category. By the end of the eighth day, the 3 million miles involved had been won. This action has allowed American Express to engage their frequent flyer target in an original way by using LinkedIn.
- Shifting from social media to social commerce. A partnership has been signed with TripAdvisor. By synchronizing cards with their TripAdvisor account, CSP+ customers can read the comments of the community of Amex cardholders and can generate them after a payment with their card. It also benefits from promotional offers and sometimes rewards in dollars.

Therefore, at American Express, including its commercial side, the customer experience is designed to be the most personalized and the easiest possible, a strategy that puts the Amex cardholder at the heart of the process.

While the human dimension is very important in a customer's experience, customer engagement can be affected by the quality of the customer's interactions with company employees (salespeople, waiters/waitresses, reception, front-desk, etc.). Thus, a good product/service alone is not sufficient, and since it does not guarantee a positive customer experience, companies need to focus on the training of their staff who are in contact with the clients and who can influence the overall customer experience. Certainly, the human dimension is a primary factor that must be taken into consideration by companies to design successful customer experiences that are pleasurable, satisfying, and memorable. Thus, several key success factors are needed to ensure qualitative training of staff in contact with customers during their experiences. The key success factors for improving the training of the staff in contact with the customers encompass four principal elements: 1) culture and the maturity of the company in terms of customer experience, 2) atmosphere of the workplace, 3) customer relationship philosophy, and 4) internal synergies for enabling a satisfactory customer experience. Considering these elements will help the company rely on a well-trained and dedicated staff who will be able to provide a memorable and satisfying customer experience.

MINI-CASE 3.7 AIR CANADA AND TOYOTA AMONGST THE BRANDS WITH REMARKABLE CONSUMER ENGAGEMENT

Consumer commitment includes both the desire to continue the relationship with the brand and the acceptance of short-term sacrifices to promote its continuation and belief in the stability of this relationship. The existence of the commitment between the brand and the consumer requires that trust reign between them; not only trust in the willingness of each partner to continue the relationship, but also trust in the loyalty of the partner. Consumer commitment can take different forms depending on the strategies and the objectives of the company. Amongst the brands that are successful in gaining consumer trust and loyalty, I can cite the following:

- Air Canada. To encourage customer engagement, Air Canada has launched a loyalty program in the form of a game accessible through a smartphone application. Each customer builds an avatar and can, as he/she travels, earn virtual rewards in the form of miles. The most loyal travelers have been featured on the company's website. This is an inexpensive operation which, according to the brand, would have generated a huge return on investment.
- Toyota. In 2003, Toyota created prepaid cards ('T') available at all dealerships. These cards are called "Our goal your satisfaction" to allow customers to give their feedback anytime and anywhere. The cards are double-folded: a red card signals a bad act; a green indicates good driving. These cards are a great success and Toyota is always amazed at the number of greetings that customers take the time to send. The key points are respect and transparency in the relationship. To build a strong and lasting relationship, Toyota should keep intact the trust that the customer has given it. Furthermore, there are other parameters that Toyota monitor, such as the processing time of incoming contacts, the service rates of the Vervins Call Center, and the Toyota Assistance platform.

o   Theming: refers to the process of creating a specific theme that allows the customer to dive into a deep thematic experience as defined by the company. Theming is a good illustration of today's contemporary societies in which the enjoyment of consumption settings can be enhanced through decors and creative contents. As stated by Baudrillard (1983), our societies are characterized by simulation and simulacra. Simulation involves service provision where the whole core product can be entirely created for the pleasure of the consumers.

The objective of the theming process is to create an atmosphere, but above all to unify the decor of customer experience. This can be done by ensuring the consistency of the theme through diverse elements of the servicescape and the physical environment that give compliance throughout the experience journey. Compliance is an essential element for successful customer experiences. It allows customers to gradually immerse themselves in the consumption and purchase experience and not escape it during the duration of the experiential process. Companies should consider theming for four principal reasons:

- Theming allows for better immersion of the consumer and can be used in many consumption areas, such as retail, services, leisure, and so forth;
- Theming also conjures a magical dimension that will make it possible to transpose the consumer into another consumption universe. The customer will, therefore, disconnect from his/her daily world characterized by external pressures related to environment and social relations;
- As stated by Schmitt (1999), themes selected by companies will be used as a mental reference by consumers and will feed pleasurable memories;
- A theme will help consumers unify the provider and organize their impressions about a place (Pine and Gilmore, 1999).

An uninterrupted themed consumption experience is considered as a new way to re-enchant the consumer during his/her purchase and consumption experiences. Marketing professionals and brand managers can apply several forms of theming that can be designed to meet marketing objectives, ranging from increasing sales volumes to creating value and the formation of branded communities. However, Gilmore and Pine (2002) argue that it is only when a theme is used that an offer (service or product) will become an experience. Furthermore, theming refers to the idea of recreating reality to make it look more real than the real object. Companies can recreate reality through two approaches:

1. Offering authentic consumption experiences to satisfy consumers with high expectations in terms of "real authenticity" (e.g., world heritage sites).
2. Offering reconstructed authenticity through hyper-real theming to meet the expectations of consumers who accept the idea of "fake authenticity" and enjoy the entertainment provided by non-authentic artifacts (e.g., Las Vegas) mixing both real and false elements.

Mossberg (2008) defines three main factors that contribute to successful theming: an arena (the experiencescape), characters (personal and other customers), and structure (construction of the story).

MINI-CASE 3.8 HARD ROCK CAFE: A THEMATIC RESTAURANT EXPERIENCE

Hard Rock Cafe is a restaurant chain founded in 1971 by Isaac Tigrett and Peter Morton. The first Hard Rock Cafe opened near Hyde Park Corner in London in a Rolls-Royce sales center where, in 1979, the walls began to be covered with ephemeral rock 'n' roll messages. There are now 139 Hard Rock Cafes in 59 countries.

The Hard Rock Cafes are enjoying a success that does not seem to be running out of steam. They all run on the same concept; the cafés exhibit on their walls unique and authentic artifacts related to the world of rock (e.g., musical instruments, photos, autographs, microphones, clothing of famous musicians, etc.). The theming of the restaurant aims to completely immerse the customer in an American universe and, more specifically, one related to the history of rock 'n' roll. Cafés usually have many video screens that loop music from the biggest rock bands with perfect sound quality. Hard Rock restaurants have a strong American flavor (e.g., hamburgers, iced tea, etc.) and the cafés are also famous for their cocktails. Souvenirs are marketed in the form of clothes, glasses, badges, etc.

○ Storytelling: a strategic tool for narrative communication that is very important for brands, especially in the field of experiential marketing. Customer experience is principally based on storytelling, which consists of telling a story to consumers in order to promote brand awareness and value by creating a universe, an identity, and an emotionally charged story. Thus, stories are made and told to reach consumers and create a strong relationship with them. Storytelling, as an integral part of customer experience design, can help companies to:

  ○ Differentiate their brands, products, and services from the competitors by sensitizing the customer to the brand's history. This will allow companies to share common values with their customers and build customer loyalty;
  ○ Place customers and their experiences at the center of the brand's history in order to create proximity with the brand;
  ○ Highlight authenticity and values as well as ideological, symbolic, experiential, and emotional dimensions of the brand.

In order to create a strong and emotionally charged storytelling, companies can also collaborate with artists and filmmakers to give more human, emotional, and historical depth to their brands, products, and services. However, the making of a story varies according to the views and goals of the company and its positioning. The storytelling can, therefore, be elaborated according to different perspectives, such as the point-of-view of the company, communication and media agencies, artists (novelists, screenwriters, etc.), sociologists, narratologists, etc. A strong storytelling can enhance customer experience by focusing on various components, such as communication and brand building, packaging enrichment, staff training (both internal and sales), and so forth. The importance of storytelling in customer experience design is twofold:

o   First, if the quality of the product is not negligible, goods necessarily require being immersed in an experiential context. Marketing and consumer researchers have shown that the happiness of customers is more linked to experiences than to products. In this sense, storytelling is able to stimulate the customer experience and can add rich references to the product.

o   Second, storytelling can provoke the narrative transport of the audience, which would lead the receivers of a story to a form of persuasion, known as narrative, something that is quite different from traditional advertising content. The specificity of narrative persuasion is related to the fact that it reduces the rational judgment of the contents of a message, and that the persuasive effects will be more resistant and marked. Thus, through brand histories, products would gain an experiential aura and would be more able to persuade current and potential customers.

Therefore, by telling a story, companies go beyond functional aspects and rational arguments often used in traditional communication campaigns. Storytelling draws its strength from the story it tells. To provide a strong and enjoyable customer experience, a good narrative story must include the following elements:

o   A strong and unique emotional content that allows the brand to be identified and differentiated from the competition;

o   A theatrical and artistic staging of the brand and the elements associated with it;

o   Visual and textual content that is significant as well as easily understood and memorized by consumers;

o   Culturally appropriate content that maintains the DNA and essence of the brand.

To create an immersive and emotionally charged customer experience, marketing managers can use several techniques. These techniques meet specific strategic objectives that highlight one or more elements of their brands.

MINI-CASE 3.9   APPLE, A GREAT EXAMPLE OF STORYTELLING

Apple, similar to other big brands, likes to tell us stories, and we often like to listen to them. Storytelling and narrative communication are subtle staging that allow the company to generate strong emotions that will make its customers more receptive to its brand. While its fans like to identify the brand as a trend rather than a company, Apple is the first example of storytelling that comes to mind. The famous "Keynotes" of Steve Jobs announcing the launch of new products (the storytelling was even renamed "Stevenotes") are the perfect expression of storytelling, as these stories were told by a charismatic leader whose admirers magnified the lyrics. Whether the stories centered around Apple's incomparable founder, the atypical creation of the company in his tiny Cupertino garage, the phenomenal success of recent years after decades of hardship and relentlessness, the launch of its new products, or the unhappy death of its creator at the height of his glory, Apple does not lose an opportunity to tell us a story that unquestionably conveys the values and philosophy of the brand. Apple creates an immersive and emotionally charged customer experience by using storytelling in its communication and advertising campaigns.

For example, in its TV commercial "Apple the Song," the brand tells consumers a story with a moving scenario. A girl discovers musical excerpts that her grandmother was holding. Over time, she will try to reproduce the piece by training on piano or guitar. The young woman manages to reproduce the notes of music, thanks to the accessories created by Apple. At the end, a grandmother who rediscovers a melody she knew in her youth may move the spectators. She then contemplates pictures of her deceased husband in a very nostalgic atmosphere. A Christmas present that can turn back 60 years of time, all thanks to a MacBook. Apple chose the right moment to unveil to the public its story: the end-of-year celebrations filled with dreams, hopes, and memories. This storytelling is like a tale or a Christmas story.

Apple knows how to make an impression for the launch of its smartphones or to celebrate the end of the year holidays, offering very simple, concise, but rich content. The company uses the talents of its customers for the benefit of the brand image. For example, the poster campaign "taken with the iPhone 6" staged photographs taken with the iPhone on giant posters and placed them in the four corners of the world.

○ Sensory marketing: is a form of marketing that appeals to the five senses (sight, sound, touch, smell, and taste) that companies use to connect their brands, products, and services with their customers on an emotional level. Sensory marketing allows companies to create stimulating and memorable customer experiences that can build emotional connections in the customers' minds by appealing to their senses. Certainly, *Harvard Business Review* (Magids et al., 2015) states that "we are about to enter an era in which many more consumer products companies will take advantage of sense-based marketing." Consequently, companies who are willing to create and enhance relationships and loyalty through the creation of memorable and touchable customers' experiences should consider sensory marketing by focusing on the translation of the five senses into practices, services, products, etc., that can induce strong emotions and feelings amongst their customers.

Most studies in sensory marketing highlight the idea that a consumer who feels good in a consumption or purchase setting (e.g., retail, restaurant, hotel, museum, gym, etc.) tends to spend more time there, consume more, and have a positive word-of-mouth. Therefore, a multisensory consumption experience based on the five senses brings together different types of marketing: olfactory, auditory, tactile, visual, and taste marketing.

ɔ Olfactory marketing: it enables the company to strengthen its identity and values. The olfactory signature is often disseminated through fragrance diffusers. It can also be integrated into products and other types of print media, such as magazines and brochures, in order to continuously reinforce the olfactory atmosphere of the brand. Companies can use the individual's sense of smell since it is appealing to the consumer's memories that can generate emotions, a sense of well-being, and nostalgia. These reactions facilitate the purchase or make the lived consumption and/or purchase experience pleasant and memorable. Thus, the sensations produced by perfumes lead the consumer to develop a strong recognition and connection with brands using their own olfactory signature to differentiate their products and services from the competitors.

MINI-CASE 3.10   HOW IS CINEPLEX USING SCENT MARKETING TO CREATE IMMERSIVE MOVIE EXPERIENCES?

Scent marketing is a form of sensory marketing that uses odors to trigger emotions in the consumer experience. Using a fragrance allows companies to immerse the customer in good conditions to buy. It is an indirect way to push to buy, by making the place more pleasant or by raising a memory, a little like the famous Madeleine of Proust. This booming form of marketing can be applied to shops, supermarket shelves, restaurants, and even cinemas. For example, Cineplex, a Canadian entertainment company headquartered in Toronto, considers fragrance as an integral part of the movie experience in which entertainment is combined with the smell of movie theater popcorn. Although it also sells pizza and other foods, Cineplex has a signature popcorn fragrance that combines with displays where movie attendees can see, hear, and smell the ambiance.

ɔ Auditory marketing: refers to special techniques and tools in choosing a product sound in a way that appears unique and attractive to consumers to buy it. The aim of auditory marketing is to broadcast sounds and music in order to influence the purchase decision-making process. Numerous studies have shown that the types of music, as well as the rhythm of the chosen pieces, have an influence on the time spent in-store and consequently, on the consumer's spending. Studies also show that consumers will go to the aisles or choose the products that are closest to the sound signal. Furthermore, the pace of diffusion and the quality of the sound also have an impact on the behavior of buyers. In customer experience design, the auditory signature is a vital element in the creation of an immersive and memorable experience. Companies must consider sound as a signature that constitutes an integral part of the customer experience design for two main reasons:

1. Auditory experience contributes to influencing customer behavior and decision-making on three levels: affective, cognitive, and conative/behavioral.
2. The auditory identity of a brand can be a collection of noises, voices, sounds, melodies, and musical compositions. Auditory marketing can be used to convey the universe, values, and identity of the brand so as to position it strongly in the mind of its customers.

The auditory/sound dimension is, therefore, an essential element to have a pleasant customer experience in immersive and emotionally charged settings.

MINI-CASE 3.11 INTEL, A POWERFUL AUDIO SIGNATURE TO BE MEMORIZED AND RECOGNIZED BY CUSTOMERS

Audio branding refers to the creation of recognizable audio signatures. It is not really a sound identity because we never hear it beyond three seconds, but it is one of the best-known brand names. The Intel jingle has been branded since the beginning with great strength and a very specific exploitation. With its audio brand, Intel was able to impose the use of its signature to all customers and partners of the brand who used its name. When Hewlett Packard or Dell made a TV or radio commercial on a computer with an Intel processor, they have the obligation to integrate the Intel audio signature.

The jingle has benefited from exceptional exposure, not only by Intel but also especially by dozens of other brands. Although the creation itself is not remarkable, it nevertheless lent itself to this game of intrusion into the communication of others with happiness. The values transmitted by this signature are the game, the good idea, and the simplicity. Paradoxically, there is nothing technological about this sound. This is its main merit, having avoided the clichés in this area to finally talk about the benefit of technology while avoiding sounding overly technological. Therefore, a strong brand must impose

(continued)

(continued)

its sound identity with force, regardless of the aesthetics or harmony of its integration into various communications.

Intel has demonstrated this perfectly. Many advertisers have cursed these four notes because they were forced to integrate them into the advertising of their own products. The fact remains that, for many, Intel is defined by this jingle. The strengths of the system: capacity for very strong memorization and an almost immediate attribution. The weak points of the system: a rather weak creation in personality – a sound that has aged quickly.

o   Tactile/touch marketing: refers to contact established between consumers and materials and elements that provide a pleasant customer experience. The sense of touch gives the consumer an impression of quality, softness, and comfort when using the product. Thus, enhancing the sense of touch through tactile marketing can influence purchase decision-making or the time spent in-store. Indeed, studies show that customers need to touch the product in order to get an idea of its quality, shape, texture, and materials. Companies must, therefore, develop a tactile signature to differentiate their products from those of the competitors and make customers want to take them in hand and buy them.

MINI-CASE 3.12   DIESEL, FOR "FUEL FOR LIFE" AND HOW TO USE TOUCH MARKETING THROUGH PACKAGING

Diesel, for "Fuel for life" offers its customers a bottle with touches of leather and straps, to perfectly match the essence of the perfume, the target, and the image of Diesel. Color code: black and gray, aged colors, and black and white. The target is young men, aged 15–35, who may want to break the rules. In terms of packaging, the bottle is shaped like a flask of whiskey, packed in brown burlap like worn jeans with apparent seams that we discover. It has a zipper to enhance the perception and feeling of masculinity.

o   Visual marketing: it refers to a visual signature that allows consumers to distinguish the identity of the brand. Visuals are important, notably through the packaging of products, decoration, layout of shops, shelving of products, etc. Colors are also important and can have a positive or negative impact on customer experience. To create a visual signature, companies should implement a set of controlled actions to create a visual identity in line with the universe and the DNA of their brands, products, and services. Brand managers and marketing professionals can use visual marketing since it has the power to act unconsciously on the customer and influence his/her perception and reactions towards the brand.

MINI-CASE 3.13 LUSH: A VISUAL EXPERIENCE IN THE COSMETICS MARKET

Sight is the most stressed sense in humans because it is the sense that is most stimulated by the environment. It should be noted that 80% of sensory information reaches the consumer through sight. In addition, visual marketing acts instinctively on the customer and affects his/her perception and his/her responses regarding the product or the point of sale. Today, it is an integral part of our consumption setting. Sight allows us, of course, to distinguish the subjective beauty of a product and to be attracted by it. Brands such as Lush can use different stimuli (e.g., color or form) by partnering with graphic designers or communication agencies to better attract the consumer to their products.

Lush's chain of stores develops cosmetics based on essential oils produced from organic vegetable materials (fruits and vegetables). The products are 100% vegetarian and 84% vegan; they are not tested on animals. The products are handmade, and all the ingredients are explained in simple language, and in the language of the country of sale. The positioning of Lush is resolutely turned towards sustainability; 60% of the product range does not contain preservatives, 62% of products can be transported without packaging, and 98% of packaging is recyclable. Black plastic, which is used in some Lush packaging, is not recyclable in domestic product circuits.

Lush, therefore, has a specific machine to transform this material into new black packaging that can be reused for additional packaging needs. The company encourages customers to participate in this recycling process by offering them a free product (a mask) in exchange for five black pots brought back into the store. Lush has also opted for transparency by providing customers with data producers of their products. In its banners, Lush has magnified the consumer experience in using all the senses of the consumer. The shops are radically changing other cosmetics brands that are rather colorfully sweet. Lush has developed stores that bring out the vibrant colors of the products. It stimulates sight in a very powerful way.

Sight is stimulated by unusual shapes of products: the colors of the products are very sharp and acidulated. These colors are highlighted by the shelving that stacks products by color. On entering the store, the customer is overwhelmed by stacks of products all more vivid in color than the last. Viewing this product presentation is an experience in itself. The products are presented as on a market stall: abundance, stacking, sale by the cut, black signs that indicate the price per kilo are planted in the products, etc.

○ Taste marketing: gustatory signature is an essential sensory element that can drive an immersive and memorable customer experience. It can also be associated with other sensory elements, such as sight or touch. Taste is not just for food, it can be used by brands to create taste experiences by combining a specific taste with a brand sphere. The aim of a gustatory approach is to seduce consumers by stimulating their taste buds and associating taste with the values of the brand.

MINI-CASE 3.14   BADOIT, THE FRENCH BRAND OF SPARKLING WATER AND THE LAUNCH OF A TASTE MARKETING CAMPAIGN

Badoit is a brand of mineral water derived from natural sources at Saint-Galmier in France. The water is naturally carbonated. Since taste marketing is more difficult to apply, most food and beverage brands conduct free tastings in the store to push the consumer to buy the product. In 2013, the historic French brand of sparkling water launched an innovative and creative taste marketing campaign in association with the gastronomic chef Thierry Marx and the French rail train company SNCF.

The Parisian subway was transformed through the "Badoit Express" operation. The trip started with a restaurant experience featuring a menu of pressed veal, lentils with foie gras, lamb with vegetables, dessert, snow eggs, and of course Badoit water – all in the subway. The 400 stunned but delighted passengers savored the meals and the media operation was a success.

The press and the news relayed the information. For Guillaume Millet, marketing director of the brand. "Badoit is historically and intimately linked to the French culinary heritage at all meals, whether everyday or exceptional," hence the idea of innovating and surprising passengers with an unprecedented operation of this kind was a great success for Badoit to show that water can be associated with a taste. By opting for a disruptive approach, Badoit surprised and took an unexpected direction by enchanting its customers in their daily transportation experience.

Markers of customer experience marketing

This part aims to identify the core markers that characterize customer experience marketing. So far, as shown in Figure 3.1, I identified five markers that illustrate the key characteristics of customer experience marketing: holistic, cumulative, subjective/personal, assemblage, and contrasting. These customer experience markers are highlighted in the section below.

Customer experience is holistic

Although the origins of holism can be traced back to philosophy, the concept itself emerged early in the twentieth century in the field of consumption, and thus customer experience. From a philosophical perspective, holism refers to the logic that certain totals are superior to the sum of their parts. This logic is supported by the anthropologist Strathern (1997) who claims that it is necessary to examine a phenomenon by mixing, crossing, and considering other domains in order to provide a profound understanding and a deep clarification of the meanings behind customer experience and an individual's functional, social, and emotional expectations.

From an anthropological and sociocultural perspective, holism refers to the study of individuals not only on a psychological level, but also by focusing on their sociocultural context, their interactions with other social actors, and their relationship to society as a whole. Whether customer experience should be considered holistic or not, is a debatable issue. From an experiential perspective, holism refers to the idea that consumers and their activities are interdependent and based on several elements: intellect, emotion, spirituality, society, and the external environment, which cannot be isolated. All are connected, related to each other, and embedded within a sociocultural consumption experience that shapes individuals' identities, behaviors, and attitudes.

Therefore, customer experience is holistic in nature as it is related to individuals with all aspects of human beings (e.g., physiological, psychological, social, economic, cultural, etc.). Thus, holism is a critical marker of customer experience that marketers should take into consideration when designing experiences, which should be embedded in a multidimensional sociocultural context in which the consumer interacts with different social actors in order to satisfy his/her functional, social, and emotional needs within a given consumption field and with relation to a specific brand.

MINI-CASE 3.15 SEPHORA CAPTURES HOLISTIC BEAUTY EXPERIENCE TO IMPROVE CUSTOMER SATISFACTION AND LOYALTY

Sephora is a French chain of cosmetics stores owned by the Luxury group LVMH that offers beauty products (e.g., makeup, fragrance, skincare, etc.). Sephora features more than 300 brands including its own private label and is present in 16 countries (e.g., France, United States, Spain, Italy, China, etc.) where the brand has been working on capturing holistic experiences to improve customer satisfaction and loyalty by launching the "New Sephora Experience," a holistically experiential and connected beauty hub that reinvents the experience of purchasing beauty products. The holistic customer experience proposed by Sephora allows its customers to express themselves by making the store an arena of freedom shaped by their own choices.

- Upon the entrance door, customers can discover the latest trends, tutorials, and new "Made in Sephora and Exclusive" signage on the table animation, renewed each month with a different theme;

(continued)

(continued)

- The path continues with the linear "Sephora Loves," highlighting the brand's favorite products as well as new brands and their iconic products;
- The "Beauty Hub," is also another great innovation that help the brand to offer the ultimate customer experience; the Beauty Hub is located at the heart of the store and offers a new way of shopping;
- The brand proposes a "Digital Look Book" that allows customers to find the inspiration to design their own beauty program with the assistance of a "Virtual Artist" that can provide them with the possibility to test thousands of looks on iPad or on a connected mirror;
- Customers can also use the "Color Profile application" that assists them in choosing a shade of foundation with optimal accuracy;
- Sephora also offers the possibility to interact and share looks, products, and opinions with the members of the beauty community through the use of a Beauty Board platform.

To enhance the holistic customer experience, Sephora set up Beauty Classes, a combination of makeup lessons and workshops delivered by beauty professionals and skin care services.

Customer experience is cumulative

Customer experience is regarded as cumulative since the experiences of the past serve to inform the present and to build future customer experiences. Cumulative customer experience means everything that follows is based on recent and past consumption experiences. The accumulative experience contributes to the sedimentation and the integration of both emotions and knowledge generated during prior and present experiences. It is thus the accumulation of all consumption experiences in various domains that creates the meanings that consumers release from all these experiences, which leave footpaths that can help other consumers decide how to approach and do things in the future. By their accumulation of consumption experiences, consumers transform their future experiences, and at the same time, they transform themselves and thus build their own experience.

MINI-CASE 3.16   HEATHROW REINVENTS THE AIRPORT CUMULATIVE EXPERIENCE WHETHER IN THE AIR, ON THE GROUND, OR ONLINE

A tourist destination with over 75 million registered passengers each year and 185 destinations served by 80 airlines in 84 countries, London Heathrow Airport is the busiest in Europe. It also has a rail link with London and many parking options. In addition, the site is one of the most profitable commercial spaces in the United Kingdom (per square meter), with more than 100 stores and restaurants in four terminals.

When the company in charge of Heathrow adopted the slogan "Make every trip more pleasant," it did not just refer to air transport. The ambition of Heathrow Airport is also to improve the **cumulative experience,** including travel to and from the airport, passenger traffic within terminals, and access to free Wi-Fi. Thanks to its progressive design, the airport also makes every digital journey more enjoyable, from organizing an online holiday to looking for shops and restaurants at one of the terminals. In order to understand the cumulative traveler airport experience and offer personalized experiences, Heathrow collects and analyzes data from all touchpoints in real time. The objective is to offer all services and useful information in one place that customers can easily access based on their needs, even though the airport, the car parks, the rail service, and the shops are all separate commercial entities, in the perception of customers, they are all part of one single experience.

Customer experience is subjective and personal

According to Weedon, subjectivity can be defined since "the conscious and unconscious thoughts and emotions of an individual, her/his sense of self and her/his ways of understanding her/his relation to the world" (1997: 32). The logic of subjectivity points out the idea of an individual's resistance to dominant discourses about consumption by adopting a personal and a subjective perspective as a response.

Customer experience is then a subjective phenomenon that is associated with a single and personal perspective. The subjective aspect of experience suggests that the perception of all objects, notions, and facts in the world differs between individuals. Across all cognitive, functional, social, and emotional dimensions, subjective experiences in the consumption field are individually unique. For instance, the same restaurant experience may be pleasant to one consumer, and unpleasant to another. Moreover, one taste may be attractive to one consumer and disgusting to another. These consumption experiences can also rapidly change and evolve within one's individual experience depending on personal factors.

Subjectivity that makes the same experience different from a personal point-of-view underscores the fact that consumption experiences are constructed from composite inputs related to a consumer's past experiences, present context, as well as the future implications and meanings of the inputs. Thus, personal subjectivity is a permanent and essential part of the consumer experience. The way customers live their experiences and view things around them involves personal subjectivity, which defines whether they like or hate the components of their customer experience, such as taste, smell, style, decor, music, atmosphere, social interactions, etc. Therefore, a subjective and personal customer experience is the outcome of the individual's mind. It is uncertain if two people could have the same subjective perceptions of their customer experience. Consumers may have comparable, but not the exact same perceptions. For instance, consumers can like the same music and atmosphere but perceive them differently. It is very common for individuals who are supposed to share the same tastes (e.g., best friends) to like a movie experience, but one may like it more or less than the other for diverse motives.

Customer experience is an assemblage

Customer experience is an assemblage of several dimensions: sensorial (five senses), physical (environment), relational (social interactions), emotional, and cognitive (functional benefit). Pine and Gilmore (1999) argue that all these dimensions can help consumers to fully live their experiences. The idea of assemblage as a framework was first introduced by French philosophers Deleuze and Guattari in 1980. Assemblage stems from the French word, which refers to the integration and connection between various heterogeneous elements and concepts that provide a coherent meaning. The composition of these heterogeneous dimensions interact with each other (cognitive and emotional, rational and irrational, etc.) forming as Bennett (2010) states, "ad hoc groupings of diverse elements of all sorts," and thus new emerging experiences.

THEORY BOX 3.6   THE FOUNDATION OF DELEUZE'S THEORY OF ASSEMBLAGE

The assemblage theory is a way of reflecting on the consumer society and its paradoxes. The main foundation of this theory is that stable and fixed components do not exist, but rather social constructions are assemblages of other composite arrangements that form more complex configurations, and thus exclude static thinking. Assemblages include mixed components or items that are not all of the same type. The assemblage theory advocates a distinctive set of interpretations of social realities, such as patchwork and liquid identities, heterogeneities, assortments, etc. For example, a country contains populations, businesses, infrastructures, administrations, government policies, political movements, etc.

Drawing on Deleuze and Guattari, I define assemblage as a key marker of the customer experience since it reflects the dynamic combination of heterogeneous elements, behaviors, and attitudes, which can be individual, subjective, social, economic, environmental, emotional, symbolic, functional, rational, etc., and that capture the heterogeneity of the experience in making and shaping numerous personal consumption experiences.

If we are to consider assemblage as a marker of customer experience, it is essential to accept the several heterogeneous attitudes and behaviors that are developed during an assemblage of consumption experiences, which encompasses, as described by Schmitt (1999), a mix of five principle categories:

- Sense: sensory experiences;
- Feel: affective experiences;
- Think: cognitive experiences;
- Act: physical experiences, behaviors, and lifestyle;
- Relate: social experiences that result from belonging to a group or a culture.

Without a particular collection of these interconnected characteristics, yet varied elements, it may be difficult to have a whole and a satisfying customer experience. Therefore, we cannot separate or isolate one element from the entire experience assemblage; as stated by Dewey in his study of art experience "in every experience, there is the pervading underlying qualitative whole that corresponds to and manifests the whole organization of activities" (1934: 204). Moreover, any reorganization of these heterogeneous elements would form a totally distinct assemblage, and therefore, a wholly different customer experience. Thus, consumption experiences are concerned with the perceptual whole, which refers to a grouping of variables that form the customer experience of the perceiver.

Customer experience is contrasting

One of the main markers of customer experience is the contrasting effect that refers to the existence of juxtaposition of opposite elements, attitudes, and behaviors that are part of the same experience and the same individual who can express both hedonic and utilitarian benefits – and can show both cognitive and emotional attitudes within the same consumption experience. While utilitarian experiences are more cognition-oriented, functional and tangible-attributes focused, hedonic experiences are more about pleasure, enjoyment, and socialization.

Consumers can have both hedonic and utilitarian motives related to several cognitive, behavioral, and affective responses. For instance, hedonism and utilitarianism are comparable in their contribution to pleasure or happiness. In contrast to prior works, as stated by Khan, Dhar, and Wertenbroch (2004), while in the domain of consumer decision-making that suggests that products could be viewed as either hedonic or utilitarian (e.g., luxuries vs. necessities, affect-rich vs. affect-poor goods), the experiential perspective states that a product/brand experience cannot be considered exclusively hedonic or utilitarian, since both of these characteristics are reflected and assessed in the decision-making process of consumers who behave in both rational and emotional ways at the same time. In particular, customer experience typically encompasses both hedonic and utilitarian dimensions, built on intrinsic product features, use, and consumption settings. For instance, when making a purchase decision concerning a sneaker, a buyer is expected to assess both its practical qualities (e.g., comfort, resistance) and its aesthetic and social characteristics (e.g., the stylishness, brand image). The importance of either one of these attributes should help decide whether the sneaker is principally utilitarian, hedonic, or both.

MINI-CASE 3.17   AIR NEW ZEALAND, DELTA, AND VIRGIN AMERICA USE OF AIRLINE SAFETY VIDEOS AS EDUTAINMENT FOR EXPERIENTIAL LEARNING

Edutainment can be applied by brands to create entertaining experiences and educate/inform their customers. The use of this strategy can help the brand to connect with its actual customers and build affinity amongst potential customers. It shows the ability of the company to use humor in creative informational and educational campaigns that are most of the time perceived by customers as useless and boring. Airline safety videos created by companies, such as Air New Zealand, Delta, and Virgin America are interesting examples that show the relevance of using edutainment, each one with its own style, humor, and storytelling, to make their passengers pay attention to onboard safety instructions.

- In late 2012 and 2014, Air New Zealand produced a themed in-flight safety demonstration video to coincide with the announcement of the film *The Hobbit: An Unexpected Journey*. The video featured passengers, cabin crew, and pilots dressed like characters from the movie, which featured famous film actors (e.g., Elijah Wood, Sylvester McCoy). Movie director Peter Jackson also made an appearance in the safety video, which ends with the slogan, "The Airline of Middle-Earth."
- In 2013, Virgin America launched an over-the-top musical in-flight safety video featuring singer Todrick Hall from *American Idol*. The video, well-choreographed and performed with dancers from *So You Think You Can Dance*, demonstrated everything related to in-flight safety by embedding the instructions in a musical and a humorous environment, from a religious dance to a kid rapping about oxygen masks.
- In 2012, Delta Airlines launched a creative retro in-flight safety demonstration video featuring the celebration of 80s pop culture in which passengers are dressed in 80s-style clothing with big hair, leg warmers, and Rubik's Cubes. The video also features well-known personalities of 80s pop culture sitting in the co-pilot's seat as a reference to an in-flight comedy.

As a result, not only did passengers pay attention to in-flight safety instructions, but they also memorized them, and tended to share their experiences with others. The idea of edutainment is to entertain while educating customers about the brand, the way they can use brand's products, and aspects of safety.

Outcomes of customer experience marketing

The focus in this part is on the four main outcomes of customer experiences: value, transformation, competency, and memorability that professionals can consider within their marketing and communication strategies. Given that goods and products are also bought for what they symbolize, it is critical for companies to know what kind of outcomes their brands and offerings (products and services) endorse in the eyes of actual and potential customers.

Value

The perception of value is essential to the enjoyment and satisfaction of consumers and is consequently of huge significance to companies. The key values companies address are reliant on the consumers' personal perceptions: economic, functional, individual, and social outcomes of their customer experiences that are strongly interconnected, but not indistinguishable from each other.

Although the four dimensions cited above are commonly used in marketing and consumer studies, the definition of customer value is still a topic of discussion. Several authors have different categorizations of customer value. The analysis of the literature led us to consider the following classification of consumer values:

- Value-in-exchange. Includes four main forms of values 1) low cost; 2) what the consumer needs in a product or a service; 3) the quality a consumer gets for the price he/she pays; and 4) what the consumer gets for what he/she gives. Value-in-exchange refers to the economic aspect of consumer value and is the most widespread in the marketing field. Value-in-exchange is also used by Kotler and Keller (2006) and continues to dominate research today; customers perceive value in the exchange of product for the price they pay.
- Value-in-marketplace. Based on Woodall's (2003) comprehensive destruction of value, which describes five forms of consumer values: net value, marketing value, sale value, rational value, and derived value.
- Value-in-time. Woodall's longitudinal perspective on value provided four temporal and staged forms. Value-in-time covers concepts over four stages that correspond with four stages of experience: 1) ex-ante (anticipated) value, 2) transaction (purchase) value, 3) ex-post (consumption) value, 4) and disposition (remembered) value.

- Value-in-use. This is related to service dominant logic and the findings of Vargo and Lusch (2006) who emphasize this idea that supports the value-in-use logic – the service. In other words, the service is what is usually traded, and goods become a unique way of service delivery. This perspective emphasizes customer-orientation and the relationships with the service provider, showing profound and more composite relations between sellers and buyers. The service attitude generating qualitative and positive connections allows suppliers to develop a full understanding of co-creating and sharing value with their customers.

- Value-in-possession. This defines material values as the propensity to place possessions and their purchase as fundamental in a consumer's life. Possessions are then seen as a means to happiness and as an indicator of one's own and others' success. Furthermore, possessions involve an extended self (Belk, 1988), demonstrate a meaning receptacle, and produce an affiliation.

- Value-in-experience. Holbrook (1994) proposed a typology of consumer value-in-experience with three dimensions:

  o Extrinsic/intrinsic: the consumer perceives value in using or owning a product or service as a means to an end versus an end in itself;
  o Self-/Other-oriented: the consumer perceives value for the consumer's own benefit versus for the benefit of others;
  o Active/reactive: the consumer perceives value through direct use of an object versus apprehending, appreciating, or otherwise responding to an object.

Transformation

What makes individuals decide whether or not to undergo certain permanent changes in their behaviors such as becoming vegan, taking drugs, getting married, having a child, leaving the county, embracing another religion, etc.? Transformative consumption experience responds to these interrogations by showing how the transforming effects of adaptation permeate the daily lives of consumers who were transformed by an intensive experience that offers a cognitive and emotional rearrangement: a new set of beliefs, values, and desires replaces previously held consumption beliefs, values, and desires in a particular consumption setting.

However, less attention has been given to the role of consumption experience as an agent of irreversible change and fundamental transformation of individuals. Thus, the main idea of a transformative experience as an outcome of a customer experience is that an experience is both fundamentally original to the consumer and capable of modifying his/her behaviors and identity in a profound and ultimate manner. Transformative consumption experience raises questions about how consumers could rationally make decisions about their future experiences when they stand at a crossroads in life. Therefore, experiences such as getting married, becoming a grandparent, discovering a new faith, immigrating to a new country, or living in a war zone are all transformative experiences that might generate irreversible changes in an individual's social life, and thus his/her future customer experiences.

Competency

Another direct outcome of customer experience is related to competency construction. More than learning from past or present consumption experiences, consumers develop creative potential and competencies by living experiences that evolve throughout their childhood, adolescent lifecycle, and adulthood. In marketing and consumer studies, the concept of consumer competence has emerged in recent works on consumption knowledge.

Bonnemaizon and Batat (2010) define consumer competence that emerges from past and present consumption experiences according to three dimensions: cognitive, or the ability to interpret marketing messages; instrumental, or the ability to use products before, during, and after the consumption process; and usage or the ability to express one's self regarding the products and services provided by the company. Very little research has explicitly utilized consumer competence as an outcome of lived consumption experiences. The majority of works, such as Alba and Hutchinson (2001), Carlson et al. (2009), and Park and colleagues, (1994) focus on consumer knowledge and skills using the concept of consumer expertise, which refers to cognitive knowledge and the process by which consumers encode and memorize relevant information to optimize their purchase. Thus, while dimensions of competence have been studied, overall competence and its creative potential as an outcome of consumption experiences have not.

Memorability

Memory and memorable experiences are also considered as one of the outcomes of the customer experience. Baddeley and Logie define memory as "an alliance of systems that work together, allowing us to learn from the past and predict the future" (1999: 1). Memory is the most important personal outcome as well as a subjective source of information through which consumers decide whether to relive an experience, repurchase the same product/brand, revisit a place, etc. However, "memory" is a more overall notion than "memorability," which, as stated by Carù and Cova (2003), refers to something unforgettable or extraordinary, whereas memory can be rather ordinary or mundane. A memorable customer experience is defined as a significant episode kept in the memory of the consumer and recalled after it has happened.

Memorability as an outcome of customer experience can be constructed in a selective manner based on lived consumption experiences that are influenced by the consumer's emotional evaluation from his/her own perspective. If the evaluation is positive, then the experience memorability can strengthen and reinforce the recall of pleasurable happenings experienced by the consumer while engaging in consumption activities, such as shopping, visiting a destination, enjoying a film, etc. That is why it is crucial for companies to ensure that their customers will have unforgettable positive experiences while in contact with the company's offerings since the memorability of a consumption experience is as critical as it is holistic in nature, and encompasses social interactions and the influence of external and environmental factors.

Summary

This chapter introduced the customer experience marketing framework and its three main stages: makers, drivers, and outcomes. The knowledge of consumer experience is very critical in determining the success of a brand. Examining customer experience marketing implies analyzing what a consumer goes through during the pre-experience, experience, and post-experience stages and seeks to identify the impact of the factors related to each stage to better design and create future experiences that are both satisfying and profitable.

PART II

The new experiential marketing mix (7Es)

4

EXPERIENCE

Experience Territory Matrix (ETM), stages, and EXQUAL tool

Purpose and context

Pine and Gilmore (1998) state that companies can achieve a competitive advantage and differentiate themselves within a highly competitive market by producing experiences instead of products. Experience should then be considered as a new category of offer that can be marketed to consumers. Also, companies can produce experiences by taking a consumer-centric approach that focuses on cognitive, emotional, physical, intellectual, or even spiritual aspects. This chapter focuses on the offer of "experience" itself as the first component of the "7Es" of the experiential marketing mix that replaces the "P" of product, which is part of the traditional marketing mix or 7Ps. Then, I define new tools, such as the Experience Territory Matrix (ETM), which can be used by companies to create and design a suitable, satisfying, and profitable customer experience, as well as the EXQUAL tool to measure and improve the quality of customer experiences.

Learning outcomes

At the end of this chapter you will learn about one of the "7Es" of the experiential marketing mix "Experience," its dimensions, stages, typologies, and how companies can use efficient strategic planning tools to measure the quality of the experience and design experiences through a consumer-centric approach that makes customers not only feel satisfied about the company's offer (products and services) but also respected, considered, and valued by the company and its employees. This will guarantee long-term loyalty through enchantment, and re-enchantment of the customer.

Experience Territory Matrix (ETM)

In this chapter, I designed the Experience Territory Matrix (ETM), a tool that helps companies manage their portfolio based on experiences instead of products. The ETM matrix (Figure 4.1) is also a long-term strategic planning tool that helps a business consider opportunities by reviewing its portfolio of experiential offerings and the way they are perceived by its customers to decide where to invest in order to improve the quality of customer experience, to renew the offer or services, and to develop new experiences to maintain customers. Other authors in marketing (e.g., Pine and Gilmore, 1998) offer a classification of customer experience types; however, that classification is dependent upon the context of consumption rather than customer perception of his/her own experience with the company. The ETM matrix introduces four typologies of customer experiences that regard a customer's perception of respect and the company's customer-centricity.

Prior works, such as Pine and Gilmore's (1998), categorized customer experiences into four core classifications: entertainment, educational, escapist, and aesthetic. These four customer experiences are classified according to two bi-polar constructs, ranging from "absorption" to "immersion" and from "passive" to "active" participation. The entertainment element encompasses experiences that involve absorption with passive consumer participation. This category includes activities where the consumer is completely absorbed in his/her activity, but his/her behavior is relatively passive since there are not various contacts with other individuals or the company (e.g. watching television, reading a book).

The educational experience also refers to consumer absorption, but he/she has the potential to be more actively involved in the delivery. This could be the case of a class or a guided tour where the consumer listens to the information given, is absorbed by the activity, but can actively contribute (e.g., by asking questions, exchanging information, working in groups). The third category, escapist, designates situations and consumption settings in which consumers are in immersion with the activity and active in its delivery. For instance, skiing or skydiving is an example of an experience where customers will learn or be entertained and will be fully immersed within their activity. The last category, aesthetic, includes identical levels of immersion, but in a more passive form (e.g., attending an exhibition).

Pine and Gilmore argue that the richest experiences involve aspects relating to those four realms. Though, in different experiential settings, the four types of experiences might be juxtaposed, transformed into other experiences (e.g., if the absorption is strong enough, the education realms can be transformed into an escapist category), and occur at different times during the whole duration of the experience.

Therefore, I contribute to the Pine and Gilmore framework by offering two new perspectives: the customer as well as the company, rather than only one perspective that focuses on consumer absorption and participation as it is the case with Pine and Gilmore typologies. The two additional perspectives led me to consider

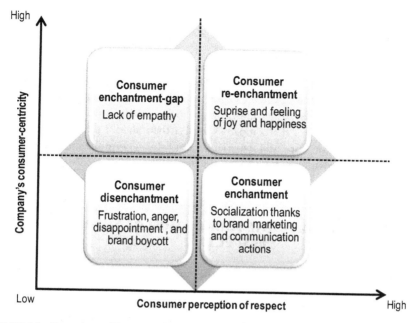

FIGURE 4.1 Experience Territory Matrix

two bi-polar constructs: consumer's perception of respect and company's customer-centricity to identify four "experiential territories," namely, enchantment, re-enchantment, disenchantment, and enchantment-gap (Figure 4.1).

- The construct of the consumer's perception of respect refers to a customer's feeling of being respected from his/her own perspective. Indeed, the question of how customers are treated and whether they feel that the company respects them plays a vital role in improving customer experience and enhancing loyalty by building quality and valued interpersonal relationships, which have a positive influence on customer-to-firm connections (e.g., Costley, Friend, and Babis 2005; Berry, 1996; 1995). Thus, this construct suggests that "respecting customers" is a major component that consumers take into consideration when evaluating their consumption experiences and reconsidering their relationships with the firm.

A consumer's perception of respect is vital in gaining and developing customer loyalty to the company. Although respect is a relevant construct for examining feelings and the quality of the consumption experience as perceived by customers – and while in the marketing field, the "feeling of respect" is assumed to be a significant factor in effective marketing relationship (e.g., Bitran and Hoech, 1990; Costley, Friend, and Babis, 2005), the concept of respect is poorly defined (e.g., Dickert and Kass, 2009) and is not broadly used in consumer research and customer experience.

Drawing upon research in service marketing literature (e.g., Ali and Ndubisi, 2011; Costley, Friend, and Babis, 2005; Dillon, 1992), consumers' perceptions of respect can be divided into three categories: attention and valuing, understanding, and responsibility. These three dimensions can be used to measure a consumer's feeling and perception of the company's respect that ranges from poorly respectful experiences to highly respectful experiences, and thus define the customer experience territory following the four boxes of experience territories.

THEORY BOX 4.1   THE FOUNDATION OF THE NOTION OF "RESPECT"

The notion of 'respect' is not unusual to most people, even if they come from different cultures. It is used very widely in people's daily lives, whether on an individual or professional level. Although the term respect does not need a definition since everyone understands it, in current human science literature, it is very difficult to find a clear definition; the concept remains very complex, even if there are several philosophical foundations. Kant (2011) argues that the notion of respect has become, for us, inseparable from that of the obligation to perform well through reverence to moral law, which is the "rational motivation" of this "moral feeling." Respect refers first and foremost to respect for the law.

The anthropological contribution to respect shows that respect is not only a matter of observing and respecting the rule or obeying the norm, it is also a matter of dealing with the consideration of things, people, or an environment. It seems then necessary to question the emergence of a right to respect or, even more, the existence of autonomy as it relates to the concept of respect. Even though the notion of respect is extensively employed in our societies, its characteristics and outcomes have to be studied. In the marketing field, in particular, service marketing literature, the "feeling of respect" has a strong impact on consumer satisfaction and loyalty, and is considered as a major determinant of successful marketing relationships with the brand.

- The second construct of a company's customer centricity refers to the ability of firms to develop a solid management commitment, organizational shift, schemes and process support, and revised financial metrics (Shah et al., 2006). Customer centricity refers to a comprehensive framework for customer feedback or customer satisfaction outcomes; however, Kroner (2017) states that making consumers happy is only a single aspect of the balance. To construct an enduring achievement, businesses should understand modern customer requirements and wants, and guarantee that there are the appropriate internal and customer-facing approaches, programs, and marketing actions in place to please and fulfill them.

According to Shah and colleagues, while the product-centric logic is based on the idea of merchandise exchange and the facilitation of the exchange of goods, the consumer-centric paradigm highlights the growing awareness of the needs of the customer by focusing on customer-connected aspects comparable to satisfaction, loyalty, the perceived quality of services (e.g., Rust, Moorman, and Dickson 2002), market-orientation (e.g., Narver and Slater, 1990), market-based learning (e.g., Vorhies and Morgan 2005), and market-driven organization (e.g., Day, 1999; 2000). Figure 4.2 summarizes the shift from product-orientation logic to market-orientation logic.

Drawing on research in service literature, especially the works of Shah and colleagues (2006), there are five main changes underpinning the need for companies to be more customer-centric:

1. Intensification of pressures to improve marketing productivity;
2. Growth in market diversity;
3. Evolution of competition;
4. Challenging and well-informed customers;
5. Accelerating advances in technology.

Companies can develop a strong customer centricity, and thus offer an ultimate customer experience by overcoming a set of obstacles that includes four main elements: organizational structure, firm's culture, process, and financial metrics.

These variables can be used to evaluate the level (high or low) of the customer centricity, and thus identify the customer experience territory. In fact, in such a competitive environment, customer centricity is the best tool for companies

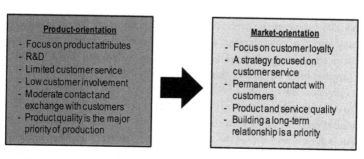

FIGURE 4.2 The shift from product-orientation to market-orientation

MINI-CASE 4.1 HOW AMAZON IS CREATING CONSUMER CENTRICITY

Amazon, a giant of the GAFA group (Google, Amazon, Facebook, and Apple), rethinks trade by implementing consumer-centric strategies and continually revolutionizing its industry since its creation in 1994. To develop consumer centricity, Amazon launched many actions and programs that focus on the impact of each action and decision of the company that may affect the product or service marketed, and, therefore, the lived consumer or shopping experience. In contrast with the traditional "top-down" modes of operation (from the management towards the final customer) by which companies remain convinced of knowing "what is good for their customers," customer-centric companies, such as Amazon, will instead favor the "bottom-up" approach and seek to collect a maximum of data produced by their customers (e.g., notices left on a forum, comments on a social network, satisfaction survey data, etc.).

The announcement of the recent acquisition of Whole Foods, a chain of large organic food distributors, and its 491 stores by Amazon, can tell us more about how consumer-centric Amazon is. Furthermore, the opening of its bookstore in New York reflects a very concrete conversion of the consumer centricity philosophy into good practices.

- Amazon Bookstore has transformed its website into a concrete reality. This new generation bookstore has been imagined as a website. The different movements in the store are like the page-to-page browsing of a website.
- A data-connected logic. One of the first tables in the bookstore is composed of a selection of the best-rated books. The selection is updated in real time through the use of data throughout the store.
- Specific space for Kindle favorites and "lovers." Amazon proposes a selection of books that Kindle readers can end up finishing in less than three days. Once again, Amazon suggests a "consumer-centric" approach by offering a selection based on the community of readers, rather than a classic highlight with the novelties and selections of booksellers.
- The "You may also like" feature. One of the most striking examples of the parallel between the website and the physical store is the selection "you may also like," which offers a selection of complementary books based on previous readings that we liked. Always in the image of a site that offers complementary products based on our previous selections, this section is its physical transcript.
- Customer testimonials for new generation product labels. Rather than just a label with the price and the bar code, the Amazon bookstore labels are true advisers and reveal the opinions of customers who have already read the book, as well as the overall score and the total number of testimonials.

- Connected loyalty. The bookstore is urging customers to join Amazon's online loyalty program, Prime. Scans recall price differences for members and non-members to bolster and encourage participation in Amazon's loyalty program.

Furthermore, the new Amazon bookstore is a fun and experiential space where physical retail and e-shopping are fused, in terms of user and customer experiences.

to create and develop close and lucrative relationships with their customers – a benefit that is tough for competitors to understand, copy, or displace (Day, 2000 in Shah et al., 2006).

Therefore, the ETM matrix is based on customer experience from a customer point-of-view, rather than on a company's offering or experience mapping; however, it does apply to both. The firm can use it if reviewing a range of experiences, mappings, or offerings (products and services), especially before starting the development of new products and services, by examining four core customer experience territories: enchantment, re-enchantment, disenchantment, and enchantment-gap. These concepts offer a reasonable justification of the paradoxes related to the subjectivity of customers and the way they perceive their consumption and shopping experiences within particular consumer cultures.

Enchantment territory

Satisfaction is not enough to retain customers who need to be enchanted, respected, surprised, and valued by the company and its employees. The concept of enchantment has been used in the field of marketing and consumer research by Ostergaard, Fitchett, and Jantzen (2013) who discussed Ritzer's (2009) enchantment theory and introduced the concept of consumer disenchantment as a critique of modern industrialized society: "societies can be described as disenchanted worlds in that they are characterized as having limited and peripheral space for enchantment, such as magic, religion, mysticism, and wonder" (Ostergaard, Fitchett, and Jantzen, 2013: 337).

In the ETM matrix, customer experience enchantment can be produced when a customer's perception of respect is high and the company's consumer-centricity is low. This means that the customer is enchanted in his/her relationships with other consumers, although the company's customer-orientation is low. In fact, strong social interactions amongst customers in experiential settings when the company or the brand is present can help the company to enchant its customers even if its customer-centricity is low since customers may show satisfaction because they network, meet and connect with new people, build social bonds, develop their social capital and social network, etc. Thus, customer enchantment is essentially related to the pleasure and the enjoyment resulting from the social experience in which the brand is present. Customers might then associate the brand with their enchantment, and thus develop a feeling of being respected by the company. Social pleasure is then the result of an individual's interactions with others or absence thereof, as in the pleasure of being alone.

Therefore, companies have to enhance the social experience of their customers by not only organizing events, but also by facilitating the interactions and the socialization amongst customers who have similar interests, values, behaviors, etc.

MINI-CASE 4.2   A GIANT SPRITE SODA MACHINE IN BRAZIL TO ENCHANT CUSTOMERS

On the Brazilian beaches of Rio de Janeiro, the temperature can sometimes reach up to 40°C (104°F). To cool off, nothing is more tempting than drinking a cold drink or taking a cold shower. Sprite, a product of the famous Coca-Cola soda brand group, decided to use this constraint to enchant its customers through a creative and experiential communication campaign.

To promote the refreshing aspect of its drink, the brand had the idea to install giant showers, drawing again from the look of fountains with soda, which one finds, in particular, in fast food signs. The holidaymakers were able to put themselves in the skin of a plastic glass and enjoy the refreshing effect of this giant shower. For the greatest pleasure of all, the concept of the "Sprite shower" is born. Some passers-by wondered whether it was water or soda flowing from these fountains. Of course, the brand has used only water throughout its operation. As a reminder, Sprite is a transparent soft drink, the confusion is far from impossible, and it has certainly had to be addressed in the spreading of the message.

To extend this action of communication, and invite other vacationers to discover this incredible giant shower, Sprite drinks were evenly distributed on the beach. This is a successful marketing operation that enchanted people and emphasized the freshness meaning of the product by embedding it within people's experience on the beach. At the same time, this operation was also a good way for the brand to experiment with its new concept. Indeed, the brand, official sponsor of the 2014 Football World Cup in Brazil, installed these showers in the locker rooms of the various stadiums throughout the country.

Re-enchantment territory

As shown in the ETM matrix, customer experience re-enchantment can be produced when customer's perception of respect is high and the company's consumer-centricity is high. This means that the customer is re-enchanted and positively surprised by the way the company treated him/her. In terms of feelings, customers might feel, not only respected by the company, but also valued, considered, and unique.

MINI-CASE 4.3   THE FRENCH RAIL TRAIN SNCF TO RE-ENCHANT ITS TRAVELERS WITH ITS CAMPAIGN "WELCOME, GOODBYE"

To compensate customers' dissatisfaction, the French rail train company SNCF produced a creative viral video with the partnership of the communication agency DDB Paris. To promote their services, SNCF has "trapped" travelers who take the train to go to work or home in different train stations across France.

The "Welcome, Goodbye" campaign installs this new brand philosophy and values of the proximity approach of Voyages-sncf.com by making it the most considerate tour operator through anticipating the needs of its customers (before, during, and after travel), and honoring their voyages with a creative idea that marks their spirit: welcoming or wishing bon voyage to travelers in a surprising and unexpected way by capitalizing on a detail of their personal life (e.g., the heavy metal fan found himself face-to-face with a group coming to play him a piece or the martial arts fan in the middle of ninjas and Shaolin monks, etc.).

Through a more personalized approach and with the implementation of new support services, Voyages-sncf.com wants to provide its customers with more than just selling them a ticket. In the first week, the campaign recorded more than 1 million views on YouTube and attracted more than 15,000 fans on the company's Facebook page.

Disenchantment territory

As shown in the ETM matrix, customer experience disenchantment can be produced when both the customer's perception of respect and the company's consumer-centricity are low. This means that the customer is frustrated, disappointed, and upset because of his/her feeling of being disrespected by the company, which does not employ a policy that is centered on its customers and their functional and emotional needs. This will produce a negative experience that leads the customer to look for other brands, products, and services offered by companies that provide them with respect and positive experiences.

MINI-CASE 4.4 H&M FACES CUSTOMER DISENCHANTMENT AND BOYCOTT OVER RACIST HOODIE ADVERTISING CAMPAIGN

For the launch of its new collection, the Swedish company H&M published a photograph of a black boy with a hoodie that reads "Coolest monkey in the jungle." This photograph was judged racist, especially when compared to a white child's hoodie where it says "Expert in survival." H&M has been at the heart of its self-made controversy on social networks.

It was a model and fashion blogger who was first to denounce the photo on her Twitter account. Her post has been shared more than 13,000 times and has been liked not fewer than 15,500 times, gaining an international scale and arousing in passing many reactions from users. While many say they are shocked, others denounce the hysteria of the web, and some even mention a voluntary provocation on the part of the brand. H&M apologized and removed the photograph from its site, leaving only a photograph of the hoodie. However, despite the excuses and the withdrawal of the photo, anger is still rumbling on social media and forums.

Enchantment-gap territory

The enchantment–gap experience is produced when a customer's perception of respect is low and the company's consumer-centricity is high. This means that the customer does not feel respected by the company, although the company's strategy is customer-oriented. This *decalage* (mismatch) between the company's approach and the customer's perception can be explained by the lack of deep understanding of the meanings customers attribute to their experiences. This leads the company to develop inefficient tools that do not capture the real feeling of customers that would otherwise help them to improve their experiences as they relate to their own perceptions of what is respectful or not.

MINI-CASE 4.5 EPSON PRINTERS AND PLANNED OBSOLESCENCE

Printers, such as those sold by the brand Epson, are emblematic of planned obsolescence. Some of these materials would have been equipped with a chip that blocks printing beyond a certain number of printed sheets. The ink cartridges may also indicate an incorrect ink level to cause the user to discard cartridges still containing ink despite the fact that these practices are prohibited in Europe. Because of these practices, the customer does not feel respected by the company, although the company's strategy is customer-oriented, in terms of product and service quality, assistance, etc. This situation creates a *decalage* between Epson and its customers who feel betrayed by the company.

Stages of customer experience

According to O'Sullivan and Spangler (1998), companies should follow five steps to design a successful customer experience:

1. User involvement: physical, mental, emotional, social, and spiritual;
2. User's co-participation in the product's offer;
3. The relevance of the product's or service's symbolic values;
4. The product's or service's multi-functionality;
5. The centrality of experience in consumption.

Following the experiential approach, consumers become active economic actors involved in their consumption experiences. Furthermore, the role of companies is to assist their customers in the production and achievement of their experiences.

MINI-CASE 4.6 THE STAGES OF THE TOURISM EXPERIENCE: EXAMPLES FROM WILDLIFE WATCHING

The experience has to be considered from the decision-making step up to the post-purchase step. While every tourism experience is different, some basic principles can be identified to guide providers.

Before the purchase

Because tourism products are intangible and can only be really appreciated *in situ*, it is important to provide as many indications as possible about the experience that individuals will live if they choose to consume the service. To this effect, new technologies, particularly, websites and smartphone applications provide a range of tools that can help consumers get a more realistic feel of their experience. Those include videos, photos, along with real-time information (webcams, meteorological forecasts, snow forecasts, etc.) and consumers' feedback (links to rating sites, blogs, consumers comments, etc.). Of course, the tone and content of the text provided in brochures, websites, and other communication support systems will also have its importance. Creating emotions, engaging various senses, and developing adequate storytelling about the product will be key points in eliciting the desire to live the experience by future consumers.

Before the experience

Once the service has been booked, it is essential to prepare customers for the experience. While it is important not to kill off the surprise effect by giving too

(continued)

(continued)

much information beforehand, in some instances, previous information can enhance the experience. For instance, when faced with a brand new subject, consumers might need to be provided with information that will help them raise their understanding of the global picture within which their experience will take place.

In Cairns, Australia, businesses have set up reef talks that visitors can book to learn about the eco-system of the reef. The talk lasts on average no more than two hours and provides visitors with knowledge regarding the reef, its balance, its various shellfish, fish, algae, and corals. This talk, which is attended before a reef dive, is an experience enhancer: it helps visitors to raise their expectations in the sense that they will start the experience with an under-standing of the meaning and variety of what they are about to see. The talk is there to give more sense to the experience and provide a more fulfilling experience. At the end of the talk, visitors can buy plasticized cards that list the different reef components and take them on the boat with them to check what they have seen during their dive.

Many attractions, such as boat trips to see mammals or seals, use the wait-ing time before departure to show films to the visitors about the area and its ecosystems. Again, these films help to give a deeper context to what will be seen, and thereby enhance the actual experience.

During the experience

As many studies have identified, the personality and knowledge of the guide are essential in the success of the experience. All the information provided by the guide during the experience will help to give a fuller meaning and provide a better understanding of what is being seen: for instance, it could address why an animal behaves in the way it does, why such flora exists in an adverse universe and the strategies it has developed to do so, etc.

When watching wildlife, such as Galapagos tortoises, sperm whales, killer whales, etc., the experience can elicit in visitors very strong emotions. These emotions are aroused by the beauty of what is being seen, its wild and natu-ral dimension, its rarity, and often its references to children's fascinations with some animals. Moreover, if the visitor is on his/her first experience, the emotions aroused will be even more intense. The guide will be there to enhance those elements by stating the rarity of the encounter, emphasizing the beauty of natural elements, etc.

However, other elements can also optimize the visitor experience. For exam-ple, making sense of the place can also be enhanced during the experience. Films shown during the trip, perhaps when customers are inside a boat, can give more information to resituate the experience within its broader context. If possible, staff will indicate to visitors when the best photo opportunities can take place (when an albatross is about to take off, when a whale is about to dive, etc.).

Involving consumers in the experience is another key point. In wildlife-watching, it can easily be done by the guide probing visitors to help them spot animals, bird songs, flower species, etc. Surprise (a strong component of satisfaction), can also be cultivated when a provider is almost certain that some wildlife can be spotted in an area but does not tell its customers in advance. One common trend is to cross dolphin schools while on a safari and let the participants enjoy, by themselves, the whole show and the great photo opportunities that it provides. At this point, the guide can retreat and let the consumers appreciate the sight and take in the intensity of what is being witnessed.

After the experience

One key point that service providers can act on is to summarize the experience at the end of the trip. Making sure they list the various elements of fauna and flora that have been seen, restating their rarity, and the chance customers have had to witness such a sight.

Providing a souvenir by taking a picture and sending it by email to visitors can be another point, although on wildlife tours visitors tend to be well equipped with photo apparatus. Sending an email afterward, encouraging members to become part of the special community of those who have witnessed those sights (joining the Facebook page for instance), and encouraging them to leave comments on rating sites, are all elements that will help visitors remember their trip and spread their satisfaction to other potential consumers.

EXQUAL tool

In order to measure the quality of customer experience from the perspectives of both the consumer and the company, I propose in this section the conceptual framework "EXQUAL" that can help marketing professionals and brand managers to improve the quality of their customer experiences. The EXQUAL tool is based on prior research in service literature, specifically the works of Parasuraman, Zeithaml, and Berry (1988) who developed the SERVQUAL scale, a multi-dimensional research tool intended to capture consumer expectations and perceptions of a service along with the five dimensions that refer to service quality.

THEORY BOX 4.2   WHAT IS EXPERIENCE QUALITY?

Experience quality refers to the degree of pleasure or annoyance of a consumer in his/her lived experience while in contact with the company. It results from the fulfillment of his/her expectations with regard to the utility and/or enjoyment of the service and the experience in light of his/her personality, as well as his/her current state.

The focus in this definition is on the personality, which means the characteristics of a person that counts as a coherent pattern of feelings, thoughts, and actions. The term "current state" refers to temporal or situational changes in a person's feelings, thoughts, or behavior. Thus, experience quality involves both current state and one's personality, a combination of factors that can influence the perceived quality of the whole experience.

SERVQUAL is an approach to quality evaluation that is very interesting since it stimulated research in this area and contributed to the advancement of services marketing knowledge. Although, The SERVQUAL scale has been broadly replicated in a diversity of contexts, such as education "EDUQUAL"

THEORY BOX 4.3   THE SERVQUAL STORY

In 1983, the Marketing Science Institute initiated an ongoing program of sponsored research to better assess service quality, much of which was assumed by Parasuraman, Zeithaml, and Berry. The authors' research on service quality was motivated by the need to provide researchers and practitioners with a conceptual framework of service quality. The issues investigated in their research included the identification of the main factors of service quality from both consumers' and managers' perceptions and the combination of these findings into a general model explaining service quality, which they called SERVQUAL.

Their innovative research was built on focus-group interviews with consumers and in-depth interviews with managers in four service sectors: retail banking, credit (cards), securities brokerage, and product repair and maintenance. The key finding of this research shows that: "while some perceptions about service quality were specific to the industries selected,

---

commonalities amongst the industries succeeded. The commonalities are encouraging, for they suggest that a general model of service quality can be developed" (Parasuraman, Zeithaml, and Berry, 1988: 44).

In other words, Parasuraman and colleagues argue that regardless of the kind of services considered, consumers used comparable factors to assess service quality, henceforth offering the opportunity of constructing a broad model of quality that would be effective throughout service industries. Conversely, expectations that had been met or exceeded perceptions would result in higher quality levels. The five SERVQUAL dimensions were named and described as the following:

Tangibles: physical facilities, equipment, and appearance of personnel;

Reliability: ability to perform the promised service dependably and accurately;

Responsiveness: willingness to help consumers and provide prompt service;

Assurance: knowledge and courtesy of employees and their ability to convey trust and confidence;

Empathy: the caring, individualized attention the firm provides to its customers.

Each of the dimensions encompasses four to six variables. The aim of each variable is to offer the highest total possible for the factors included in each of these five dimensions, which can also be an average.

(e.g., Mahapatra and Khan, 2007), health "HEATHQUAL" (e.g., Lee, 2016), and art (art museums) "ARTSQUAL" (e.g., Higgs, Polonsky, and Hollick, 2005), and found to be relatively valid, it has encountered some limits: the complexities of using the gap measure; the difficulty of developing scales when services group multiple encounters; and whether customers, while experiencing shopping or consumption, have similar evaluation processes as when they are in their everyday life.

Drawing on prior exhaustive research in service literature and the recent development of the SERVQUAL instrument, I developed EXQUAL (Table 4.1), which is a tool that allows companies to consider various elements to measure the quality of the perceived customer experience as it is measured through the dimensions that are believed to represent customer experience quality.

TABLE 4.1 The EXQUAL tool

Dimension	Element	Type of consumer needs
Human	*Empathy*. The delivery of caring, customized attention to customers through:	Functional, emotional, social
	• Polite attitudes of employees; • Explaining the details; • Listening to the customer; • Understanding and considering the customer's situation and feeling; • Developing a sense of closeness and friendliness; • Understanding the customer's problems as empathy; • Informing and communicating with the customer; • Knowing the customer.	
	Courtesy. Refers to the consideration for:	
	• Customer's property; • A clean and neat appearance of contact personnel; • Manifesting as respect.	
	Competency. It is the ownership of the needed abilities and knowledge to deliver the service	
	Reliability. The aptitude to deliver the promised service consistently and perfectly	
	Assurance. The acquaintance and politeness of staffs and their aptitude to convey trust and confidence	
	Responsiveness. The disposition to help customers and to provide prompt services	
Offering (product/ service)	*Tangibility*. The presence of physical facilities, equipment, personnel, and communication materials	Cognitive, rational, functional
	Efficiency. Elements, such as attitudes about not using unnecessary medication, degree of efforts for proving appropriate service and offer, reasonable prices; appropriateness of cost for services provided	
	Credibility. Involves aspects, such as trustworthiness, belief and honesty. It includes holding the customer's best interests in the highest regard	
	Access. Refers to the approachability and ease of contact	
	Security. Allows the customer to feel safe without any risk or doubt, including physical safety, financial security, and confidentiality	

Environment	Considering external elements: is the environment enjoyable? Is the environment stimulating the five senses? Is it surprising and enchanting? Does the atmosphere affect the consumer's state of mind?	Sensorial, physical
Value	Does the experience allow sharing values with customers? Does the company show and express social justice and eco-friendly behaviors through its products, stores, the attitudes of its employees in contact with customers, its communication, etc.?	Spiritual

Summary

This chapter has examined one of the components of the experiential marketing mix "E" as "Experience" that replaces the "P" of Products in the 7Ps of the marketing mix. It has explained how the experience can be designed, applied, and measured through the integration of strategic planning tools, such as the Experience Territory Matrix (ETM) and the EXQUAL tool, to improve the quality of customer experiences through difference stages. These tools are very critical for companies and brands that want to implement the experiential marketing mix by applying its 7Es in order to guarantee a satisfying, enjoyable, and profitable customer experience.

5

EXCHANGE

Co-creation and collaborative marketing

Purpose and context

Involving consumers in the co-creation of supply and consumption experiences is not an end in itself. A company would engage in the co-creation process if the participation of the consumer is considered as a value. The involvement of the consumer requires favorable conditions allowing the transformation of ideas into innovation and products as they respond to existing needs. Today, more and more actions are being taken by companies to engage the consumer and benefit from his/her knowledge and creativity by involving him/her in the company's offer and its improvement. For businesses, it is therefore important to understand: at what stage should they involve the consumer? For what type of work? And what is the interest for companies? This chapter focuses on the value that emerges from the "Exchange" between the customer and the company as a second component of the "7Es" of the experiential marketing mix that replaces the "P" of price, which is part of the traditional marketing mix approach, or the 7Ps. I'll show, in this chapter, how "Exchange" of value between customers and companies can be the focus rather than price in designing suitable, satisfying, and profitable customer experiences.

Learning outcomes

At the end of this chapter you will learn about one of the "7Es" of the experiential marketing mix "Exchange," the typologies of value creation and its processes, and how companies can use different strategies to involve their customers in the co-creation process of value by putting customers to work and using their creative potential in designing unique and valuable experiences.

Co-creation as value-in-exchange in customer experience

The idea of co-creation has been a rather new conception in the services marketing domains that supplement a relevant understanding regarding the difficulties of the

experience and exchange value expected by customers. This perspective
a clear vision about the participation of customers who can also be co-cr
or even employees who are remunerated, and thus play an important role in
production and the delivery of offers. In the recent years, consumers have becom
more integrated in the process of designing products and services: innovations are,
therefore, more consumer-oriented.

THEORY BOX 5.1 THE CO-CREATION CONCEPT

In their seminal article, Prahalad and Ramaswamy (2004) describe the value
of co-creation as a joint initiative through which providers (companies) and
recipients (consumers) create value together. In the co-creation process, value
is created reciprocally for each of the market actors (consumers, organizations, and networks) who engage in the process by interacting and exchanging their resources. The interactions take place on an engagement platform
where each market actor shares its own resources, integrates the resources
proposed by other actors, and potentially develops new resources through a
learning process.

This definition emphasizes the importance of the Internet and online
platforms in the construction of the relationship between companies and
customers. Thanks to the development and democratization of technology,
today, companies no longer have the monopoly on information, nor even
an exclusive benefit from access to information. Consumers and businesses
have the same information, which reduces the power that firms hold over
consumers. As stated by Prahalad and Ramaswamy, the Internet has enabled
consumers to "[. . .] step [. . .] out of their traditional roles to become consumers and consumers of value" (2000: 80). The Internet has allowed consumers
to express themselves and engage actively with businesses, thus becoming a
new source of competence.

In a more recent article, these same authors emphasized the idea that
today's consumers are more connected, informed, empowered, and active,
and they do have new tools that help them to make choices, resist, collaborate, or even negotiate with the companies. Therefore, maintaining
a dialogue between the company and its customers in the co-creation
process is very important to guarantee a positive and satisfying customer
experience.

Values–in–exchange can encompass different elements (e.g., self-fulfillment,
confidence in skills, joy, fun, belonging, accomplishment, relational, self-respect,
excitement, interpersonal, etc.) that are dependent upon the context in which the
co-creation process is implemented, the objectives of the company, and the outcomes sought by customers.

1Y STARBUCKS IDEA," A PLATFORM ENCOURAGE CO-CREATION WITH TOMERS

ɔn idea box, "My Starbucks Idea," where com-
ɔnare their ideas about the brand, its products and
ɔrrers, etc. "My Starbucks Idea" is a collaborative platform that
ɔtarbucks customers access to a great ideas box where everyone can submit its ideas and wishes. Customers can also vote for suggested ideas and comment on them. As a result, this online collaborative space allowed an abundance of ideas while giving the floor very easily to its customers who can track the status of their ideas and their implementation. Amongst popular ideas developed and launched thanks to co-creation with customers, I can cite the following: including Wi-Fi in all Starbucks, having a free birthday drink, or offering coupons to offer drinks to friends in any room.

Customers as employees

The shared production of goods and services amongst the firm and the client is not a novel idea. For example, fast food or supermarkets have increased certain achievements through enhancing the participation of their customers to cut production costs. Consumer participation in service creation was first considered as an approach to increase efficiency by using the client as a free workforce, and thus attaining an inferior price (e.g., Fitzsimmons, 1985; Mills and Morris, 1986). In the consumer culture paradigm, most works suggest enlarging consumer participation and expanding it in the experiential sphere, since it benefits to lead the consumer towards a consumption experience and provide him/her with satisfaction, values, and reward. In this perspective, co-creation is connected with a dynamic participation that suggests consumer engagement helps in determining the firm's offerings, which is perceived by the customer as a value in exchange since he/she plays an active role in the creation process, and thus is considered as legitimate and competent.

The value produced through a co-creative process can be achieved through the implementation of the "DART" (Dialog, Access, Risk-benefits, and Transparency) model developed by Prahalad and Ramaswamy, in 2004. This model provides companies with guidelines for co-creating value with their customers. It is primarily designed to encourage a constructive dialogue between the company and its consumers. To enable this dialogue, the company must give consumers access to certain devices. It should also manage the dialogue in such a way that it allows reducing risks (risk-benefits). Finally, creating a value with consumers requires transparency, and, therefore, the sharing of information.

Beyond products and services, companies offer their consumers a real experience of co-creation. Value is no longer unilaterally created by the company, but co-created with the consumer. This model is consistent with the theorization of Da Silveira and colleagues (2001) because, regardless of the level of mass customization, and, therefore, the degree of consumer involvement in the process, in order to co-create value with the consumer, the company will always engage in a dialogue with the consumer by making certain tools available, generating interest, and sharing information.

To date, not many cases show a "true" co-creation if the process implies that consumers are being actively involved by a firm in the co-creation of its offerings (products and services). The example of *IReporters* cited underneath is very relevant in this respect.

MINI-CASE 5.2 IREPORTERS: CNN USE OF CITIZENS AS REPORTERS TO CO-CREATE MEDIA CONTENT

In the audiovisual and media sector, a number of the internationally renowned US TV channels, such as CNN, have implemented the "IReporters" concept, which describes a type of citizen journalists who produce and disseminate documentaries and reports. On the CNN website, Internet users are invited to share their experiences, comments, and videos on current news or other matters.

The best stories will be broadcasted on the CNN TV news channel and the IReporter is often invited to join the journalist and participate in the debate. Thus, CNN benefits from the expertise of these citizen journalists and reduces the costs of its professional journalists because to produce a report that requires travel would inevitably generate financial and management expenses for the company.

IReporters are different because there is no cost – they work for free because they are passionate about the issues and topics. This participation in terms of production and dissemination of information is becoming essential for media groups and the audiovisual sector that attempt to enhance the collaboration with the consumer, who is, himself/herself, able to produce, disseminate, and influence information through his/her online social network. However, this ideology has some limits in terms of the relevance and the value of the information produced by a consumer who is not paid for this work. Indeed, in the fashion and haute couture sector, designers and luxury brands pay influential bloggers to attend their shows and provide feedback and information on their blog to the online community through Twitter, or Facebook. These users receive remuneration in return and are considered as employees, which is not yet the case in the media and audiovisual industry.

In the service business (e.g., hotel and restaurants), the processes of co-creation are more informal than in other sectors. In fact, the indirect service provision that characterizes the service industry naturally suggests that consumers will, deliberately or not; contribute to the co-creation process. Perhaps the best approach to consider for businesses is offering a set of facilities and services so that customers can easily pick which ones they prefer to use in their experiences.

MINI-CASE 5.3   MCDONALD'S "CREATE YOUR TASTE" TO CREATE A UNIQUE BURGER EXPERIENCE

The "Do It Yourself" (DIY) McDonald's strategy is based on the customization of sandwiches by involving customers. Like automatic kiosks installed in all restaurants around the world that allow customers to compose and send their order directly to the kitchen, the American firm now offers a "customization" of burgers.

Customers can create their own burgers by choosing the ingredients and naming their creation to earn a serving of French fries and a free drink. Some people imagined sandwiches that were impossible to realize without seeing a list of ingredients and gave them strange names, such as "Bag of lettuce," composed only of salad; "The Carbonator," with only bread; or the "Atheist's Delight," without any ingredients.

McDonald's has already launched a new control system called "Create Your Taste" (create according to your taste). Twenty-two fittings are thus proposed to be integrated into restaurant terminals to allow customers to build their own burgers. After a successful first test in the Los Angeles area in 2013, this control system was expanded to three more franchises in August 2014 in the US and then the concept has been exported to Australia, New Zealand, and Europe. This co-creative strategy replies to an increasingly popular trend in the United States: that of DIY.

From service-dominant logic to experience-dominant logic

Vargo and Lusch develop a new vision of consumers in services by introducing the concept of service-dominant logic (SDL) in 2004. They defined a new approach that underlines the shift in the marketing thinking from products towards a greater attention to services and facilities. Vargo and Lusch state that entire economies are service-based in which knowledge and specified skills are the fundamental source for creating a sustainable competitive advantage. These authors view organizations according to two main foundations:

- Operand assets refer to elementary resources existing in a consumption setting that is proceeded upon to market them to potential customers. They contain physical incomes, such as decors, design, or landscapes.
- Operant assets refer to physical and mental skills, as well as knowledge used to convert operand assets by including, for example, the knowledge of a waiter to explain and serve wine, the relational competencies of employees in contact with customers, etc. For Vargo and Lusch, the key to a competitive business lies within operant assets.

The most significant contribution of the SDL is the idea that consumers are co-producers. Vargo and Lusch (2004) state that resources do not have value as such, but their value is co-created with customers when they are used, which means that the value exchanged is defined and co-created within the customer experience rather than being embedded in output. Kelley, Donnelly, and Skinner (1990) state that since consumers participate in the on-going experience and service delivery process, they play an active role that places them in the position of "partial employees."

The common idea of co-creation is that a service only develops value (interactive value) when it is used by consumers and that this use requires an active customer participation (e.g., Carù and Cova, 2006; Gummesson, 1998). The firm and the customer cooperate in order to create unique offers, and value-in-exchange can be seen as a flow of experience co-created by the customer. Minkiewicz, Evans, and Bridson (2009) state that it is the consumption experience itself that is co-created rather than the value. Therefore, the knowledge, skills, and motivation of employees in contact with customers are primary determinants of the ability of the company to co-create and share value-in-exchange with its actual and potential customers (e.g., Maglio et al., 2009).

Since its creation, the SDL has been well recognized by marketing scholars, but it remains a new field that is in continuous evolution. Indeed, several recent articles have questioned some of the issues associated with the SDL. On one side, Edvardsson and colleagues (2011) have published several articles stating that service experience and consumers do not exist in isolation and need to be considered within their broader social system. For instance, Edvardsson et al. look at the idea that within a service experience resources should be integrated into their broader social constructions, since they point to what is acceptable or not within transactions and within a specific culture. This aspect as such is not new and has been dealt with by consumer culture theory scholars (Arnould and Thomson, 2005) who also looked at the meaning created within a social context.

The evolution brought by Edvardsson and colleagues is particularly interesting since it brings a wider and more meaningful vision of the experience context, integrating more sociological and psychological dimensions that were missing in the original SDL approach. By integrating those dimensions, this field is moving towards bridging the gap between quality-centered cognitive approaches and more experiential approaches, thus, shifting the focus from service-dominant logic to customer's experience dominant logic (CDL).

MINI-CASE 5.4 TRIPADVISOR, VALUE CO-CREATION THROUGH SHARING TOURISM EXPERIENCES

According to TripAdvisor, its site is the world's premier travel site. TripAdvisor provides advice for travelers and a wide-ranging variety of travel selections and planning features with whole relations to booking tools. TripAdvisor encompasses the greatest travel community worldwide with more than 60 million single monthly visitors and over 75 million reviews and opinions in 2012. The site operates in 30 countries, including China under daodao.com.

The website provides a listing of accommodation, catering facilities and activities, with reviews and more. A forum allows visitors to ask and answer questions while "goLists" indicate catalogs of destinations and activities collected by users that they advise: travel themes, must-see attractions, stops on a walking tour, or ideas for a rainy day. The collaboration with Google Maps provides customers with an easy tool to geolocate the sites of interest.

TripAdvisor is the site most recognized and the first one to meet such success. It works on a very basic principle: customers, after registering, can leave evaluations of as many locations as they wish. Evaluations cover hotels, restaurants, activities, and destinations. What constitutes the strength of TripAdvisor is that it is based on an exchange of genuine evaluations from consumers. The success of this site is associated with the fact that word-of-mouth is the source that has the most powerful impact upon tourists' choices due to its high credibility. Also, the quantity of comments left on the site is a guarantee, to some extent, that even if unfair or non-genuine comments are left (by owners, for instance) the sheer volume of comments neutralizes this bias.

TripAdvisor could be seen as a site of consumers' exchange only, but the comments are co-constructed with the service providers since owners can give an answer to some of the comments posted on the site. The care tourism actors take in formulating this response is also a good exercise of customer relationship management and, more simply, a good exercise of co-creation: customers and providers collaborate to give an evaluation and explanation of the services provided (especially when negative comments are voiced).

On the provider's side, TripAdvisor for Business provides services that can help managers monitor their service. For instance, property ratings and review snippets provide managers with updated detailed information about their property: overall rating, popularity index, and recent review snippets. Hard copy certificates of excellence and travelers' choice hotels can be displayed on tourism service providers' walls and an award plate can be displayed on their front desk. Award badges can also be downloaded from the TripAdvisor website and displayed on their website and Facebook pages. This service also applies to destination managers who can help their visitors find the best attractions, restaurants and hotels near them (as recommended by TripAdvisor travelers) and display chosen pictures. They can also identify the 'best of destinations' (with suggestions for holidays, day trips and short breaks) and organize a forum where customers can exchange on their experience. TripAdvisor also offers free online educational seminars to learn about online marketing strategies, increasing direct bookings, and free TripAdvisor tools.

Research on value-in-exchange led some scholars, such as Heinonen and colleagues (2010), to take a consumer perspective, as it relates to his/her experiences, in examining the concept of co-creation. Heinonen and colleagues offered an enhanced vision focusing on the individual rather than the service: customer dominant logic (CDL) in response to the limits identified in the SDL. For Heinonen and colleagues, while SDL views the consumer as essentially passive in the service experience, the CDL approach takes into consideration a broader framework to understand fully the consumer experience that can have implications in terms of service design and service quality development. For instance, consumers' personal goals need to be better understood to then analyze how the service provision fits with those personal goals. Rather than looking at the service transaction alone, the company and its employees need to consider customers' intentions and resultant activities (Helkkula et al., 2012; Minkiewicz et al., 2009). The value exchanged is then shaped by the experience lived by customers when they interact with the company, its products, services, and employees.

According to Helkkula and colleagues, the value produced within the customer experience paradigm and which results from the exchange between the consumer and the producer can be defined as follows:

> we consider value in the experience to be the value that is directly or indirectly experienced by customers within their phenomenological life/world contexts . . . customers make sense of and experience value in an interactive way, based on their previous experiences or understanding.
>
> *(2012: 61)*

In other words, the company should focus more on what the customers are doing and how particular products and services can be adequate with their experiences in the way they can enhance the benefit perceived as well as improve the well-being of customers.

In the CDL, Heinonen and colleagues (2010) also argue that companies should consider that value-in-exchange can also emerge from both cognitive and emotional experiences that include all the stages of consumption from pre-decision all the way to post-purchase. They also contend that customers' discussion of their experiences (directly or over the Internet) might renegotiate the evaluation of the value exchanged. Certainly, one aspect that should deserve further attention is the fact that co-creation and the value-in-exchange deserve greater attention by describing the role of firms in the co-creation process and identifying what are the outcomes and the value-in-exchange expected by customers. In fact, the role of firms is, therefore, to facilitate access to resources through designing, delivering, manufacturing them, etc., in order to be fully considered as a value facilitator; however, the firm only co-creates value when there is an interaction (exchange value-creation).

MINI-CASE 5.5   NIKE CO-CREATES VALUE THROUGH JOGGERS' EXPERIENCES

When Apple launched the iPod in 2001, Nike brand managers noticed that many runners used their iPods to listen to music and playlists when jogging. In 2006, Nike launched Nike+ in partnership with Apple. It is a smart sensor, inserted into the runner's shoe, able to communicate with an Apple receiver (iPhone or iPod). The sensor records the length of the race, the number of kilometers/miles traveled, and all kinds of other data.

Nike has developed an Internet platform to co-create with its customers. Members upload their personal data: goals, distances traveled, duration, number of calories burned, etc. The key to success lies in sharing opportunities with other members of the network. Applications derived from Google Maps allow members to map new routes, view them, and distribute them around the world. Members can also organize challenges and compare their performances. The amount of data generated by users enabled Nike to learn more about the average duration of a jog, to know the different types of courses, the temperatures and weather conditions during the outings, and the type of music most suitable for this or that experience, and so forth. All kinds of information helped managers and marketers to design new products that fit with different running experiences, and thus offer the ultimate running experience to their customers who also participated in the co-creation process.

Collaborative marketing: the art of putting consumers to work

Collaborative marketing is linked to the arrival of a new consumer with creative potential and his/her ability to co-create and co-produce offerings with the company. Collaborative marketing is applied to the fields of innovation, services, and design in which users/consumers are involved in improving products through their opinions, ideas, and suggestions. The collaborative marketing approach refers to a focus on consumers, especially their skills, in order to involve them in a collaborative process. Companies should, therefore, consider their customers as partners and economic actors capable of carrying the values of the enterprise or the brand, to communicate them, and to propose creative solutions to improve the quality of the experience, including products and services.

Collaborative marketing allows companies to differentiate themselves from the competitors, and thus retain their customers by involving them and sharing values with them. In fact, collaborative marketing aims to engage customers in the creation process of the offer, which can take several forms. For example, consumers may be involved in product development (design, logo, packaging, etc.) or in the communication policy (promotion on social networks, participation in an advertisement, creation of a video, etc.). Consumer participation depends on the degree of his/her creative potential and the level of involvement: consumers can vote for the design, name, or logo of a new product; animate a group of consumers around a brand; or co-create the product with the company.

The levels and the factors identified suggest that the brand should apply a strategy of prioritization of co-creation practices that will facilitate their choice according to the degree of co-creative engagement and competence expected from the consumer. The three levels of co-creation (DIY, collaboration, and co-innovation) imply a certain level of commitment and competence on the part of the consumer. The strength of engagement in the co-creative process and the required skill dimensions vary depending on the level. Thus, a simple action, such as personalization, is DIY. That collaboration or co-innovation requires the consumer to possess certain skills and knowledge of the product in order to successfully innovate.

1. DIY. It is characterized by simple tasks, such as customizing objects based on the options available and offered by the company. It is an effective way to help consumers take ownership of the marketed product by transforming their appearance or functions. It is, for the consumer, an extension of his/her own identity.
2. Collaboration. In this phase, the consumer's collaboration can take two forms: passive or active. Passive collaboration of consumers is a form of co-creation that consists of giving one's opinion. Active collaboration brings together all practices aimed at involving the consumer in the design or in the promotion of a product (e.g., Amazon, etc.). The project, as is defined and framed by the company, will then give instructions that consumers should follow in their collaborative process.
3. Co-innovation. It is defined by technical contributions. Consumers should ultimately have strong and creative knowledge, skills, and ideas, which the company can integrate to establish its specifications, launch, and commercialization of the innovation (product and/or service).

Today, collaborative marketing is booming thanks to the democratization of the use of social media and technologies, which contributed to the development of creative exchanges between consumers and businesses. So, the exchange between a company and its consumers is rewarding for both of them as consumers feel invested with an important mission, and companies can use the creative potential of their customers to innovate and differentiate themselves from competitors. From a company point-of-view, there are three main advantages in using collaborative marketing:

- To benefit from the creative potential and ideas of customers;
- To better know and retain them in the long term;
- Consumers who co-create can also talk about their actions and the new products they created.

More and more companies are integrating collaborative marketing in the co-creation of their offerings with their customers who can feel valued since they are part of the creation or the communication process. For example, Walt Disney World parks involve their visitors at different levels. In the following scenario, consumers can be regarded as a partner through their involvement with Disney's communication campaigns. The company asked families to film the real reaction of their children to the announcement of a trip to Disneyland Paris. The videos were then posted on the website and put to the vote of Internet users. The winner will be awarded a VIP stay at the park and the family will get to make an appearance in an advertisement on television.

**MINI-CASE 5.6 THE FINNISH AIRLINE FINNAIR
CO-CREATES WITH TRAVELERS THROUGH
THE "QUALITY HUNTERS" PROJECT**

Given the benefits of co-creation, it is not surprising that many companies use it. This is how the Finnish airline Finnair solved one of its problems. Its high fixed costs and its organization did not allow it to adapt to this new market context. To stay competitive and simply survive, Finnair was dependent on a strong global presence. This is why Finnair set up the "Quality Hunters" project, a recruitment campaign that received more than 5,300 applications from 90 different countries. At the end of this campaign, two women and two men were selected.

The new recruits had the mission of traveling around the world and visiting Finnair's destinations while writing blog articles on a given subject. The main objectives were to evaluate and propose ideas to improve the quality of the trip. At no time did Finnair intervene: bloggers were free to express themselves as they wished. Throughout the campaign, bloggers and members of the Finnair community were able to submit ideas for new services. The successful co-creation campaign generated 260 new ideas, some of which have since been implemented.

Customers who are willing to collaborate can be involved at all stages of the offer development of the company: production and proposal of ideas, testing and validation of products and prototypes, communication and promotion, etc. The profile, knowledge, and status of the customer can guide the company in its choice to involve the customer upstream, downstream, or throughout the creation and production processes, at the launch of a new product as well as during the different stages of the customer experience.

MINI-CASE 5.7   LAY'S OFFERS ITS CUSTO╱
TO CREATE THE NEXT C╟

"Do Us a Flavor" is Lay's co-creative campaign tha'
propose the next flavor of chips. Lay's invites potatc
to its next innovation by offering its customers the ability to ⌐..
they would like to see on supermarket shelves and, as stated by the bra⌐⌐,
can be absolutely anything; customers are free to propose creative, original,
and crazy flavors.

The project was widely relayed on social media since it is necessary to connect
to Facebook to submit a creative idea and then to Twitter, Vine, or Instagram to
get votes. The entire campaign was designed to engage as many fans as possible
to create the buzz around Lay's chips. This marketing campaign has accumulated millions of visits in just a few months. More than 14 million proposals have
been submitted. Fans appear eager to share their ideas and participate in the
launch of a new product into the market. Internet users have made their suggestions on a page provided for this purpose on the official website, and the least
one can say is that many of them have rather curious tastes.

In the soft category, we find rather tempting combinations, such as
tomato–goat cheese, sausage–mustard, or basil–pepper. But some have not
hesitated to propose sweet flavors that are completely improbable: vanilla ice
cream, candy, apple pie, pork–pineapple, chocolate–marshmallow–bacon,
waffle–chicken, or chicken–cake. If the project has a fun side, the issue is very
serious: the one whose flavor will be selected will not only see his/her "creation" marketed, but will also win one million dollars. But for that, it will be
necessary to convince a jury of culinary experts who, one suspects, will carry
out a meticulous sorting of ideas.

Collaborative marketing, as a process to value exchange with customers, can
be considered by companies attempting to meet the needs of their customers who
want to be part of a creative and/or a productive process. Customers consider that
they also have a role to play in the company and that if the brand is a success, it is
also thanks to them and their collaboration. Collaborative marketing can, therefore, help companies seek ideas, suggestions, or even personal data to improve their
products, services, and brands, and thus adapt them according to the expectations
of their customers. Therefore, by collaborating with their customers, companies
create a competitive advantage, retain their customers, and attract new ones.

Summary

This chapter has examined one of the components of the experiential marketing mix "E" as "Exchange" that replaces the "P" of Price in the 7Ps of the

eting mix. Beyond the price, in Chapter 5, I highlighted the importance thinking in terms of value exchange rather than price. This chapter has ntroduced two ways of generating value-in-exchange: co-creation and collaborative marketing. These two strategies are very relevant for companies that would like to involve their customers and use their creative potential and exchange value with them within their experiences.

6

EXTENSION

Experience continuum and intra/extra-domestic experiences

Purpose and context

Customers' perceptions and evaluations of their experiences frequently change through a series of interactions, buying, and consumption occurrences with the company over an extended period of time, and taking place within different settings (e.g., in-store experience, online experience, in-door experience, etc.). Experiences are variable and inconstant, and companies need to understand how the customers' expectations vary and what new or emerging requirements, services, and products can meet those needs. To understand the fundamental triggers of the experience over a period of time, marketers need to design customer experience as a continuum that includes both extra- and intra-domestic experiences and explores the dynamic between the two consumption spheres to guarantee customer satisfaction and loyalty.

This chapter focuses on the customer experience offer as an "Extension," which is an integral part of the "7Es" of the experiential marketing mix. This approach influences companies to broaden their vision by shifting the focus from the "P" of "Physical environment/Place" in the traditional marketing mix logic to a more extended consideration of customer experience that is dynamic, evolving, and goes beyond the physical environment. In this chapter, I will explore two main dimensions of customer experience extension: the customer experience continuum and the intra/extra-domestic consumption experiences. I will then introduce tools and strategies that companies can use to design the ultimate customer experience and avoid disconnections in the experiential process, and thus, limiting customer disappointment.

Learning outcomes

At the end of this chapter you will learn about one of the "7Es" of the experiential marketing mix "Extension" and how companies can use efficient marketing design tools to create a continuum to guarantee the quality of the consumption experience by taking into account the dynamic between intra- and extra-domestic customer experiences in order to avoid the discontinuity in the experiential process, which is often a source of customer disaffection of the brand or the company.

Experience continuum

Jean Liedloff (1975) introduced the concept of continuum to refer to the fact that human beings aim to achieve optimal physical, cognitive, behavioral, and emotional development, which requires a long-term evolutionary process from childhood to adulthood based on a continuum of experiences. What is the experience continuum? One way to answer this question is to ask another question: Why is there a continuum related to customer experience and consumption knowledge? If I advocate the experience continuum today, it is because there has been a finding of "discontinuity" somewhere between consumption experiences and the knowledge accumulated from them as well as the way it affects the lived experience. Therefore, there is a need to restore this link and define customer experience as a continuum that goes from physical to digital, from in-door to out-door experiences, and exists as an evolving process in which the assembled knowledge will affect present and future consumption experiences. One of the consequences of this discontinuity is that, as at the end of the process, a large number of consumers will not live the ultimate consumption experience they were expecting because of the discontinuity in the experiential process that has negative consequences.

THEORY BOX 6.1   THE CONCEPT OF CONTINUUM

Jean Liedloff introduced the concept of continuum for the first time in 1975 in his book *The Continuum Concept*. This concept is intended for anyone who wants to know what has not worked in our evolution and learn how to return to principles more suited to our nature. The author has made several expeditions to the South American jungle and has observed, amongst other things, the way of life of the Yakwanas tribe. He found that their sense of happiness, work, and effort was very different from our Western conceptions. He explains it by the fact that this tribe has not moved away, like modern societies, from its continuum, especially in relation to babies. By living with the Yekwana people in the deepest jungle of South America, Jean Liedloff has learned the lessons of this simple life and the importance of the "bond of attachment" to the mother at birth. A newborn child is welcomed as "naturally good and sociable," but at this stage, being in the arms of the mother is of huge importance for its development. Thereafter, he makes his own experiences from which he draws the consequences himself. The relation to human feelings is totally different from what is currently practiced in our culture.

Liedloff defines the concept of continuum as a series of experiences that correspond to the expectations and tendencies of our species in an environment of the same logic as those born of these expectations and trends. In other words, our "ancestral programming" pushes us to certain appropriate behaviors and induces in us certain expectations. Thus, from birth, the baby expects to receive from his mother a "maternal" behavior: his continuum indicates that his place is in her arms, against her body, and this is where he will live and evolve during the first few months of his life, until he is ready to try other experiences.

The rupture of the continuum in our modern societies has negative consequences for individuals and society: the unfulfilled expectations of the baby remain for the rest of his life as children, and then as adults. He will seek to fill them and to find the maternal figure and experiences "in the arms" that he missed. His sense of happiness will be profoundly altered: his quest for something else, at best, will be permanent and prevent him from enjoying the present moment, and thus finding happiness in the present moment. Some diseases, addictions, and sexual disorders can be explained by this non-respect of the continuum. Indeed, the journey to happiness must be done step by step, and if the first of them is missed, one has to start from scratch in a potentially infinite quest. In terms of the consumption experience continuum, companies have to stay connected and as close as possible to the continuum using common sense by meeting the expectations of the new consumers and novices who do not have knowledge or who are living their first experience, such as one's first time driving a sports car, first time dining in a gastronomic restaurant, first time traveling by plane, etc.

In philosophy, Dewey developed the "experience continuum theory," which states that each experience includes aspects from those experiences that have occurred in the past, and adjusts in some manner the value and the quality of those experiences that happen in the future. In applying the experience continuum theory to the experience of education, Dewey states that "educational experience involves both continuity and interaction between the learner and what is learned" (1938: 10). Thus, Dewey's idea is that experience results from the interaction of two principles:

- Continuity, which refers to almost all experiences (previous and current) that are accepted onward and affect upcoming experiences and choices;
- Interaction, which is defined as the neutral and inner circumstances of an experience.

THEORY BOX 6.2 DEWEY'S EXPERIENCE CONTINUUM THEORY

John Dewey is the initiator of "learning by doing" based on the idea that one comes to do things and use tools for simple construction; it is in this context and on the occasion of these acts that activities are arranged. For Dewey, experience is the key to understanding nature and reality. Experience is also a necessary means to understand failure and to preserve it; it is not definitive but dedicated to the continuity of construction.

According to Dewey, experience is a process of self-renewal through interaction with the environment and this process unfolds continuously. But, the continuity of the vital process is not ensured by the prolongation of the existence of an individual, but rather, it unfolds through the social group. The bridge between the individual and the consumer society is consumption experiential learning, which is the process by which the customer experience renews itself continuously (e.g., the first experience of wine tasting is different from the second since it is based on prior learning or the first purchase experience of a luxury item online is different from the in-store shopping experience, but does incorporate elements from what the customer learned in the virtual experience). In other words, consumption experiential learning is an essential process for the very evolution of consumption experience and the satisfaction process. The renewal of consumer experience is accompanied by the re-creation of beliefs, ideals, hopes, happiness, and consumption habits. The continuity of any consumption experience through renewal can also occur by means of a social group or the consumption context.

Therefore, experience continuum is the only way for companies to guarantee successful experiences for their customers because their experiences are embedded within a social environment and are part of a continuing process that allows renewing present and future consumption experiences.

Drawing on Dewey's research, I argue that customer experience should at each stage build on what has been learned in the previous stages well as in the alternative, and informal stages. In fact, experience and consumption do not directly relate because some experiences are not related to shopping or consumption (e.g., personal or family experiences that prevent or alter the development of future consumption experiences). So far, I have identified four main forms of experiences that should be connected to create a customer experience continuum (Figure 6.1).

The challenge for the experience continuum is to provide customers with quality consumption experiences involving all the senses that will result in advancing their learning and their creative potential in their forthcoming experiences in order to create an experiential continuum. Therefore, the continuum of experience

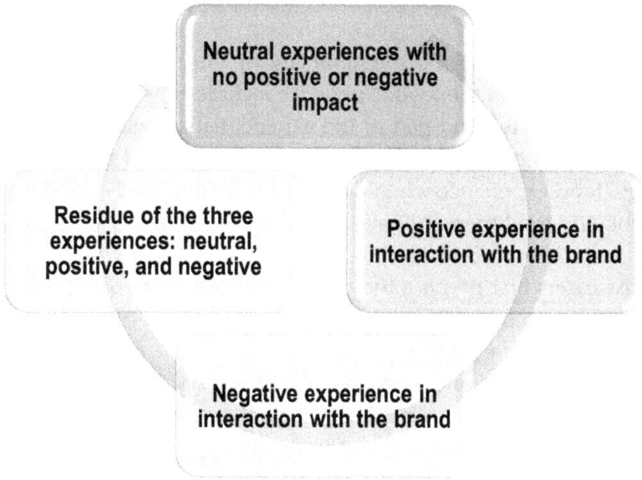

FIGURE 6.1   A continuum through the connection of four forms of experiences

includes all cognitive (intellectual), affective (emotional), and behavioral changes during a lifecycle as new experiences adjust and change existing models.

Furthermore, the experience continuum integrates the idea that any experience that is high in indirect service provision is also the one that generates more opportunities for co-creation up to auto-creation. In their book *Consuming Experience*, Carù and Cova (2006) define this approach as an "experience continuum." The experience continuum indicates that consumers vary in their reliance on a service provider to co-construct their product. For instance, the ski experience in a resort can produce a continuum ranging from self-organized activities to business-organized activities. Thus, customers define, understand, and operate on resources in service systems in different ways depending on what they want to achieve, the resources they have available, and their capabilities, as well as their financial situation. Therefore, the continuum in ski experiences shows that tourists build their value by referring to the various activities they engage in and depicting themselves as active organizers of their holiday.

MINI-CASE 6.1   THE CONTINUUM IN FOOD EXPERIENCE: THE "TOURIST-EATER" EXPERIENTIAL JOURNEY

By eating the food of the destination visited, the tourist has an intimate encounter with local cultures, which he/she incorporates both physically and symbolically within his/her food tourism experiences. The discovery of foods and iconic drinks of the destinations visited and the food experience continuum

(continued)

(continued)

contributes to enhancing the memorability of the experience. As a tourist-eater, the continuum in the food experience includes three main stages that all together are connected and part of the experiential knowledge that will allow the tourist-eater to be fully immersed in his/her travel and in the overall food experience: food experience when the travel is getting ready, food experience on the spot, and food memory.

1) Tourist-eaters first prepare their trip from various media (tourist guides, cinema, food travel guides, testimonials, etc.). They mark the start of the future food journey and participate in the development of the preliminary image of local and iconic foods of the visited destination. The food experience at this stage is mainly cognitive and helps the tourist-eater to get familiar with the context by learning about the popular dishes, foods, and drinks.

2) Food experience on spot: at this stage, tourist-eaters incorporate places and activities during their lived experience. The time of stay offers different opportunities for interaction with native food cultures through physical elements that are clearly recognizable in the tourist zone (plates, ingredients, vegetables, or animal elements) as well as other components that are more in the immaterial (symbolic of food, social values, hierarchies and codes, social bonds, culinary, cultural, and artisanal know-how, and so on). The food leads the tourist-eater to learn, often through his/her complications and the limitations of his/her own food culture. The categories of the eatable foods, the level and kind of cooking, the structures of meals and food intake, table manners, food codes, the daily temporality, the places of supply, the rules of hygiene – all are elements from which the boundaries of one's own food culture are drawn. Eating the food of the "Other" like him/her or with him/her is a journey and an experiential learning process in itself.

3) The food experience memory: the memory is an essential element of the tourist-eater's food experience continuum. By the "food experience memory," individuals stay connected with the destination and the world of holidays in their daily ordinary life. The action of buying and bringing home, for example, local products (wines, farm products) extends and strengthens the trip beyond the holidays. In addition, tourist-eaters can also acculturate new food practices and cooking habits, whether they do it for themselves or to share with others as symbols of their food experience enchantment, discovery, or experiential learning in their country of origin. With this practice, they tend to create a continuum by extending the experiential food journey on their return where meals are the occasion of a second assimilation and simultaneously allow the consumer/visitor to integrate into everyday objects, receptacles of memory, and emotions of lived

past food experiences. The reported object, thus, allows the imaginary link between the here and the elsewhere while at the same time making the everyday a "new elsewhere." It magically narrows the distance between the last journey and the next through reviving the images, moods, flavors, and scents of travel by introducing them into the monotonous ritual of everyday life. The tourist-eater is not only transformed into an accumulator of unusual items, he/she also blends domains and cultures: distant world and ordinary realm, free and forced, novel and usual.

This assumption is consistent with the views of Grönroos (2008) and Heinonen and colleagues (2010), who argue that, essentially, customers "create" value for themselves (auto-creation) and do not exactly "co-create" value with goods or service providers. The outcomes of the customer experience continuum also indicate the importance of social interactions, the pleasure in acting as a group or as a family (e.g., the ritual of picnicking), and the transmission between people (e.g., swimming instruction of children at the swimming pool). The idea of a continuum stems from the recognition that customer experiences have very different facets and can either be totally, partially, or very marginally co-created.

On one side, the continuum depicts experience services and situations where most of the customer experience is organized and controlled by the provider/company. And from the vast offer, customers will organize their own experiences according to their needs (functional, emotional, and social). These situations can involve fairly large actors of the marketplace whose major objective is to design and organize a customer experience with the aim to serve customers often in an isolated location (within the vicinity of a store, mall, restaurant, resort, or a cruise ship, where the customer experience can be fully managed and customers' spending localized).

On the other side, settings, whereby the consumer seeks less support from the provider/company, will depict situations, such as staying in one's flat and reading a book. For instance, some very important times of a holiday might take place in close intimacy: family togetherness can be achieved through playing cards, as a family unit, building a sand castle with one's grandson, riding a bike together, etc. Customers are also in demand for those times when they will live intense, but yet simple moments, without any intervention from the service provider and even with limited contacts with the marketplace. However, scholars have not often recognized this simple but fundamental dimension of the consumption experience. For instance, in the tourism sector, because tourism experience is viewed as an extraordinary time of one's life, one in which it can involve exotic and luxurious destinations, it is somehow reasonable to think of it as an extraordinary experience.

However, this aspect does not necessarily mean that the experience, itself, always has to be extraordinary. In fact, customers, whether they are tourists, visitors, or shoppers, need time to themselves, such as moments where they will spend nice moments with their friends and family without any connection to the service provider or the company's employees. This dimension is extremely important and one aspect that consumers will aim to have is freedom of choice (e.g., selective moments where they want to be in contact with the service provider). At times, they may not want to have any form of activity or timing imposed upon them.

THEORY BOX 6.3   FROM ORDINARY TO EXTRAORDINARY CONSUMPTION EXPERIENCES AND VICE VERSA

Consumer experiences are numerous in the daily lives of individuals and can counterbalance the extraordinary offers. They are classified as ordinary or even intraordinary, which refers to the everydayness that requires idealistic and excessive attention. The difference between an ordinary experience and extraordinary experience can be emphasized by a pleasure that is described as evanescent. This degree of pleasure flows from the intensity of the interaction, or even from its exceptional character in the life of the subject which makes the experience extraordinary. The extraordinary experience makes sense only when it is compared to more ordinary moments of consumption. It then seems necessary to preserve the unequal densities of life with all force, if only for benefiting from the pleasure of contrast. Yet, sociological studies underline the fact that daily passions show the intense dimension lived through a visibly ordinary experience. These experiences are massively shared, individually assumed, morally accepted, and experienced intensely. They bring the consumer to a desired re-enchantment as legitimate aspirations for self-realization and re-enchantment of the world. Therefore, the daily experience becomes here, not a passion of extraordinary essence, but passion experienced in an extraordinary way by the individual who makes sense of it in his/her life.

The intense situation does not emanate from the exceptional nature of the experience, but derives from a relationship of closeness that evolves between the consumer and the experience. It is the practice of consumption under this angle, which challenges the questioning of whether the consumer experience is extraordinary or rooted in everyday life.

Intra- and extra-domestic experiences

Customer experience is a global process that integrates two spheres: extra–domestic and intra–domestic. Although the quality of customer experience is often studied in the extra–domestic context through the quality of services in stores, hotels, or restaurants, the domestic dimension is even more important when it comes to improving the global customer experience and should stay in step with the values and DNA of the company. For example, the DNA and the quality of service delivery should be coherent from the beginning to the end of the process in the same way that for example, the purchase of designer furniture in a store is defined by the store experience itself and the relationship with sellers, which is complemented by a home delivery service that is often supported by external service providers or partners.

These providers will be responsible for delivery and home installation. If providers are not trained according to the company guidelines, the home-based experience is likely to be negative (e.g., indiscretion of the service provider, failure to meet delivery deadlines, lack of uniforms, very poor service, etc.). This example highlights the issues related to the continuity of the customer experience from the extra-domestic sphere to the private one, which must force retailers and companies to look beyond the quality of service experience in stores, and focus more on their personal training, or on the selection of reliable partners who can extend the quality of customer experience from extra- to intra-domestic spheres.

MINI-CASE 6.2   UBER EATS, AIRBNB, AND AMAZON: FOOD DELIVERY APPS TO EXTEND EXPERIENCE FROM EXTRA-DOMESTIC TO INTRA-DOMESTIC

If 2016 and 2017 have been demanding years for innovation in the restaurant industry, the following years promise to be even more dynamic. Foodservice innovations that revolve around the quest for more and more services, especially at home, and the renewal of the customer experience, whether it is extra or intra-domestic, are becoming very promising. New market actors, such as Uber, Airbnb, or Amazon have entered the world of foodservice with ambitious strategies, such as providing food delivery service to individuals' homes, that will make them key players in on-demand services.

- Uber Eats, the home meal delivery application is part of a strategy to turn the brand into a service platform. Besides the delivery of meals, possibilities through applications available in cars could include booking a restaurant, listening to a made-to-order music playlist, etc.
- In 2016, Airbnb presented a major evolution in its positioning. The platform now offers more services, including new experiences, placing it in direct competition with certain travel agencies.
- As for Amazon, with AmazonFresh, and soon its ability to deliver meals at home, its plan is to occupy the marketplace and grow a customer base already acquired.

Therefore, for these digital pure players, extending the customer experience and challenging the traditional restaurant and delivery service model can

(continued)

(continued)

be achieved by focusing more on the continuum between the experience in restaurant outdoors and the food experience indoors by reproducing the food experience lived by the customer at the restaurant. Restaurants and fast food brands are trying to reproduce the atmosphere of a restaurant at home, so there is a lot of potential for suppliers to develop and innovate by offering disruptive containers that fit with the in-door food experience. For traditional restaurant actors, it is also about exploring other worlds to provide continuity vis-à-vis the brand by offering the ultimate delivery experience.

Summary

This chapter has examined one of the components of the experiential marketing mix "E" as "Extension" that substitutes the "P" of "Physical environment/Place" in the 7Ps of the traditional marketing mix. It has explained how the experience can be designed as a continual process to avoid disconnection and rupture in the experiential process that is often a source of customer disappointment. In this chapter, I investigated two main dimensions of the customer experience extension process: the customer experience continuum and the intra/extra–domestic consumption experience. I also introduced a number of examples, tools, and strategies that companies can use to design the ultimate continuum in consumer experience.

7

EMPHASIS

Brand culture emphasis and storytelling

Purpose and context

In the marketing mix logic, communication applies with a push and platform or medium logic to deliver messages to the audience. However, due to an increase in traditional and digital communication platforms, as well as the rise of experiential expectations, efficiency has been reduced and brands have had to compete with creative originality to get their message across. That is why I propose in this chapter to shift the focus from a traditional communication policy focusing on brand content and media to a more holistic approach that allows the humanization of the brand by bringing its personality to life to create a strong relationship with its customers and thus differentiate the brand from its competitors.

This chapter focuses on "Emphasis" as one of the "7Es" components of the experiential marketing mix that replaces the "P" of "Promotion" part of the traditional marketing mix or 7Ps. I define emphasis through two key communication strategies: the creation of a brand culture and brand storytelling to make the transition from brand promotion, its know-how, and its products and services to an emphasis on brand personality, myth, and values that can be captured, created, and shared with its actual and potential customers within their experiences with the brand.

Learning outcomes

At the end of this chapter, you will learn about one of the "7Es" of the experiential marketing mix: "Emphasis," what it means, and what its dimensions are. I also answer the question: can brand managers create a satisfying customer experience by implementing an emphasis on the brand's personality and culture, which goes beyond its products and services? You will also learn more about storytelling and brand culture as two major strategies and approaches that companies can implement to design customer experiences in which customers will feel strongly connected to the brand.

Brand culture emphasis

A brand culture emphasis refers to the way companies should use consumption culture elements to connect with their customers. Instead of using brand promotion as in the Ps of the traditional marketing mix, the emphasis on brand cultural meaning provides a necessary complement to promotional strategies by including a focus on the meanings that are embedded and shaped by particular cultural settings and the meanings that the brand shares with its customers. This section will expose the shift from brand content to brand culture, the theory of brand culture, and cultural branding management, which are important components of the experiential marketing mix.

From brand content to brand culture

Brand content refers to editorial content created by a brand, which injects symbolic, cultural, historical, and artistic elements that represent the basis for creating original content, in the form of short films, documentaries, books, and various visual and textual elements. There are several theories and models of communication that describe the process of brand content, but what most theorists find paramount is the importance of conveying a message that aims at the clarity of it, the duty to convince prospects as well as to bring a certain notoriety to the product or service offered. The transformation of branded content into cultural branding is a consequence of three main changes that have affected communication strategies and the content of messages to fit with the emerging consumption trends within a digital and experiential era:

- **The media context**. With the rise of the Internet and digitalization of societies, access to advertising is becoming easier and consumers are more and more involved. Thus, it becomes difficult to reach a large number of consumers with a multiplicity of media that results in the fragmentation and the dispersion of audiences. Previously, there were only few media sources (e.g., television, radio, cinema) that exposed a large number of people to the content of advertisers. Today, the viewer has changed and developed new and powerful attitudes that can be summarized in four points:
  - Consumers decide about the selection of the type of medium (e.g., TV, web, etc.);
  - They select the place, time, and content, which can also lead to advertising avoidance;
  - They decide if they want to react (e.g., comments, criticism);
  - They can produce, publish, and share content because the essential technical and financial means are less important than in the past.

The democratization of technologies gives ideas to marketing and communication professionals, who occasionally ask their consumers to create their advertising. For instance, in 2006 the Dorito's brand of chips broadcasted an advertisement, made by anonymous consumers, during the Superbowl final.

- **The socioeconomic context.** In recent years, society, more specifically Western society, has begun to develop certain feelings that communication cannot ignore. The movement for ecology enhanced by the disbelief of capitalism and the global economic crisis of 2008, led to the rise of new behaviors. Consumers today are expecting a more "responsible" communication content. The social and environmental responsibility of the companies is a crucial element that should not be neglected because today's consumers are very sensitive to social and ecological issues. For instance, the Kit Kat brand of chocolate bars has been warned by Greenpeace, an environmental Non-Governmental Organization, about deforestation to produce palm oil for chocolate bars. By parodying an advertising of Kit Kat (Nestlé) and using social networks (e.g., Facebook and Twitter), Greenpeace has strongly caused damage to Nestlé's brand, which at the time saw the price of its shares fall.
- **Historical context.** The evolution of communication can be divided into three stages: modernity, postmodernity, and alter-modernity. Modernity is a way of communicating that aims to value the brand as an agent of humanity's progress towards the satisfaction of its desires. In the postmodern era, communication and advertising were marked by self-deprecation, derision, and mockery; the brand made fun of itself. The current era refers to alter-modernity that shows that communication is no longer conceived as a message centered on the brand, but as a service, a content for the experiential benefit of the consumer.

The shift from brand content to brand culture can be explained by the motivation of consumers to live experiences with the brands that are charged with meanings. The principal differences between brand content and brand culture are summarized in Table 7.1.

TABLE 7.1 The shift from brand content to brand culture

Brand content	Brand culture
Messages are translated through a speech	Creating a place in which consumers can immerse themselves and live unconsciously their experiences with the brands
Brand reality is affected by the media that carries it	Reality goes beyond the media that expresses it
One of the modes of brand expression	A complex system of elements that make up the brand
Affirms the positioning and the expertise of the brand	Creates a universe of the brand in which values are captured, created, and shared with actual and potential customers

The theory of brand culture

Culture is a legacy; it is what links the brand to the company and to its customers. It is also the historical and cultural systems that support the brand. The culture of the brand refers to the roots, the heritage of the brand. For instance, Lacoste is a brand that finds its roots in the French aristocracy of the 1920s and in a class sport, tennis. We can define brand culture as a historical and embedded system, a collective imagination built on ideology, myths, rites, norms, and beliefs of a brand and often inspired by the culture of the organization that holds the brand.

An increasing stream of consumer research underlines the strong relationship between cultural elements and brand meanings from a consumer perspective. For instance, Wernerfelt (1990) argues that brands are viewed as a symbolic language allowing consumers to communicate their types and values to each other. Drawing on research in the anthropology of consumption literature, some scholars, such as Muniz and O'Guinn (2001) and McAlexander, Schouten, and Koenig (2002), define brands as the reinforcement of communities building beyond social and geographical boundaries. Therefore, the brands are not only seen in terms of their symbolic resource for the construction of personal identity, but also as a foundational element that helps individuals to get together beyond their differences and share social experiences that can improve their well-being.

Brand culture signifies the cultural norms of brands that affect brand significance and value in the market. The brand culture concept captures the theoretical gap between brand identity as a strategic concept and consumer understandings of brand persona (e.g., Schroeder and Salzer-Mörling, 2006). From a cultural standpoint, brands can be considered as communication items that the brand manager desires customers to purchase into – a symbolic setting as expressed by the brand personality. Therefore, theoretically, brand management refers to delivering messages, which are expected in connection with the brand owner's objective (Kapferer, 2004). Nevertheless, this perspective does not take into consideration consumers' effective re-appropriation of brand significance and external elements related to the cultural and experiential settings, such as time, space, past experience, personality, history, etc. Holt (2002), who examines brands in relation to the evolution of marketing practices and consumer culture in the current marketplace, argues that marketers struggle to incorporate their brands into different groups of popular culture. Brands that effectively achieve this cultural emplacement can, consequently, make consumers produce unique and distinct identities and, surprisingly, resist conformist business influences.

THEORY BOX 7.1   DOUGLAS HOLT'S CULTURAL BRANDING THEORY

Holt's vision underlines the idea that the market is not segmented by socio-demographic criteria, but by cultural tensions. Douglas Holt's approach is particularly interesting since it refers to the process of brand identity construction that companies need to implement in order to create meaningful and valuable consumption experiences in interaction with their customers and other market actors. According to Holt, a brand's equity does not come from the richness of its mental associations, but from the myth it delivers to resolve cultural contradictions within the society. There is, what Holt calls, myth markets that arise from contradictions between a "dominant ideology" and the "identity project" of individuals.

Holt's cultural branding theory is based on the observation of consumption cultures to identify the brand myths and to reconstruct the tensions and desires of individuals on a certain number of themes. For Holt, the brand tells a story with characters and a plot. Of course, the brand does not have the same influence on society that a film or political speech may have. In contrast, the strength of a brand lies in its ability to make its story accessible through the ritual of consumption. Therefore, the goal of brand managers and marketers is to identify the most appropriate myth market for their brand and to invent a myth addressing a cultural contradiction by borrowing and enriching the stories already conveyed by other more powerful cultural actors.

The second contribution of Holt's cultural branding theory is that branding refers to the collective nature of a brand. According to Holt: "marketers like to think of brands as psychological phenomena that frame the perceptions of each consumer, while what gives the brand its power is the collective nature of these perceptions" (2004: 3). Thus, the brand is not only a marketer–consumer dialogue, but rather it includes many different market actors who participate in the emergence and influence of the brand. As a result, the meaning of the brand is dynamic and evolving since it is the product of the interactions between all these elements. For Holt, marketers and brand managers do not have to think of a brand as a sum of elements but as a "symphony" where it is the interactions that give the brand its strength.

Brand culture is then a central element in building a strong brand since it is co-constructed by injecting cultural meanings embedded within different consumption experiences. Even if the company is at the initiative of the brand and defines the first outlines, it cannot alone generate values, attitudes, and shared behaviors amongst consumers in their experiences with the brand. The brand community is an integral part of this cultural construction because brand culture can, therefore, escape the company. To be able to influence this culture, the brand manager should understand the mechanisms of the emergence of cultural meanings in consumption experiences. Holt (2004) states that the brand should then be viewed as a cultural narrator who delivers identity value by addressing a collective meaning embedded within individuals' consumption experiences:

> a brand becomes iconic when it delivers an identity myth: a simple story that
> responds to cultural tension by tapping into an imaginary world rather than

the everyday lives of consumers. The aspirations expressed in this myth are the imaginary expressions of the identity desire of individuals.

(2004: 8)

To do so, marketers have to identify the mechanisms behind brand culture in a community and the characteristics of these cultural elements to design suitable and meaningful customer experiences.

MINI-CASE 7.1   NIKE: THE CONSTRUCTION OF THE "JUST DO IT" MYTH

If we take the example of Nike, the myth used is that of the anonymous and lonely hero who manages to succeed by the sheer force of his/her determination. This story told by Nike is for anyone who remembers the new economy of the 1980s, a world where competition between individuals has become the rule. In the field of sports, this evolution is also visible with the development of individual sports practices and the abandonment of stadiums for the benefit of the street. Nike identified this myth market before its competitors and developed an identity myth inspired by the struggle of black Americans for equality. Many films, political speeches, and magazines were already dealing with this fight, but Nike has reused the cultural codes of the black community to associate them with the sport and give them a narrative dimension of the fight for the surpassing of oneself.

In his second book co-authored with Douglas Cameron, *Cultural Strategy*, Douglas Holt looks closely at the Nike brand and reveals that the success of this brand is not related to better technology of its products, but to a cultural approach to the brand "Nike has proposed a sports myth about self-transcendence that has served as a powerful motivational metaphor for the ideological anxieties of Americans struck by globalization and its consequences on the US labor market" (2012: 20). Holt explains that Nike has built its success on an ideological opportunity, that of "combative individual will." In the 1970s, all sports brands communicated in the same way, by highlighting the superhuman qualities of great champions. But this "cultural orthodoxy" was undermined by the severe economic crisis that hit the United States in the late 1970s. The ease with which these athletes were shown winning no longer matched the concerns of individuals. From now on, it is the rigor and the mental and physical strength that are the essential values. It is in this social context that the practice of jogging develops: sports come out of the stadiums and invades our daily life; it becomes a necessity to keep pace with professional life by ensuring a balance in our lives. Running represents the new values of the American society.

To address this emerging new ideology and embody the "Just Do It" myth, Nike turned to the Black-American community to build its brand story. Indeed, the living conditions of the black community in the United States are difficult. Historically, black Americans have often lived apart from others, some grouped together in community ghettos like Harlem in New York. This frame of reference offers a powerful analogy with the American labor market: life is a permanent and violent struggle. Thus, Nike has diverted the cultural codes of the black-American community to tell its brand story about the strength of the individual will in sports.

The cultural angle chosen by Nike for its communication was that of social discrimination. All the discourses of the brand are made from the angle of the struggle to overcome social discrimination by individual effort:

- The first Nike TV commercial shows Michael Jordan with Spike Lee on a basketball court. "Spike and Mike" highlights Michael Jordan's success story told by Spike Lee, who plays a fictional character living in the ghetto. Illustrating the two characters highlights Michael's success in overcoming social discrimination.
- The second TV commercial is still in the world of basketball but features no star this time. "Hardrock Miner" shows young black men improving their shooting skills on a basketball street. The universe is dark, the tone is messianic, and the music explicit. Everything embodies the struggle to beat social inequalities.
- The third TV campaign is aimed at the female target of Nike, a segment of the population still little seduced by the brand at the time. Once again, it is the angle of discrimination that is used in a spot called "If you let me play sports."
- The fourth TV campaign of Nike is built around Tiger Woods, a global star of golf – a sport that is at the antipodes of basketball and its street art. Yet Nike will use the previous cultural codes and apply the same tactics to give an image of Tiger Woods that is that of the oppressed American black who managed to rise to the top of the social ladder, by hard work and perfectionism without equal. Thanks to this bold treatment, Nike has been able to extend its myth to sports other than basketball.

To extend the brand to other countries and enter the coveted football market, Nike adapts its myth by replacing the black American ghetto with Brazilian favelas. In the eyes of the public, each brand has a legitimacy to tell a certain type of story. For example, Nike has authority over the personal motivational stories of athletes in their daily workouts. All Nike commercials have the same style of narration and construction: they start with the athlete in a situation of effort, a repetition of training-related events, and a modest success but which has great value for the athlete. The voiceover is often discreet and represents the athlete's inner voice. This unity in the style of history and form gives authority to the brand by giving it an exclusive right of ownership over these cultural codes.

Furthermore, Holt argues that brand cultures are collectively formed and shared. To become iconic, brands should anticipate avant-garde consumption and social trends. In order to do so, Holt recommends a methodology following six steps to develop an effective brand culture strategy. Table 7.2 summarizes the six steps to help brand managers and companies define and implement a brand culture strategy.

Therefore, within the cultural branding framework, brands are not seen as mere intermediaries of cultural significance, they become, themselves, moral standards that form cultural practices, commercial activities, and public rules regarding the individuals who belong to a particular consumption culture. For instance, robust brands continually advance referent models to define consumers' goals, desires, and thoughts as well as the way they behave and the way they might feel. Furthermore, brands may anticipate cultural aspects of faith, ideology, politics, and legend, as they normally endorse a philosophy and thought related to religious and political systems that associate consumption with happiness and well-being.

TABLE 7.2 Six steps for implementing a brand culture strategy

Step	Definition
Examine the cultural orthodoxy of the setting and the competitors	Brand managers should first study the cultural context that an innovation should circumvent, what we call cultural orthodoxy that refers to the conventional cultural expression (both ideology, myths, and cultural codes) used by the competition
Identify the social disruption that will move out orthodoxy	At every instant, societal changes take place and they end up disrupting consumer identification within conventional expression categories. Whether driven by technology, the economy, the media, or even something else, these changes will drive consumers to desire a new ideology
Uncover the ideological opportunity	It is necessary to evaluate how the disruption will act on the consumers. What are the new cultural expressions? How do they evolve? To which emerging ideology do consumers' values gravitate?
Collect appropriate source of materials	A cultural innovation is usually about cultural expressions coming from subcultures, social movements, or even the content of the brand. This is the source material that will be used by brand managers to respond to the ideological opportunity
Apply cultural tactics	Many techniques can serve as tactical improvements to a cultural strategy. For example, it may be to provoke ideological fighting, to mythologize the brand, or to revive a dormant ideology
Shape a cultural strategy	A cultural strategy needs to detect a precise occasion that is practical at a specific instant, in a certain social setting and replies to that occasion with a specific cultural manifestation. In fact, for a brand, to surf on a cultural precursor is certainly a paying strategy of innovation and development

MINI-CASE 7.2 NIVEA, DOVE, AND L'OREAL: DISTINGUISHED BRAND CULTURES?

Nivea is a German personal care brand specialized in body-care. Nivea is seen as a "protective brand" that focuses its communication on the success of its flagship product: Nivea Cream. Launched in 1911, its recipe remains unchanged and still contains no endocrine disruptors. Since then, Nivea continues to focus its efforts on the care and protection of skin. It has also developed a brand culture characterized by an ideology about what beauty is that emphasizes the idea of natural beauty and that all women are naturally beautiful.

For **Dove**, a personal care brand created in the 1950s and owned by Unilever, the brand culture refers to the commitment of the brand to fight for female's self-esteem and acceptance. The brand highlights female models that do not meet the traditional standards of beauty imposed by society, proposing instead the philosophy "beauty is inside you." The photographs they use have not been retouched, they are the images we greet each morning in the mirror. The brand is very active in viral marketing about the photoshopped lie. Its videos denounce an inaccessible idealism of beauty and the female body, which often create a media buzz. The brand also frequently produces testimonial films that lead women to think about why they are so critical of themselves. Its products promise no other miracle than that of offering a feeling of moisturizing well-being – and this is where the brand differentiates from all the others.

As a world leader in the cosmetics market and owner of 44 brands (up to date) with specific communications, the **L'Oreal** group relies on innovation and is now a major player in research and development. At the heart of its laboratories, the group has managed to recreate human tissue to abolished and move beyond the practice of testing cosmetics on animals, one of its greatest and yet subtle innovations. Furthermore, L'Oreal brand culture is characterized by an ideology relevant to the nature of beauty based on the idea that beauty is cultural and the brand should integrate cultural features in the commercial discourses and the products.

Storytelling

Storytelling has been the subject of a lot of attention in recent years; it is an approach that has been used for many centuries and was developed heavily by politicians and marketers alike. The idea behind storytelling is to influence the consumer through his/her feelings by using the solid expressive associations that stories deliver. The purpose is, by telling stories, to provoke feelings (rationality will only come in later to motivate the purchase) that should lead customers to be more open to the communication carried. The stories are created to capture the consideration of consumers and the tale will help consumers be more profoundly immersed than by using conventional communication modes.

- Emotions are seen as the key element, as they engage consumers and create involvement with the place/product;
- Narratives will use anecdotes, entertaining stories, details about a brand/destination, and portrays authentic pieces of information (even if legends are often brought in);
- The message has to convey sincerity. It needs to be seen not as a commercial message, but as a communication in which a consumer/local inhabitant/destination share its story with other like-minded customers;
- Memories are triggered when context and relevance are created through the story wherein the emotions elicited will also feed into long-term and meaningful souvenirs.

For example, a hotel room could be described using a traditional communication mode: description of the location, standards of service, and amenities. A storytelling approach will aim to describe the place by explaining, for instance, what the visitor will see from the hotel room (describing the landscape and nearby sights) and what can be undertaken close by, for example, a visit to a local farm that produces a memorable food product (it is even better if the owner is named personally, as a friend). The narrative may also have suggestions for types of activities that can be undertaken nearby (for instance, if it is cycling, brief explanations of the type of roads available, degree of difficulty, etc.). The description does not need to be too long but if it involves references to various senses, it will necessarily elicit emotions from the reader. The idea is to give the basis from which the reader can project him/herself into the experience. It is not so much a promise (as a traditional advertisement would be) but rather a sincere description of a rare and emotional moment.

THEORY BOX 7.2   STORYTELLING AND NARRATIVE: WHY DO BRANDS NEED TO TELL STORIES?

Storytelling is the art of telling stories and it is used in many fields and disciplines, such as communication, politics, movie, art, etc. Narrative is a representation of the facts or an event that is subjective in essence. Every representation is already an interpretation. The issuer represents, in some way, the knowledge of his/her speaker who has expectations that correspond to gender, context, and discourse.

A story requires at least two propositions: the first having a cause-and-effect relationship with the second. The listener or the reader should be able to follow the order of the episodes, as well as be able to grasp their meaning by judging and reflecting which is why the narrative activity combines a chronological order and a configurational order. A story is a series of events that, thanks to the concept of peripeteia (a sudden change in a story), connect to make sense. Thus, the story begins when an unexpected event occurs. Characters animate these stories, generating representations. History always has an intention and an illocutionary force. Then comes the coda, or evaluation. The reader or spectator analyzes the narrative and extracts its meaning.

> For the brand, both fictional and real narratives help shape the brand experience to connect and share values with its customers. In order to describe the brand identity, brand managers can use a character from literature; fiction gives a structure to reality. These narrative patterns known to all are unifying, composing a collective imagination such as "telling the brand story of the self-made man."

Storytelling is a strategic tool for narrative communication. Its approach is characterized by an emphasis on cultural, experiential, and emotional aspects that is very important for allowing brands to communicate in order to immerse their customers in meaningful experiences and share common values with them. Instead of promoting brands, products, and services by using traditional communication tools (e.g., advertising, sales promotion, direct marketing, etc.), customer experience should incorporate storytelling that consists of telling a story to consumers to promote brand awareness and values by creating an emotionally charged universe, identity, and story. In fact, stories are made and told by companies to reach their customers and create a strong relationship with them. Storytelling is an integral part of the building process of customer experience since it allows companies to:

- Differentiate themselves from the competition by making the customer aware of the brand's history, allowing him/her to share common values, and build loyalty;
- Place the customer and his/her lived experience at the center of the brand's history to create closeness;
- Highlight authenticity and values as well as ideological, symbolic, experiential, and emotional dimensions of the company's brand, products, and services.

Furthermore, in some cases, in order to create a strong and emotionally charged storytelling companies do not hesitate to call on artists and filmmakers to give the brand more human, emotional, and historical significance that consumers can capture and share. Additionally, the making of a story varies depending on the vision and the objectives of the company. Storytelling can be developed from the point-of-view of business, communication, media, and artists (novelists, writers, etc.) as well as from the perspective of social sciences, especially in the mythology field.

MINI-CASE 7.3 STORYTELLING IN LUXURY EXPERIENTIAL BRANDING: *INSIDE CHANEL*

For many communication agencies, Chanel represents the perfect illustration of the way storytelling can emphasize the brand identity and share cultural meaning with its customers. The brand, created more than a century ago by Gabrielle Chanel (aka Coco Chanel) and regarded as a symbol of French luxury, is indeed a master in the art of telling its story. Through videos, short films,

(continued)

(continued)

or photos, the products, values, and know-how of the house are scripted, allowing the universe of its brand to be always more accessible.

Chanel's storytelling strategy is reflected, for example, in the web series that the brand has created to trace the story of its creator: *Inside Chanel*. I note, in particular, Chapter 16, which focuses on the passion of Coco Chanel for the camellia, a flower that became symbolic of the luxury brand. The voiceover is a feminine voice embodying the personification of the camellia, which narrates throughout the video the place of the camellia in the life of the creator, how she used it, how she was inspired by it, and how it is found in her creations (in jewelry or later with the wedding dress imagined by Chanel's famous designer Karl Lagerfeld – entirely covered with embroidered camellias). The anaphora "I remember" allows the luxury brand to establish a relationship of intimacy, a dialogue, with the spectator (customer) – as if the latter returned to the life of Gabrielle Chanel.

In telling a story, the company goes beyond the functional aspects and rational arguments often used in traditional communication policies. In fact, storytelling draws its strength from the story it tells. To provide a strong and enjoyable customer experience, a good narrative story must include:

- Strong and unique emotional content allowing the identification and differentiation of the brand amongst its competitors;
- A theatrical and artistic staging of the brand and the elements associated with it;
- Visual and textual content that is memorable and easy to understand and memorize by consumers;
- Culturally appropriate content without losing the DNA and the essence of the brand.

In order to create an immersive and emotionally charged customer experience, marketers should know how to build a storyline that responds to their specific strategic objectives, which can emphasize one or more narrative elements related to the company's brand, products, and services.

By analyzing the literature in both marketing and narratology (narrative studies), I identified two main pathways that marketers can follow to construct the story of their company or brand: 1) the transformation of brand positioning into a history, and 2) the building of a storyline that retraces the "hero's journey," a model developed by the Joseph Campbell in his book *The Hero with a Thousand and One Faces*, first published in 1949 and reissued in 2008.

Transforming a brand's positioning into storytelling

To transform a brand's positioning into an emotional story, the brand manager should start from the DNA and the essence of the brand and then build around the narrative elements that highlight the values and positioning of the brand. In order to achieve a successful transformation process, several elements should be taken into consideration:

- The values and DNA of the brand and the history of the company;
- A narrative that can include the history of the founder and the brand, customer experiences, anecdotes, and tales, etc.;
- The temporal and spatial dimensions of the narration process;
- The roles assigned to each character in the story;
- The articulation of episodes with a common thread – several related stories that constitute the final story, stories interrupted by negative or positive events, etc.

The transformation of the brand DNA and its positioning into a strong storytelling requires four main steps: identity, relation, story, and incarnation. These steps are presented in Figure 7.1 following a methodological logic highlighting the main issues and objectives related to each step.

The hero's journey

The hero's journey is a concept and a tool established by Joseph Campbell in 1949. It is a classic of narratology extensively used even today in narrative communication to build stories with myths. The hero's journey is about building a story by describing the initiatory journey of a hero who goes through several phases during which he/she is likely to meet moments of happiness as well as difficulties that he/she will have to overcome during his/her initiatory journey. By passing from a known world to an unknown universe, the hero is realized and creates a myth that fascinates, inspires, and touches the audience. The hero's travel method is often used by novelists and filmmakers, and recently in video games (e.g., Tale of Dragon Age: Origins).

This model is particularly relevant in the development of narrative communication, as it is based on the study of the main myths in different cultures that have survived through time and have retained their status of myth in our contemporary societies

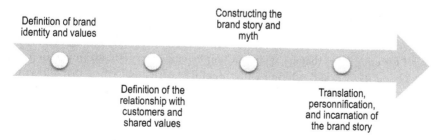

FIGURE 7.1 Four key steps in storytelling construction

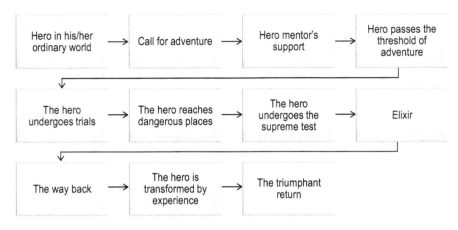

FIGURE 7.2 The hero's journey model

(e.g., the myth of Beauty and the Beast). Figure 7.2 summarizes the principal characteristics related to each phase of the hero's journey of travel that brand managers can take into account in their communication to tell a story and create a strong myth around the founder of the brand, his/her story, his/her personality, etc.

As shown in Figure 7.2, the construction of the brand's storytelling based on the narrative of the hero's journey can be achieved by following five main steps:

- The hero's dream of flight and the beginning of the transition from the known and ordinary world to an unknown universe;
- The decision to leave and the doubts and fears associated with it;
- The discovery of the extraordinary world;
- Mixed feeling due to the hardships encountered during the trip;
- Triumphal return to the known world with a transformed identity giving the hero the status of a myth.

Summary

In this chapter, I have examined one of the components of the experiential marketing mix "E" as "Emphasis" that replaces "P" of promotion in the 7Ps of the marketing mix. I have explained how brand managers and marketers can implement and emphasize two strategic communication approaches: the creation of a brand culture and brand storytelling. These communication strategies are very critical for companies that are willing to implement an experiential marketing mix by applying its 7Es, and offering a meaningful experiential setting that allows the brand to capture and share values with its actual and potential customers.

8

EMPATHY CAPITAL

Empathy concept, empathy experience, and empathy capital formation

Purpose and context

Empathy is the ability to take the perspective of others, to understand their reasoning and their emotional state. For a marketing manager, more specifically, it is the ability to take the customer's point-of-view and put him/herself in his/her place. A provision that should go without saying, but that is not so widespread, especially in the field of services. This chapter focuses on the component of "Empathy capital" as part of the experiential marketing mix that replaces the "P" of "People" in the traditional marketing mix or 7Ps. I explain in this chapter how "Empathy capital", its formation, and empathy experience capital can help companies in designing emotional and suitable customer experiences with employees who are able to empathize with customers and efficiently respond to their needs.

Learning outcomes

At the end of this chapter you will learn about one of the "7Es" of the experiential marketing mix "Empathy capital" that replaces the element "people" in the traditional marketing mix, its definitions, typologies, functioning, and how companies can use different empathic strategies to offer a good customer experience, which is achievable from the moment employees can develop an adaptive empathy capital that helps to identify the profile and the needs of their customers.

The empathy concept

This section will introduce the concept of empathy, its definition, the empathy tools, and marketing actions that can be taken into account by companies to construct, improve, and enhance the empathy of their employees, and thus translate their offers (products and services) into memorable and satisfying experiences. I will focus on the empathy of people who deliver the experience and who are in contact with customers. The empathy capital of people is a critical component of the experiential marketing that goes beyond the P of people in the marketing mix that only focuses on interpersonal skills and customer service in order to improve customer satisfaction.

A good experiential marketing mix is then based on the idea that with a strong empathy capital, employees, who are in contact with customers, would think "customer" first at both emotional (how does he/she feel today) and cognitive (what does he/she need according to his/her feeling today) levels. This can be achievable from the moment employees can develop an adaptive empathy capital that helps them use their social and interpersonal intelligence to identify the profiles, moods, aspirations, and expectations of the client's experiential moment.

What does empathy mean?

Most of the time, empathy is referred to as "I feel your pain," a shared emotional state that goes beyond "I know how you feel." In other words, empathy is the ability of the individual to put him/herself in the other person's place, to understand his/her reasoning and his/her emotional state. Empathy is a multidimensional concept and involves both emotion and cognition. Applying empathy to experiential marketing mix highlights the idea underlined in Greenson's definition (1960), which suggests that a company's employees should have the ability to put themselves in the shoes of their customers. The capacity to put oneself in another person's position allows us to understand his/her feelings, or to imagine his/her emotional, psychological, and intellectual representations. Consequently, empathy can be studied as a different concept, such as altruism, projection, inter-subjectivity, compassion, or identification. Since empathy is a complex phenomenon, this section will focus on the origins, definitions, and the evolution of the concept of empathy. It will also distinguish empathy from other closely related but confusing constructs in order to provide a definition that is easy to implement in the experiential marketing mix.

THEORY BOX 8.1 EMPATHY AND ITS RELATIONSHIP TO EXPERIENCE

Empathy is a complex phenomenon – a very human one that is found in the heart of one's self and is linked to emotions and experience (narrative empathy). It is through the shared experience of the world corroborated by the presence of others that objectivity can be constituted. Empathy is deeply rooted in the experience of our lived body, and it is this experience that allows us to recognize others, not as spirit-endowed bodies, but as like-minded people. There could be no perception without consciousness of the acting individual.

> Empathy is what makes one recognize others not as a single object, but as an alter ego that, despite its persistent difference, aims at the same world as us. Inter-subjectivity is then the starting point of an understanding of empathy. Stein (1964) states that the concept of empathy is not simply limited to the feelings or emotions of others within experiences. There is a more elementary connotation of empathy: the "other" is experienced as other than oneself through the recognition of similarity. An important part of it lies in the common experience of action. This shared experience then turns out to be the pillar of shared identity. Depraz (2001) distinguished four complementary levels of empathy:
>
> - The involuntary coupling of one's "living" body with the "living" body of the other in perception and action;
> - The imaginary transposition of oneself into the situation of the other;
> - The interpretation of others as an other for oneself, and of oneself as others for others;
> - The ethical and moral perception of others.

Empathy: origins and evolution

A primary consultation of the Oxford dictionary shows that empathy is the "ability to identify with others, to feel what they feel." This definition raises questions about the components of empathy, its process, and its relationship to sharing affects and feelings. Etymologically, the word "empathy" derives from the Ancient Greek word *empatheia* (physical affection or passion). It is a combination of two words "em" for "in" and "pathos" for "feeling." Drawing on the Greek definition, two German philosophers, Hermann Lotze and Robert Vischer, proposed in 1858 a German word *Einfühlung* ("feeling into"), a term from a philosophy of art aesthetics that states that the appreciation of a viewed object depends on the viewer's ability to project his/her personality into the object. In other words, Vischer (1873) refers to *Einfühlung* as the relationship of a subject with a work of art, allowing him/her to access its meaning.

Moving from a theory of art to philosophy, the notion is taken up by Lipps (1903) who states that the individual's access to something by experiencing the situation on the mode of "feeling in the thing." Later, Lipps claims that we can attribute feelings and emotions to others similar to ours by only recognizing their forms (e.g., the observer of a pride situation, can at the same time feel pride him/herself).

The British psychologist Edward Titchener (1909/2014) translated the original German term *Einfühlung* into the English term empathy (Gallese, 2003). By taking up the thesis developed by Lipps, Titchener refers to empathy as the amalgam of visual and kinesthetic imagery through which certain perceptual experiences become possible. Titchener attributes to empathy both a perceptive and a social function.

In the modern era, empathy is the ability to identify with others and to marry the subjective perspective of others. It is a distinctive trait that makes us so deeply human, which is at the source of social reasoning and moral behavior. It allows us to access the subjectivity of others through a mode of thought of implicit knowledge. Decety (2002) describes empathy as being based on neurobiological systems shaped during our evolutionary history. From a Neo-Darwinian perspective, empathy would have a role in social relations between members of the same species, or even interspecific members.

Empathy is not a mechanism in itself, but a process of communication whose purpose is to specify the mechanism(s). Freud (1920) states that the process of empathy identification shows the way to get into the feelings of the other without being emotionally involved. According to the iconic North American humanistic psychologist Carl Rogers (1980), empathy is about capturing as accurately as possible the internal references and emotional components of another person and understanding him/her as if she/he was that other person. In the phenomenological tradition, empathy represents the apprehension of the affective dimensions of others.

Rogers established a relationship between empathy and experience by developing a permissive, person-centered psychotherapeutic relationship. Through a series of interviews, the individual gradually acquires an understanding of him/herself to a degree that makes him/her able to deal with the realities of life in a more constructive way, and to discover with relief his/her own solutions to his/her problems. Then, Rogers theorizes his psychotherapeutic practice, which refers to empathy as a significant variable in the helping of relationships. In other words, empathy is a matter of perceiving from the inside the personal reactions, and the essential feelings of the individual as they appear to him/her and communicating this understanding to him/her. As written by Rogers,

> to be empathic, is to perceive the inner frame of reference of others as precisely as possible and with the emotional components and meanings that belong to them as if one were that person, but without ever ignoring the condition of "as if."
>
> *(2004: 59)*

Therefore, empathy allows the professional to participate as intimately as possible in the customer experience while remaining emotionally independent. For Rogers, empathy is a process of entering into the perceptive world of others, which allows it to become sensitive to the affect movements that occur in the latter, while keeping the awareness of being a separate person from him/her. For the French psychosociologist Mucchielli (1995), empathy refers to the "cold intelligence" that allows one's immersion into the subjectivity of the other: "it is this effort that we call 'empathy,' an effort of *decentration* in relation to oneself in order to enter the universe of the other, and thus understand him/her in a humanistic manner" (1995: 10). In phenomenology, Edmund Husserl refers to empathy as the decisive phenomenon from which intersubjectivity emerges to elaborate a common world.

Also, the concept of empathy should be distinguished from sympathy. Unlike sympathy that refers to sharing a feeling or a belief allowed by the phenomenon of "affective contagion," empathy reflects the representation of the feelings, desires, and beliefs of others, and thus does not simply address only the conscious subjectivity. To be in sympathy with the other is to be concerned about his/her well-being. Empathy, thus, appears as a conscious mental simulation of the subjectivity of others. In other words, the mental simulation allows individuals to understand what another person thinks and feels in a present, past, or even in an anticipated situation (Decety, 2004). In summary, the discussions related to the emergence and the development of empathy trace back, as Stotland and colleagues emphasize, to "the beginnings of philosophical thought" (1978: 11). However, despite widespread contributions in different disciplines, empathy is not a well-defined concept and is most of the time confused with other notions.

Empathy and areas of confusion

Given the numerous definitions of empathy that were outlined over 100 years ago (Cuff et al., 2016), several points of confusion resulted from the multiplicity of these definitions and their outcomes that can make the understanding and application of empathy in customer experience compromising. While Batson (2009) states that several significant efforts have been made by scholars to distinguish empathy from a variety of related concepts, Preston and de Waal (2002) describe empathy as an overall set encompassing all related concepts, such as sympathy, emotional contagion, inter-subjectivity, and compassion. Ickes (2003) offered a relevant categorization in order to distinguish empathy from these frequently associated notions by proposing a discussion on the concept based on the identification of six associated notions, including empathy (Figure 8.1).

For Ickes (2003), the six identified notions vary through three main levels:

- The degree of cognitive representations of the target's emotional state;
- The degree of emotion sharing;
- The degree to which a self/other distinction is maintained.

FIGURE 8.1   Classification of empathy-related constructs

For Ickes, empathy is situated in the middle of these three levels, which makes it clear that empathy is a debatable concept and, as stated by Ickes "it has an inherent ambiguity that invites the kind of definitional debates that have continued unresolved since the term *Einfühlung* was first introduced nearly a century ago" (2003: 64). Thus, the concept of empathy invites more research on how and why empathy can be distinguished from other overreaching constructs.

However, the most common debate with regard to empathy is related to its differentiation from sympathy that appears in several studies. While some scholars empathize the connection between both concepts, others, such as Hein and Singer (2008), claim that empathy and sympathy should be disconnected. Eisenberg and colleagues (1991) define sympathy as a distinctive construct. They refer to sympathy as a vicarious emotional reaction based on the apprehension of others' emotional state or situation, which involves feelings of sorrow or concern for the other. This definition is close to the definition of empathy, but does not incorporate all its dimensions. Furthermore, two other concepts are frequently associated with empathy:

- Compassion: refers to the sensation that results from observing others' distress, and which provokes a consequent wish to help;
- Tenderness: an extensive friendly and comforting feeling frequently provoked by vulnerable behaviors.

In order to distinguish empathy from other constructs, Cuff and colleagues (2016) examined 43 distinct definitions, and thus identified seven themes reflecting the essence of empathy: 1) cognitive or affective; 2) congruent or incongruent; 3) subject to other stimuli; 4) self/other distinction or merging; 5) trait or state influences; 6) behavioral outcome; 7) and automatic or controlled. These themes are developed in Table 8.1.

TABLE 8.1 Empathy themes

Theme	Characteristic
Cognitive or affective	A highly debated characteristic of empathy is if it is a cognitive or affective notion. Cognitive empathy is the aptitude to appreciate others' feelings, linked narrowly to the theory of the mind. Affective empathy is related to the experience of emotion, caused by an emotional motivation. Certain definitions are grounded upon merely affective or cognitive mechanisms. However, numerous definitions include both
Congruent or incongruent	Certain scholars have clearly claimed that the empathic emotion of the observer has to be corresponding with that of the observed individual, with numerous suggesting this to be the situation in a "sharing" of emotions or "experiencing" the other's emotions vicariously. For others, correspondence may happen but is not essential, and some authors propose that the emotion is congruent with the observer's perception of need

Subject to other stimuli	Some authors suggest that an emotional other exists for the observer to observe. With rare exceptions, almost all scholars make this statement. Yet, certain ones claim that straight perception might not be essential, and empathy can either be in reply to the emotions or other emotional stimuli
Self/other distinction or merging	Authors refer to a clear definition of self/other distinction: the observer is conscious that his/her emotional experience originates from an exterior source. The principal reason for a self/other distinction derives from the need to distinguish empathy from emotional contagion
Trait or state influences	Authors refer to empathy as an "ability" or "capacity," suggesting an unchanging characteristic concept. Though, others recommend that empathic replies may be setting-specific. The attribute interpretation suggests that some individuals are more empathic than others, with this aptitude being steady throughout time
Behavioral outcome	Authors question if empathy automatically has a behavioral consequence. Although it is suggested that empathy is frequently followed by a behavioral response, many authors have claimed that empathy has no related behavioral result in the instant appreciation. A few definitions comprise behavioral responses to empathy and some stage models of the empathic process cover some shapes of behavioral outcome
Automatic or controlled	Authors have questioned if empathy is instinctively provoked or subject to control. Some of them claimed that empathy, like other characteristics of the mind, can be created and shaped by variables beyond one's control

The forms of empathy

Drawing on French human psychology literature, in particular, the works of Boulanger and Lançon (2006), empathy, as a component of the experiential marketing mix, can be implemented through five principal actions:

1. Dynamic coupling of the living experience of oneself (e.g., salesperson) and the customer. It refers to the pre-reflexive level of perception and action, which is the foundation of empathy creation and expression. When implementing or observing dynamic coupling by living a purchase experience, two identities may emerge from the coupling of seller's and buyer's lived experiences: a social identity, as seen by others, and a shared identity when the new-shared meaning emerges. The shared identity between sellers and buyers is a form of pre-reflexive and implicit comprehension of the other, and is based on a strong sense of identity connecting individuals to each other. This coupling or pairing represents a link between the self (e.g., salesperson) and the other (e.g., customer) on the basis of their experience similarity.

2. Imaginary transposition. Empathy can be expressed through imaginary transposition, which refers to the lived experiences of others through the efforts to access their consciousness. Instead of coupling experiences, a cognitive process is employed by the company's employees to mentally imagine or transpose themselves into the role of the customers. This mediation is the result of the imagination, which relies on

perceptions but in a deferred way: everything happens "as if" one could be in the place of the other without going there. This transposition reflects the "spatialization" of the imagination: I am here and also, in a certain way, there (I'm a seller, but, in a certain way, a customer).

3. Interpretation of customers through communication and language. Expressing empathy involves gestural or verbal communications that allow companies' employees to show to their customers that they are able to perceive themselves from the client's perspective.

4. Recognition of the other (customer) as a person who deserves attention and respect. From an evolutionist's perspective, moral understanding begins to emerge as children perceive others as intentional agents. Moral understanding does not come from any rules imposed by the adult world, but rather from the ability to experience empathy. Employees' ethics here should be regarded as a responsibility to a person who feels emotions. Thus, the conception and expression of empathy emphasize the fundamentally ethical and emotional nature of the experience lived by customers.

5. Altruism marketing. Altruistic marketing practices refer to a company's willingness to take an interest in others in order to create an empathic identity. An altruistic brand is characterized by behaviors oriented towards others who benefit from it and for which no advantage is hoped by the brand. Altruism encompasses three types of motivations that can encourage brands to develop an altruistic attitude:

   a. Charity, commitment motivations, and positive contribution to society;
   b. Motivations related to the brand's self-image or brand's ego-altruism;
   c. Motivations that reflect an idealistic vision of the world, which can take two forms: personal pleasure and solidarity.

Empathy in customer experience

Definition

Drawing on previous definitions and discussions of the concept of empathy in human psychology, I can now define the empathic customer experience:

> An empathy experience is a multidimensional concept that has emotional, cognitive, and motivational facets. It combines both mental and affective dimensions, and is reliant upon the interaction between personal feature capacities and sociocultural influences. Empathy has a vital role in facilitating interpersonal relationships within consumption experiences, in which relations between customers and company's employees are essential to offering enjoyable, satisfying, and profitable customer experiences. The emotions of the customer and company's employees in contact with the latter (salespeople, front desk, etc.) are alike but not indistinguishable because a self/other difference is an integral part of empathy development and expression. Creating an

empathic customer experience can be either unconscious, or generated by a controlled practice and learning process. Furthermore, other stimuli, such as the capacity of salespeople to develop their imagination about customers, can create empathy in customer experience.

Following previous discussions, the conceptualization I offered above acknowledges the significance of both mental and emotional aspects embedded within a shared customer experience. Creating an empathic experiential setting can be achieved, either through a controlled process, or through an instinctive mode that leads to behavioral outcomes. Empathy in customer experience is then the ability of salespeople to perceive and be sensitive to the emotional states of their customers, often combined with motivation to worry about their well-being.

Empathy experience functioning

The empathy of companies' employees (e.g., salespeople, waiters, front desk, and others) who have direct relationships with customers refers to a complex mental state in which different perceptual, cognitive, motivational, and emotional processes interact with each other. Empathy is deeply embedded in the lived customer experience, and it is this shared experience that allows employees ranging from front-line staff to managing directors to recognize customers, not only as clients, but as like-minded people who wish to be treated according to the logic: "I treat customers the way I would like to be treated."

Since the concept of empathy is by nature nomadic and unstable because of its continued migration from one discipline to another – formerly from aesthetics, philosophy, and then to psychology to end up in marketing – I propose a categorization of empathy in customer experience marketing, which includes the following ideas:

- Empathy takes place in a state of consciousness;
- Empathy implies the relationship;
- Empathic understanding occurs at different levels of accuracy;
- Empathy has temporal dimensions limited to the present moment;
- Empathy requires energy that varies in intensity;
- Empathy implies objectivity;
- Empathy means validation of the experience;
- Empathy requires being free from a value judgment or evaluation.

Components of empathic customer experience

Drawing on prior sections and works in the social neuroscience field, especially those of Decety and colleagues (2016), who refer to empathy as a driver of prosocial behaviors, I propose hereafter three main components of empathic customer experience: cognitive, emotional, and motivational. These three components are somewhat independent, although they can interact with each other. In other words, one can understand the feelings of the other without feeling the same emotions.

- Emotional–empathic experience. It refers to the ability of salespeople to share the emotional state of their customers in terms of intensity and the intrinsic attractiveness and/or averseness of the shared experience. This key component of customer experience empathy plays an essential role in nonverbal communication, especially in experiences of distress, disappointment, or dissatisfaction. The emotional aspect of empathic customer experience is independent of the cognitive dimension of empathy that allows one (buyer) to understand other's (customer) own mental states (desires, beliefs, intentions, and attitudes). Though, emotional–empathy is not shared by others. In other words, emotional sharing does not necessarily or automatically lead to concern for others. Indeed, it can trigger a distress response from the observer (salespeople) but then be associated with withdrawal behavior rather than helping others (customers).
- Cognitive–empathic experience. It allows the salesperson to consciously put him/herself into the mind of the customer to try to understand what he/she is thinking about an offer (product or service) or feeling about his/her lived purchase experience. This perspective underlines the fact that salespeople have to develop skills related to social thinking from a customer standpoint. The customer perspective can then help salespeople to understand the subjective state of their customers, and thus anticipate their tacit emotional and functional needs. Therefore, cognitive empathy can be stimulated or reinforced by various means, such as reading or watching movies. In doing so, whether in an implicit or explicit way (as in reading a novel), another person's perspective can be adopted.
- Motivational–empathic experience. It refers to the concern of the other (customer) and reflects the motivation of salespeople to care for the well-being of their customers. This component of empathic customer experience is also very natural and appears in the context of parental care for many animal species. Motivational–empathy is, therefore, a biological necessity for survival and development as well as an integral part of humans' social interactions.

Empathy in the experiential marketing mix

Empathy is not an easy element of the experiential marketing mix to consider in creating memorable and satisfying customer experiences. Indeed, empathy is a complex element that involves several human, social, and environmental factors. For instance, a salesperson who speaks the same language is always better suited to create empathy, and thus facilitates sales. However, that alone is not enough when it comes to dealing with a customer who has just had a bad day and who is probably in a negative emotional state. This customer will strongly appreciate being looked after with more attention and understanding. The customer will also be demonstrating behaviors that will show that he/she will request other additional services, perhaps even gifts. The lack of empathy can generate consumer frustration, and thus dissatisfaction. Indeed, marketers should think as persons and not as professionals in order to develop their empathy. In so doing, salespeople will improve customer experiences and interactions with the brand, products, service providers, salespeople, etc. By understanding the interactions between the emotional, cognitive, and behavioral aspects of consumer needs, companies, too, will be better armed to offer enjoyable consumption/shopping experiences, and thus a durable satisfaction for their customers.

In his book *'Empathetic' Marketing: How to Satisfy the 6 Core Emotional Needs of Your Customers*, Mark Ingwer uncovers an empathic marketing framework that can help companies identify human needs and include this logic into marketing strategy, communication tools and campaigns, and customer experience design. To do so, Ingwer (2012) identified eight key dimensions that constitute an integral part of 'empathetic' marketing: 1) the capacity to identify emotional needs behind decisions; 2) the need for continuum; 3) the need for control; 4) the need for self-expression; 5) the need for growth; 6) the need for recognition; 7) the need for belonging; and 8) the need for care.

MINI-CASE 8.1   EMPATHY IN SERVICES: THE CASE OF THE CAR RENTAL SECTOR

The car rental industry is a highly competitive sector where there is a need to apply empathy, which requires taking into account different aspects. First, the level of prior knowledge of the client. It may be the first time he/she goes to this city. It may be useful to give him/her a plan to easily leave the agency and come back with as much ease as possible. Also, taking into account his/her abilities in different situations could be appreciated (e.g., are the car's list of options configured according to the language he/she uses? Another question: if the customer arrives late, he/she is probably in a more or less strong state of fatigue. He/she may then appreciate a drink or help loading his/her luggage).

These simple elements are factors of differentiation in an industry where many elements of the service are generally strictly aligned. They require to go, like the customer, through different stages of access to the service, in similar circumstances, or to be able to imagine them. The advantage of being empathic is having the ability to accurately observe the interior setting of reference of the customer, the emotional mechanisms, and the senses attached to it, as if the seller or the service provider was the customer him/herself. Someone who needs more than just a car rental: perhaps empathy regarding his/her situation, whether he/she is coming from far or not, etc. Car rental employees in contact with customers should be trained and able to project themselves into the clients' situation, and feel what they feel and do, feel their fatigue or suffering at the same time as them, identify with them, understand their fears.

Thus, empathy at all levels can transform the customer experience and provoke positive emotions. For instance, the interaction with a passionate seller who values the customer and his/her company's philosophy, culture, history, know-how, etc. who also is an expert of the brand and its products, and has a listening and understanding approach, will generate a consumer's happiness and make him/her want to spend more time in a store, or come back next time, possibly with family and friends as he/she appreciated the human exchange and the discussions about the brand and life in general.

In a highly competitive context, empathy allows marketing managers to meet two fundamental needs: functional and emotional. These elements constitute an integral part of a relevant experiential marketing mix application for designing successful and memorable customer experiences and, as a result, allows the company to create an ultimate competitive advantage as well as customer satisfaction and loyalty.

Drawing on social neuroscience literature, especially Zaki and Ochsner (2012) who developed an empathy process framework, I then suggest an empathy experience logic based on distinction between: *perceivers* (a company's employees in contact with end-consumers focusing on the customer's internal state) and *targets* (consumers who are the emphasis of a perceivers' consideration). The aim of empathy in customer experience is then more about helping customers rather than selling products to them. The dynamic and the relationships between the two market actors shape the empathy experience in a particular consumption setting.

Further, the empathy experience framework assembles a set of processes that generate empathy that fits into three comprehensive categories:

- Experience sharing: vicarious sharing of customers'/targets' internal conditions;
- Mentalizing: clearly seeing (and possibly examining) customers'/targets' mental conditions and their foundations;
- Prosocial concern: conveying stimulus to advance customers'/targets' experiences (for instance, by decreasing their anxiety).

MINI-CASE 8.2   IKEA'S RETAIL THERAPY TO CREATE EMPATHY

In 2016, IKEA completely changed its communication strategy by renaming its products based on people's search on Google. It is no longer a question of simply promoting the furniture of the brand, but, especially highlighting family situations that we all know to communicate in a much more subtle way. The brand noticed that many people used Google to answer existential questions: "My children go out too much," "He cannot manage to tell me that he loves me," etc., therefore the furniture brand decided to associate these questions with its products, which becomes:

"How to succeed in a long distance relationship" for carton transportation, "My partner snores" for a sofa, or "My mother cannot cook" for a microwave oven.

All these search words gave IKEA an idea for implementing the "Retail Therapy" operation. On the website, the brand has assigned each of its products a Google query name that appears in the top searches. Users who continue to query the famous search engine to answer their existential questions can be found on the brand's website. It was a brilliant and relevant idea that allows IKEA to express its empathy and its proximity to its consumers, and, especially to generate many more purchases on the web.

Empathy capital formation

Empathy capital is important for companies, and particularly for customer experience design, because it allows marketers and brand managers to truly understand and decode the hidden needs and emotions of the customers they are designing the experience for. As such, companies can design customer experiences that go beyond the three dimensions of an offering (product or service): attractiveness, viability, and sustainability by developing the empathy capital of their employers, from engineers to salespeople, and training them to develop and practice their empathy potential. It is, thus, obvious that marketing professionals and brands who demonstrate empathy provide better customer experiences with higher satisfaction. The best approach to training professionals in developing their empathy skills is to make sure that their professionalized empathy is customer-centric, focused on customer well-being, helpful, intentional, self-conscious, self-inspiring, and maintainable. In order to help professionals develop their empathy capital, two approaches can be applied: an empathy map (business-based framework) and McLaren's empathy model (research-based applied to business).

Empathy map

Following this idea, the development of empathy capital of perceivers (e.g., salespeople) can be achieved through the use of the experience empathy map – a collaborative tool developed by David Gray in 1993, the founder of XPLANE, which is a global consulting agency that provides businesses with a human-centered design toolkit.

The empathy map can be used by professionals to develop their empathy skills, and gain a deeper understanding of their customers. A very easy tool to use, the empathy map represents the customer (target) in the center and is surrounded by main boxes that include the following questions:

- What would customers be thinking and feeling?
- What are their doubts and ambitions?
- What might it be possible for their networks, associates, friends, and superiors to say while the client is consuming our product/service?

- What would the customer catch or perceive in these situations?
- What would customers see while consuming our product/service in their setting?
- What might the customer be telling and/or doing while consuming our product/service?
- How would that be modified in both public and private spheres?
- What are certain of the customer's discomfort facts or worries when consuming our product/service?
- What improvements might the customer experience need while consuming our product/service?

McLaren's empathy model

Using an innovative model, which was developed by Karla McLaren (2013) while working in the area of health experience, makes the development of empathy capital achievable and all of the practices in customer experience empathy easily manageable. By applying this model, marketing professionals and brand managers can learn how to develop and work with their empathy; and learn how to become knowledgeable and happy empathic market actors. Drawing on McLaren's model, empathy capital can be developed by focusing on six essential aspects (Figure 8.2).

As shown in Figure 8.2, the six aspects of empathy build upon each other and while emotion contagion tends to occur automatically, the other elements are

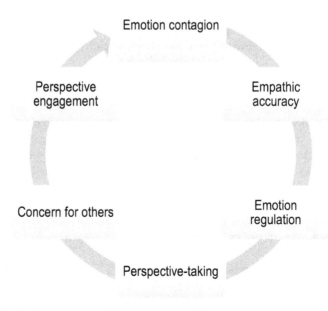

FIGURE 8.2 Six key aspects of the empathy model

more deliberate and can be advanced with the empathic skills one can learn and develop throughout life.

- Emotion contagion: before empathy can be implemented, consumers need to feel that an emotion is happening – or that an emotion is expected of the service provider or the salesperson. The entire process of empathy relies upon the capacity of the company's employees in contact with customers to feel and share emotions with them by developing emotional skills.
- Empathic accuracy: refers to the ability of employees in contact with customers to precisely identify and understand emotional states and intentions in themselves and in the customers.
- Emotion regulation: in order to be an active empathic responder, company's employees should develop the ability to understand, regulate, and work with their own emotions; they have to be self-conscious of their own emotions in order to regulate them, and be able to respond skillfully to the needs of the customers in the occurrence of strong emotions, rather than being overwhelmed by them.
- Perspective-taking is a competency that helps employees who are in contact with customers put themselves in the place of the customers; and see the situations through their eyes in an attempt to sense what might be their feelings, needs, and fears.
- Concern for others: empathy is not enough to provide a satisfying customer experience: employees have to show their ability to care about their customers in a way that displays compassion and concern.
- Perspective engagement allows employees to make perspective decisions based on their empathy and to respond and act in a way that is in accordance with their empathy while offering solutions for customers. It includes both the capability to feel and precisely identify the emotions of customers, regulate their own emotions, assume the perspective of customers, focus on them with care and concern, and then act in a skillful way based upon their perceptions.

Therefore, McLaren's framework applied to empathy capital formation to improve customer experience can help professionals to:

- Define strategies that create, support, and maintain empathy capital;
- Help employees develop emotional skills and mindfulness training;
- Develop, practice, and apply the six aspects of empathy in designing appropriate customer experiences;
- Identify strategies to involve or disengage certain facets of empathy, depending on customers' states and requirements;
- Understand the role of emotions either positive, negative, or both in the workplace and their impact on empathy, communication, performance, customer experience, and outcomes;
- Developing practical skills to encourage and support an emotionally well-synchronized customer experience.

MINI-CASE 8.3   PROCTER & GAMBLE PROMOTES SELF-CONFIDENCE OF TEENAGE GIRLS: ALWAYS #LIKEAGIRL

"You run like a girl!" is the supreme insult on the playground, which means someone is running badly. This derision is supposed to mean girls are not fast, they are not even strong, and not even good enough to drive. The "Always" promotional campaign speaks to and defends women by carrying out a movement that goes against this phenomenon. The brand Always uses several participants, male or female, small or taller, to put into practice certain phrases like "running like a girl," "throwing like a girl," and "fighting like a girl." Thus, the expression "like a girl" loses its power and becomes less often (if ever) associated with silly and weak behavior. Casual aggressions like these, especially when made to girls, could be a good explanation for the loss of confidence in teenage girls, which affects one in two girls during puberty.

Studies on young American girls aged 16 to 24 show that at puberty, girls are afraid of failure and feel that the pressure of society is enhancing this fear of failure. They do not dare to try new things for fear of failing. Yet failure is a respectable thing; it helps us learn, grow, and ultimately build our self-confidence. For more than 30 years, Always has been working to educate millions of teenage girls by instructing them about puberty and its effects to give them confidence. In its promotional campaign, a video displays ten-year-old girls who were interviewed without knowing the answers of the other participants and, therefore, without being influenced. Always asks young women to show what it means to "run like a girl." Their interpretations of actions are immediately degrading to their gender. But when the same request is made to little girls, they give the best of themselves. A contrast pointing to the decline in self-confidence suffered by girls during puberty. Always chooses to change this mindset by encouraging the men and women of this video to see things from a different perspective. This is a very empathic initiative and a moving video that allows the brand to establish a strong connection with its customers through showing and sharing its empathy.

Summary

This chapter has examined one of the components of the experiential marketing mix "E" as "Empathy capital" that replaces "P" of "People" in the 7Ps of the marketing mix. Beyond focusing on people and their training, in Chapter 8, I highlighted the importance of empathy capital formation in designing positive customer experiences that are suitable to customers and allow companies to use different empathic strategies to train their employees to sense, feel, and act like the consumer throughout the purchase experience by putting themselves in the customers' shoes and seeing the world through their eyes.

9

EMOTIONAL TOUCHPOINTS

From customer touchpoints to emotional touchpoints and emotional touchpoints toolkit

Purpose and context

Customer touchpoints are the points of contact between the company (products and services) and customers who can interact with service encounters that can affect their experience in a positive or a negative way. Thus, touchpoints are one of the essential characteristics and one of the most important pillars of the customer experience design. However, in the actual definition and practices of experience touchpoints, emotions and the way they are generated and expressed by customers are not considered in the process, and the focus is more on the tool or the platform of contact rather than on the emotion generated by the tools. We know that a successful contact that emotionally engages the customer is a fundamental part of the success of the customer experience design. Therefore, the starting point for identifying customer experience touchpoints should focus more on emotions to define the touchpoint and not the other way around. That is why I propose, in this chapter, an approach to emotional touchpoints that offers a very tangible input to the customer experience design and shows how to support such customer emotional engagement in practice.

Chapter 9 focuses on "Emotional touchpoints" as a component of the "7Es" of the experiential marketing mix that replaces the "P" of "Physical environment," which is part of the traditional marketing mix or 7Ps. I show, in this chapter, how companies can shift the focus from the logic of a physical environment that includes the examination of the main physical and digital touchpoints to a more holistic and customer-oriented logic based on the idea of emotional touchpoints to help companies design customer experiences with emotional touchpoints that are suitable and can match the needs of customers through different stages in their journey.

Learning outcomes

At the end of this chapter you will learn about one of the "7Es" of the experiential marketing mix "Emotional touchpoints," the shift from a touchpoints logic to emotional touchpoints approach and its toolkit cards, as well as the way companies can use this new tool in designing suitable and profitable customer experiences.

From customer touchpoints to emotional touchpoints

Emotional touchpoints go beyond the idea of customer journey touchpoints (Figure 9.1) in which customers might find a brand online or in an advertisement, see evaluations and reviews, ask friends who already had an experience with the brand, visit company's website, shop at a retail store, or contact customer service before, during, and after their experiences. In the journey touchpoints, companies only focus on the individual transactions through which customers interact with parts of the business and its offerings in a very functional and optimized way. It is relatively easy to apply and control in order to ensure customers' satisfaction by connecting them with the company's services, products, salespeople, etc.

Despite being a central part of customer experience and service literature, research into touchpoints is very limited and the existing works are either practice-based or, in the marketing field, authors studied it under CRM (customer relationship marketing) literature, which mostly focuses on the need for integrative approaches to multiple channels, a term often used instead of touchpoints. Rather than focusing on customer experiences and emotions, CRM uses technologies as the main tool to develop efficiency, organize, and optimize relationships with customers by transforming them into automatic and integrated relationships. As stated by Payne and Frow: "CRM is a management approach that seeks to create, develop, and enhance relationships

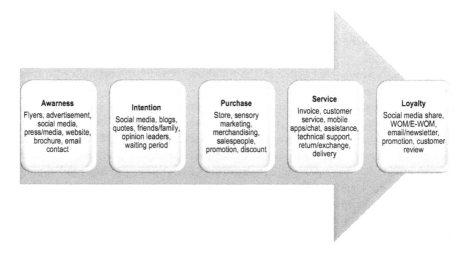

FIGURE 9.1 Customer journey touchpoints

with carefully targeted customers to maximize customer value, corporate profitability, and thus, shareholder value" (2004: 527). Therefore, the logic behind using CRM is purely functional and economic (e.g., maximizing profitability). Although certain works on CRM (e.g., Choy, 2008) demonstrate an interest in rethinking touchpoints by reintegrating them into the customer experience approach, little literature is available regarding how we can apply touchpoints to improve customer experience at both the functional and emotional levels. There is, therefore, a strong need for developing research on how to identify the appropriate touchpoints that really count in the customer experience, what kind of points of contact companies need to set up, how they could be related to customer experience, how service providers could use them with other touchpoints, and for what kind purposes.

Using touchpoints in service literature is not new. It was introduced by Shostack as part of service design under the term "service blueprinting," which refers to: "everything the consumers use to verify their service's effectiveness. The setting, including color schemes, advertising, printed or graphic materials, and stationery, all proclaim a service's style. The design should not be carelessly delegated to outsiders or left to chance" (1984: 137). Shostack used the term "orchestration" to explain how service blueprinting and its points of contact should be designed to offer a satisfying service experience.

However, connecting customers with offerings, products, salespeople, and services is not enough to create a satisfying customer experience at functional, emotional, and social levels. Indeed, the explosion of customer interaction points both offline and online, as well as the growth of channels and applications in a context with multi-touchpoint, multichannel, and hypercompetitive environments make the reliability of satisfying customer experience across these touchpoints difficult and unmanageable. Further, integrated marketing (e.g., Iacobucci and Calder, 2003; Fortini-Campbell, 2003), which takes a holistic approach of service delivery by emphasizing the importance of touchpoints and linking them to customer experience by better understating consumer behaviors and creating brand identity, did not really focus on emotional touchpoints as connectors.

Therefore, while customer touchpoints refer to the brand's points of customer contact from start to end of the customer journey in a very functional way, emotional touchpoints primarily focus on the emotional impact of the moments where customers interact with different services and people. Thus, customer touchpoints, as described in prior works focusing on services and customer journey, has a narrow view since it focuses only on those moments where a customer/user interacts in some way with the company's services or products, such as arriving at the store, talking with a salesperson, or having a dinner at the restaurant, etc.

The idea of using emotional touchpoints leads companies to develop a deeper understanding of the emotions related to the experience by focusing more on the moments where the customers' memories are being activated. Are customers touched in an emotional way (feelings) or a cognitive way (profound and long-term memories); independently or whether the moments were profound in a customer's contact with the company (e.g., living a dinner experience or a hotel experience); or within small and short-term interactions. All can have the same significance for the customer in terms of emotional and cognitive impact.

Emotional touchpoints were first used in the medical field, especially in nursing research, to improve the patient and family experience in hospitals and for supporting doctors, nurses, and other people to deliver compassionate, empathic, and dignified care (e.g., Dewar et al., 2009). Dewar and colleagues used emotional touchpoints as a method to understand compassionate care in hospital settings.

MINI-CASE 9.1   THE USE OF EMOTIONAL TOUCHPOINTS TO IMPROVE PATIENT AND FAMILY EXPERIENCE

The study of Dewar and colleagues in the care field shows how emotional touchpoints can be used as a technique for exploring patient and family experience. The study was conducted in the UK and was part of the "Leadership in Compassionate Care Program," which focuses on improving the experience in hospital and training staff to provide compassionate care. The study used an action research method to embed compassionate care in practice and education.

Data were produced using the touchpoint method from 16 patients and 12 relatives from a variety of care situations that comprised medicine for the elderly, older people's mental health, and a stroke unit to describe patient and family experiences and learn more about compassionate care in hospital settings. The first objective of the study was to examine what compassionate care means to different stakeholders, including staff, patients, and their families. The emotional touchpoints method was used to address the following topics:

- The focus on the experience of being in a hospital;
- Reinforcement of reflection and sharing of emotion;
- The use of emotion with patients on a busy inpatient ward;
- Promotion of confidence in staff using a method in their everyday practice.

The use of emotional touchpoints tools by the patient or family story was a method that addresses these requirements, highlights the process of using emotional touchpoints, and discusses the benefits of this approach in terms of improving patient and family experience.

Dewar and colleagues state that the benefits of using the emotional touchpoints approach is relevant since the method shows its ability to help practitioners understand in a more well-adjusted and sensitive way both the positive and negative aspects of an experience. It also has the power to help service users take part in a meaningful and realistic way in developing the service thanks to the substantial knowledge that results from the real stories of people (patient, family, and staff) and that has directly influenced change in the field.

The benefits of using this approach in defining customer experience touchpoints, as stated by Dewar and colleagues, incorporate its capacity to help practitioners examine from a more well-adjusted mode both the positive and negative sides of an experience and to help service users take part in a significant and accurate mode in improving the service. Significant knowledge resulted from these personal stories that had directly induced change in the area. The conclusions of Dewar et al.'s research show that the changes are not only related to practical solutions, but have also focused on the complex sociocultural dimensions that are part of compassion care delivery. It is, thus, obvious that using emotional touchpoints rather than touchpoints in the experiential marketing mix is essential to improving interactions with customers by being more customer-centric and providing them with satisfying experiences at both emotional and cognitive levels.

Furthermore, evidence suggests that focusing on subjective experiences as customers define and perceive them are a successful approach to analyzing and understanding the changes in the touchpoints tools as well as marketing and communication practices. This allows for the development of innovative techniques, the creation of new tools, and staff training to better interact with customers. Thus, establishing a contact and a conversation with customers through the use of emotional touchpoints is very helpful for companies to guarantee customer satisfaction and loyalty, and thus create a durable competitive advantage.

Emotional touchpoints are different from one customer to another, although it is within the same experience. The sector of activity, whether it is highly experiential, such as the service and tourism industries, or relatively experiential (e.g., supermarkets, stores), can also affect emotional touchpoints regarding the way consumers' emotions are expressed and the point of contact that generates them. The use of emotional touchpoints in designing meaningful customer experiences can help companies to:

- Get access to the way customers feel using the company's services and products;
- Help customers become more involved in designing suitable services in a meaningful and deliberate way;
- Capture both positive and negative aspects of customer experience. Both feelings are necessary to improve the quality of the experience and the emotions generated;
- Develop an innovative approach by allowing customers to share their stories and experiences, which can help professionals learn more from daily practice;
- Detect applied transformations that can be made to improve the experiences of customers;
- Take into consideration the impact of sociocultural factors and their impact on emotional touchpoints identification;
- Allow employees to improve their empathy capital by developing their understanding of how it feels to be part of the service and the whole customer experience.

Using the emotional touchpoints method relies on the art of using storytelling and the ability of each market actor (consumer/buyer and producer/seller) to tell his/her story related to the lived and shared experience.

In other words, the producer/provider listening to the story invites the customer/receiver to tell his/her story in his/her own words. This will help the company focus on one, or a set of touchpoints, that are significant to its customers from their own point-of-view, and then select an assemblage of emotional experiences (through manners, behaviors, attitudes, words, facial expressions, etc.) that narrates each touchpoint. The method of storytellers recounting their own experiences invites customers as well as a company's employees to talk about their emotions and why they felt this way in a very reflexive manner. Accessing reflexive data about experiences can help customers to share experiences that are important to them using emotional touchpoints that incorporate both emotion and cognitive aspects. However, using emotional touchpoints is dependent upon the ability of the person in contact with customers to develop a strong capital of empathy.

Freshwater and Stickley (2004) suggest that usually, individuals do not have a rich emotional vocabulary in relation to action and a situation involving an emotion word. Furthermore, offering examples of ready emotion words to apply in the emotional touchpoints method can allow customers to express, through visuals and a selection of words, what they feel and think about their experiences, and how each touchpoint has affected in a positive or a negative way their consumption or shopping experiences. Thus, companies can approach their customers by identifying the emotional touchpoints related to their experiences before, during, and after four stages: preparation, carrying out, following, and moving into action. The sum of all experiences from emotional touchpoint interactions illustrates customers' feelings (positive and negative), and thus satisfaction or dissatisfaction about the whole experience.

Therefore, emotional touchpoints are one of the fundamental facets of customer experience design, and an important component of the experiential marketing mix. They represent the connection between the service provider or the company's employees and the end-user or the customer. In this way, emotional touchpoints have to be first considered in terms of the emotions they generate and the identifications of the point of contact that generates them and not the other way, as in the traditional logic of customer touchpoints. The emotional touchpoints approach is based on the use of empathic and ethnographic methods combined with other tools, such as a card-based toolkit (e.g., Bate and Robert, 2007; Dewar et al., 2009; Dewar, 2013).

Emotional touchpoints toolkit

Drawing on the emotional touchpoints toolkit developed in the medical field by Dewar et al. (2009), I offer a touchpoints toolkit that could help companies, service providers, and employees in contact with customers to gain precious information about their experiences and the emotions related to them. The emotional touchpoints toolkit can be applied to both customers and a company's employees.

The toolkit follows a very simple and obvious process, and incorporates the use of visual cards to help individuals (customers and employees) to express their emotions when in contact with a particular touchpoint, starting first with the identification of the journey each market actor (customer and employee) went or will go through.

Thus, companies can use the emotional touchpoints toolkit to identify significant points in their clients' experiences. It is then used as a framework for collecting stories based on subjective data and personal feedbacks from both customers and employees. The use of the emotional touchpoints toolkit requires the four following dimensions:

- Mapping the way customers find out about the company's service or product to create a touchpoint from the company's perspective;
- The process is based on the touchpoints that are part of the customers' journey. The company's mapping is then presented to the customers who will be asked to pick up one or more touchpoints they should talk about (e.g., customers can talk about their experience and how it made them feel, and what they thought about it – customers can also be asked to focus on either a negative or a positive emotion produced by one of these touchpoints and explain what made them feel this way;
- Capturing the emotions related to each touchpoint as expressed by the customer in his/her own emotion words;
- Decoding and understanding what is important to customers about the way they are treated, or how services are functioning for them. It is a way of going beyond "it's ok" statements and accessing a more comprehensive feedback about what works or fails.

In the design field, Clatworthy (2011) employed the emotional touchpoints framework developed by Dewar and colleagues to rethink service design through a collaborative work involving both consumers and service providers. Clatworthy used a card-based approach, or emotional touchpoint cards as an innovative support tool (e.g., Brandt, Messeter, and Binder, 2008). Based on the use of the emotional touchpoints toolkit and cross-functional collaboration, Clatworthy developed a card-based tool with the following seven functions for facilitating new service development. These seven functions are related to the three main stages in which different card-based tools were used (Figure 9.2).

The toolkit includes emotional touchpoint cards that can help open the conversation about customer experience. It is composed of visual cards for both customers and the company's employees, and is classified as follows:

- Emotion cards (e.g., joy, happiness, anger, sadness, etc.);
- Touchpoints cards (e.g. Internet, phone, TV, call center, salespeople, etc.);
- Neutral cards to be filled by either customers or employees.

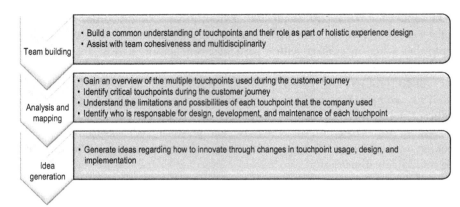

FIGURE 9.2 Functions in card-based tools

MINI-CASE 9.2   THE USE OF "EMOTIONAL TOUCHPOINT CARDS": HOW DOES IT WORK?

For marketers, using the "emotional touchpoint cards" is fundamental for learning about customer's experiences and considering future actions in terms of staff training, communication, store design, etc. Through the conversations generated by the use of different cards, customers will feel encouraged to deliver their real and deep feelings about their experiences with the brand since they can feel valued, supported, and enabled to play a role in driving forward real improvements in the company's offers (products and services). Marketers can use "emotional touchpoint cards" by following these steps:

- Prepare cards with different emotions with visual expressions as well as visuals for touchpoints that connect customers with the company (e.g., salespeople, website, store, product, call center, etc.);
- Invite customers and take enough time to break the ice, introduce the purpose, and make customers feel comfortable and valued;
- Spread the suitable set of "Touchpoint" cards and ask participants to select one;
- Spread out the "Emotion" cards and ask participants to select the emotion word that best expresses their experience of the "Touchpoint," and then ask them why they felt that way;
- Discuss together what could be done in the future to improve their experiences;
- Agree to some actions and thank the customer for sharing.

TABLE 9.1 Emotional touchpoint cards stages

Stage	Definition	Objective
Mapping an existing situation	The cards help to map out a current experience. We can go through each phase of a service or customer journey and pick out the touchpoints that are significant to each phase. Various features can be debated, such as which touchpoint is most vital to the customer, which are used in order, which are most often used etc.	It helps to advance the discussion about how customers view the company's offer (product and service) through touchpoints, and how they frequently jump between them
Identifying the pain points	Once the customer experience has been designed and journey mapped, we can classify the touchpoints along the experiential journey that do not operate principally well from a customer standpoint and identify why	This stage can be a valuable resource for refining the uniformity of the customer experience throughout the journey
Identifying the company's teams and functions in charge of the touchpoint	Different departments can be responsible for the design of different touchpoints. This often can be a source of confusion but should be defined and identified from the customer perspective	Identifying who is in charge of each touchpoint and defining ways of organizing different touchpoints is very helpful to assist a company to coordinate activities around the customer experience
Touchpoint migration	As firms might not define procedures for updating their touchpoints, a touchpoint might become, over time, out of date or there could be a better touchpoint alternative that can be used as a replacement or addition	This stage is critical when it comes to the use of technology and considerations regarding self-service. Applying a touchpoint cards tool can stretch thoughts for new touchpoints and can help map out a migration strategy from one touchpoint to another
Touchpoint addition or subtraction	This stage refers to the challenge of removing important touchpoints to find a better replacement. If it cannot be replaced, then the firm has gained a deeper understanding of the touchpoint's importance and role	This step can be a useful task in many ways, particularly to help challenge today's situation, which might have deep historical roots and need updating
Forced association to create new services	In this stage, the firm is forced to create a service based upon random cards. Forced association is an idea generation technique to force one away from logical thinking. Doing this with the touchpoint cards forces the team to overcome pre-conceived understanding	It is an entertaining and challenging way to examine the touchpoints, and often uncovers useful reflections regarding the customer experience and journey

Drawing on works in the design field (e.g., Clatworthy, 2011), the construction process of the emotional touchpoint cards includes several touchpoints that can be defined from two perspectives: consumer and company's employees (amongst different teams: marketing, communication, digital, etc.). In developing emotional touchpoint cards, companies can follow three key steps:

- The first set of cards can be a selection of images representing different touchpoints;
- The second category of cards can be selected as an innovation game for the company offer in order to involve customers and the company's employees in collaborative design of unique customer experiences;
- The third category includes cards related to both the images in the first set of cards along with the names of the corresponding touchpoints to enable rapid recognition of the touchpoint. Both customers and company employees will form an inspirational source for idea generation.

Therefore, the emotional touchpoint cards can be used in different ways, depending on the objectives of the company (Table 9.1). In this way, the customers and the company's employees participate in the conflicting phase during the customer experience design based on the implementation of emotional touchpoints.

Summary

This chapter has examined one of the components of the experiential marketing mix "E" as "Emotional touchpoints" that substitutes the "P" of "Physical environment" in the 7Ps of the marketing mix. This chapter highlighted the importance of shifting the focus from a customer touchpoints approach to an emotional touchpoints logic that includes the examination of human interaction as well as physical and digital touchpoints that are involved in the customer experience design. It has introduced the emotional touchpoints toolkit cards as a new tool that companies can use to design an efficient customer experience, and define the relevant touchpoints that connect customers with the company's offers (products and services). Furthermore, this chapter shows how emotional touchpoints can help to emotionally engage with customers, to understand experience at a profound level, and provide an accurate way in which both employees and customers can be involved in experience design.

10

EMIC/ETIC PROCESS

Emic/etic perspective and sociocultural customer journey

Purpose and context

The process applied in the 7Ps of the traditional marketing mix refers to the idea that the value delivered to the customer follows a top-down (etic) logic in which meanings are created and delivered by the firm throughout the customer journey. Using an emic/etic approach fundamentally involves the observation of a single cultural group of consumers and offers structured and embedded observations about consumer behaviors that help the company in the design and the adaptation of the customer experience that matches different consumption cultures and subcultures.

This chapter focuses on one component of the experiential marketing mix "Emic/etic process" as a replacement of "P" of "Process" in the traditional marketing mix logic (7Ps), which extends the vision of process from a one way and a top-down logic to incorporate consumer values into an iterative process that integrates both consumer and company visions, which are embedded within a particular cultural setting. In this chapter, I explore the shift from the logic of customer journey mapping to the sociocultural mapping of customer journey that follows two key approaches: the emic/etic perspective and the sociocultural definition of customer journey. I will then introduce tools and strategies that companies can use to design the ultimate customer experience.

Learning outcomes

At the end of this chapter you will learn about one of the "7Es" of the experiential marketing mix "Emic/etic process," and how companies can use efficient emic/etic tools to create a continuum in terms of the quality of the experience by considering the dynamic and iterative aspect of the experiential process and the cultural dimension of the customer journey mapping.

Emic and etic perspectives in the experiential marketing mix

This section introduces two main approaches: emic and etic. Both are relevant in the study and the design of customer experiences. In this section, I will focus on the origins of this new and innovative perspective, its challenges, and the opportunities for companies to implement it in order to design suitable customer experiences.

Emic and etic perspectives: origins and definitions

In the field of anthropology, the linguistic anthropologist Kenneth Pike (1954) developed the emic and etic approaches that were then extended in 1967 in his book *Language in Relation to a Unified Theory of the Structure of Human Behavior*. Pike established a differentiation in linguistics between phonemic and phonetic (emic and etic are derived from the suffix of these two words). While phonemics suggests the study of sounds for their significant functions in a certain language and the meanings of words (e.g., Helfrich, 1999; Yin, 2010), phonetics refers to the examination of common sounds present in different languages. In other words, phonetics involves studying the sounds that are generally utilized in human language regardless of their senses.

Applied to the examination of individual social behavior, Pike's definition highlights "etic viewpoint studies behavior as from outside of a particular system, while the emic viewpoint results from studying behavior as from inside the system" (1967: 37). Drawing on Pike's definition, the cultural anthropologist Marvin Harris (1964) suggests cultural lenses to define emic and etic perspectives. For Harris, rather than concentrating on the senses and the principles of the insider (emic), it is more relevant to study the way individual and macro variables (e.g., cultural, social, spiritual, ideological, political, economic) affect and shape those meanings and beliefs.

THEORY BOX 10.1 ETIC AND EMIC APPROACHES TO UNDERSTANDING CUSTOMER EXPERIENCE DESIGN AND CULTURAL DIFFERENCES

As important as the conceptualization of culture and the determination of cultural dimensions, it is equally essential to clarify the approach used to design customer experiences that are embedded in a particular cultural setting. The debate about etic and emic approaches to examine cultural differences in designing customer experiences cannot be ignored.

The etic and emic approaches to studying consumption culture have attracted the attention of many researchers in the past (e.g., Berry, 1996; Irwin et al., 1977; Triandis et al., 1972), and they continue to arouse the interest of researchers today (e.g., Harris, 1999; Morris et al., 1999) in the fields of anthropology and psychology. Etic and emic represent opposite epistemological approaches, specific to the fields of anthropology of consumption and intercultural consumer psychology.

The emic approach prevails especially amongst anthropologists, who consider that: a) each consumption culture has unique ideas, consumer behaviors, and concepts; and that (b) cultural specificity should be the object of study. The etic approach is often adopted by researchers doing cross-cultural consumption research who consider that: cultures have both specific dimensions and universal dimensions; and that the universal dimensions are at the heart of customer experiences lived in different cultural settings.

While emic and etic perspectives in understanding and organizing social behaviors were first applied in the cultural anthropology field (e.g., Pike, 1967), the use of these conflicting approaches has developed since 1970 and become prevalent throughout several fields, specifically in studying consumer behavior, consumption cultures, and consumption meanings. Though, as the use of emic and etic perspectives became more widespread, a number of definitions have been raised and were either contradictory or confusing. Headland and colleagues state that "authors equate emic and etic with verbal versus nonverbal, or as subjective knowledge versus scientific knowledge, or as good versus bad, or as ideal behavior versus actual behavior, or as private versus public" (1990: 21).

Emic and etic perspectives in consumer research

In using emic and etic perspectives in the understanding of consumer behavior, attitudes, and cultural consumption schemes as well as using them to generate consumption experiences that are both intellectual and perceptual, these two thoughts underline conflicting standpoints, as they analyze behaviors by considering either the perspective of the insider (observed: consumer) or the outsider (observer: company). Therefore, the distinction between etic and emic can contrast the knowledge produced on behaviors of a community or a social group (etic) and the knowledge produced by the members of the community themselves (emic).

TABLE 10.1 Emic vs. etic

Emic	Etic
Study of consumer behaviors from inside the system	Study of consumer behavior by taking up a position outside of the system
Examine a single consumption culture or subculture	Examine several consumption cultures and compare them
Hidden meaning of consumption practices revealed by the analyst/observer	Consumption meaning created by the analyst/observer
The criteria are considered valid inside the system	The criteria are considered universal

Assuming the subjective description of the customer experience, emic and etic viewpoints play an important role in defining the process that the company can use to deliver a meaningful customer experience. However, before considering emic and etic perspectives that help companies think about the suitable process to design and deliver the customer experience, we first need to distinguish between the two approaches, and thus discuss the conflicting aspects between both as shown in Table 10.1.

- **The emic perspective.** Merriam (2009) defines the emic perspective as the meanings and the linguistic elements of a specific culture in which the members who belong to it share common characteristics (e.g., the culture of consumption, the teaching culture, the managerial culture, the youth culture). The emic process captures individuals' original meanings of real-life situations within their own consumption cultures and from a subjective perspective, as stated by Willis, the emic approach: "looks at things through the eyes of the members of the culture being studied" (2007: 100). This will provide the company with valuable insights about the way consumers will redefine the meanings of its products and services, the process by which this has been operated, and why it has been done (outcomes).

Thus, scholars from different disciplines acknowledge the important role of the emic approach in the interpretation of the tacit and the emerging meanings of a consumption culture and experiences within a specific group of individuals. Therefore, the foundation behind the logic that the emic perspective is more appropriate is based on the fact that it is difficult to accurately understand the distinctions of a specific consumption culture and/or customer experience unless we immerse ourselves within that particular culture, which cannot be comprehended by the etic perspective, which does not allow a full immersion that would, otherwise, help to capture both implicit and explicit meanings related to consumption experiences. Therefore, as stated by Helfrich: "what is emphasized in this approach is human self-determination and self-reflection" (1999: 133).

THEORY BOX 10.2   THE EMIC APPROACH TO UNDERSTANDING CUSTOMER EXPERIENCE

The emic approach is an inductive approach similar to that used in the field of anthropology. Companies can examine the cultural system, and thus consumption experiences from the point-of-view of its members (customers) in order to identify characteristics and behaviors of their own. This can be accomplished by using ethnography, whereby we try to apprehend a specific consumption culture from the perspective of its members. The anthropologist–ethnographer spends long periods in a cultural context in order to learn the language, habits, values, and beliefs of consumers in a specific consumption field. The goal is to discover phenomena specific to this consumption culture.

The emic approach is often associated with the interpretive paradigm. It is closely related to cultural anthropology of consumption and focuses on the study of consumer behavior within a single consumption culture. According to this approach, we study behavioral phenomena and the social interrelations through the eyes of consumers from a particular consumption culture or sub-culture. We try to avoid imposing notions and ideas a priori. Companies who favor this approach try to understand the specific cultural characteristics of a group of consumers. They do it in the terms specific to this group or subgroup. The approach here is based on interpretation, and is generally predominantly qualitative. Companies who adopt an emic approach can get a fairly accurate description of a consumption culture from an insider perspective.

Having the emic process applied to customer experience conception and design starts by settling within the consumption context by immersing and socializing one's self within a specific context. There is then a need to learn about the words used, the behaviors, and even other fields and dimensions that are not directly related to the studied consumption context. The investigator needs a set of skills that are by nature ethnographic and exploratory. In ethnography, Schensul, Schensul, and LeCompte (2013) recommend critical skills that the investigator needs in order to be a good ethnographer that is, to be a full member of another culture, and thus allows the design of suitable customer experiences by:

o   Getting familiar with the consumption culture and the culture of the group;
o   Learning about the consumption culture, its norm, history, codes, meanings, social interactions and rules, etc;
o   Developing strategies and skills to approach and experience the new consumption culture without being intrusive;
o   Developing a proactive role as listener and connecting;
o   Building empathic relationships with the members of the group.

- **The etic perspective.** It refers to the outsider's perspective, which is in contrast to the emic one. The etic perspective includes an external interpretation and understanding of a consumption culture and its meaning produced by the consumers that belong to the same setting and have the same experiences. Overall, in consumer behavior studies, the etic viewpoint is connected with that of the perspective of the scholar and the way he/she sees things. The research question will structure and define his/her fieldwork and then he/she will approach the consumption culture with a set of variables defined outside the culture.

For Willis, this etic approach used to comprehend a specific consumption culture highlights: "structures and criteria developed outside the culture as a framework for studying the culture" (2007: 100). This occurs when consumer researchers use established theoretical schemes regarded as meaningful and appropriate to study an alternate consumption experience. The variables, hypotheses, and perspectives that are part of ready-to-apply frameworks are then used in the analysis of a totally different consumption setting or consumption experience. The use of an etic perspective to explore and understand customer experience is helpful, as etic-oriented research examines the cross-cultural perceptions and allows comparisons through various consumption experiences, which change according to the cultural setting; however, it certainly cannot completely apprehend what it actually means to be part of the consumption culture.

THEORY BOX 10.3   THE ETIC APPROACH TO UNDERSTANDING CUSTOMER EXPERIENCE

By following the etic approach, researchers try to have a "universal" understanding of the consumption phenomenon being studied. On the basis of absolute or standardized criteria, they can then construct tools and methods in advance in order to identify cultural characteristics that are universal in scope to design suitable customer experiences. The tools are tested in selected cultures to study variations in the criteria considered universal. For example, we can evaluate the equivalence of an experience and service quality measurement model in order to determine universal aspects as well as aspects specific to the cultures, which constitutes an important challenge in terms of designing a universal customer experience with high standards that speak to almost all customers within different cultural settings.

Companies adopting an etic approach examine several cultures by making comparisons between them. From this point-of-view, culture is considered as a variable. In this perspective, it is argued that the social world can only be understood from the point-of-view of the individuals actively involved in the social activities studied. This paradigm refutes the independence of the subject/object relation and states that the reality (the object) is dependent on the subject.

- **Tensions between the emic and etic orientation.** Although the two perspectives can be used separately to explore customer experiences, in practice they are, however, inseparable since the process will mix both emic and etic viewpoints. Many scholars of consumer behavior emphasize the struggle between the two logics. By considering the inevitable subjectivity of the investigator/scholar who is already charged, and thus influenced by his/her own consumption experiences, thoughts, and feelings, an exclusively emic perspective is problematic to follow in order to get a deeper understanding of a whole customer experience. The same applies for the etic perspective, which will hide nuances, meanings, and feelings within a particular consumption culture, and thus will not allow access to deep knowledge through an accurate customer voice.

Therefore, I suggest that the process by which companies can understand and design meaningful customer experiences should incorporate the two perspectives: emic and etic because they are complimentary and valuable to the study of a specific consumption culture in which the experience is shaped and embedded (e.g., Patton, 2010). The use of both emic and etic processes is supposed to be an advantage instead of a constraint, or a source of confusion when it comes to customer experience design, as the anthropologist Agar argues "etic and emic, the universal and the historical particular, are not separate kinds of understanding when one person makes sense of another. They are both part of any understanding" (2011: 39). Though, differences between etic and emic processes exist, and can be underscored by acknowledging the variables that can affect the understanding, and guide the design of customer experiences. Amongst these variables, I can mention the following: the investigator's own system of values, target's age, gender, sexual orientation, ethnicity, etc.

THEORY BOX 10.4   THE ETIC/EMIC APPROACH TO UNDERSTANDING CUSTOMER EXPERIENCE

Researchers show that the use of both approaches allows a better understanding of the effects of culture on consumer behavior. Berry and Parasuraman (1991) suggest a model based on three steps. The first step refers to the use of "imposed" constructs and tools that are imported (without any modification) from the consumption culture in which they were designed. In a second step, the constructs are enriched by incorporating aspects derived from the particularities of each consumption culture. Then, the constructs in the model are refined to eliminate aspects that are not equivalent in different cultural contexts. The factors that survive this cleansing are called "derived etics."

Brett et al. (1997) describe another method, still in three stages, that integrates both perspectives. Unlike Berry and Parasuraman's model (1991), they clearly distinguish cultural factors from ecological, and economic factors in the analysis of intercultural differences. However, as in Berry's model, the last phase is the design of a customer experience following an etic approach. In both cases, the emic perspective is present in the initial stages, but it is not

(continued)

(continued)

retained in the final explanation. Thus, there may be a synergy between these two approaches, which allows for a better understanding of the impact of culture on certain aspects of consumer behaviors. In this perspective, companies can evaluate the role of culture and determine the quality aspects of customer experiences that are universal, and those that are specific to each cultural context.

Emic and etic perspectives through CCT lenses

While customer experience design should follow a dual process including both emic and etic perspectives to better design suitable and satisfying experiences, which have to be embedded within a predetermined consumption culture, it is important for companies and marketing professionals to consider customer experience as an integral part of the framework that encompasses the Consumer Culture Theory (CCT) developed by Arnould and Thompson in 2005. CCT invites consumer researchers as well as marketers to focus more on both emic and etic reasoning by taking into account the social and cultural representations, as well as the meanings consumers attribute to their consumption practices and experiences.

THEORY BOX 10.5   CONSUMER CULTURE THEORY (CCT) AS A FRAMEWORK TO BETTER UNDERSTAND CUSTOMER EXPERIENCE

CCT has been growing in the United States since the 1990s to gain a better understanding of consumer practices. It has been theorized by CCT researchers, like Russell Belk, Craig Thompson, and Eric Arnould, who use interpretative approaches to get closer to the lived experience. The fundamental principle of this theory is that consumption is not a purely market phenomenon, but a culture with its myths, rites, and stories. Individuals, thus, use consumption as a factor of social integration as well as for the identity resources it provides them. They will develop relationships of attachment with products and brands. More broadly, consumer goods serve as a vehicle of communication of signs and symbols between individuals.

Consumer societies have an anthropological significance. They offer their members structures through which they can exchange and produce meaning together. CCT is also an interdisciplinary field that uses emic/etic and critical approaches to understand the consumer experience. It focuses on social representations and cultural practices to explain consumption practices. To interpret consumption experiences, the CCT approach examines the ideological, social, cultural, and symbolic dimensions of consumption. For example, Schouten and McAlexander's (1995) study of consumer subcultures, specifically bikers, or Kozinets' (2002) analysis of the Burning Man festival in the Nevada desert, are emblematic of CCT approaches.

Sociocultural mapping of customer journey: emic/etic perspective

The customer journey is the process by which customers access and evolve through different experiential stages in which they are in contact with different touchpoints. The traditional customer journey mapping is based on a one-way process over time, and includes a purchase cycle (Lemon and Verhoef, 2016) that usually encompasses three stages: prepurchase, purchase, and postpurchase. The sociocultural mapping of customer journey based on both emic and etic perspectives is an **iterative, bi-directional,** and **culturally embedded process** that allows professionals to view from both sides, as well as from inside and outside of the customer experience within a particular consumption culture (Figure 10.1).

In their journey, consumers embark upon several pathways in quest of objectives and in reply to many opportunities and difficulties. Consumer journey is connected with consumption experiences in which customers are in a relationship with companies (e.g., when consumers search information, use products and services, choose brands, engage in online or offline consumption experiences). However, consumers do take further journeys that do not focus on consumption as their main ambition, but yet associate brands, products, and services with their experiences (e.g., patient journey in healthcare). For Verhoef and colleagues (2009), during a customer journey, the consumer is connected to both tangible (e.g., products) elements and intangible elements, such as feelings, emotions, novelty, etc. These two aspects shape customer experience before, during, and after, and are evaluated by the customer throughout his/her whole journey.

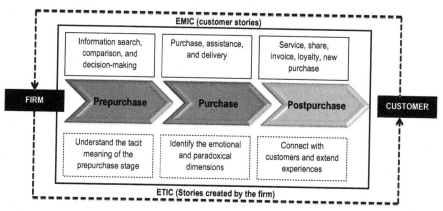

FIGURE 10.1 Customer journey sociocultural mapping

According to services marketing literature, experience is viewed as an integral part of the customer journey that includes the entirety of the shopping process. Drawing on this idea, Pullman and Gross (2004) state that customer journey is the engagement of customers in acts that incorporate both anticipation and emotions, which evolve throughout time. Other authors, such as Lemon and Verhoef (2016) and Shaw and Ivens (2005), suggest that examining the customer journey process, specifically, all connections and interactions between the customer and the company's brand, product, technology, employees, and service can help companies to obtain a better understanding of customer experience by considering both tangible and intangible aspects. In fact, the customer journey, as a process that incorporates various consumption experiences, includes interactions with different market actors and larger social and environmental components. In their research, Lemon and Verhoef theorize customer experience as

> a customer's journey with a firm over time during the purchase cycle across multiple touchpoints . . . it is a dynamic process. The customer experience process flows from prepurchase (including search) to purchase to postpurchase; it is iterative and dynamic. This process incorporates past experiences (including previous purchases) as well as external factors. In each stage, customers experience touchpoints only some of which are under the firm's control.
>
> *(2016: 74)*

Beyond understanding customer journey mapping, it is fundamental to understand the multifaceted and complex emotional and experiential journey consumers engage in with the support of brands, products, services, and technologies, and which is shaped by a specific consumption culture. Therefore, the use of "sociocultural mapping" as a framework to explore the complexity of customer journey helps companies to capture additional and new experiential dimensions and touchpoints that can improve customer experience throughout the customer journey.

The concept of "sociocultural mapping" is often used in culture and governance literature, which is an emerging interdisciplinary field of research, covering a range of approaches used in varied contexts as a tool and method of analysis, organization, and interpretation. The evolution of sociocultural mapping links academic and artistic research with policy, planning, and advocacy contexts. For Duxbury and colleagues (2015), sociocultural mapping is a development tool embedded in communal engagement and the creation of spaces to incorporate multivocal stories. Thus, in order to improve customer experience, it is vital to use customer stories to map customer journeys, as it is a more effective approach than creating journey maps based on the stories created by companies.

Therefore, sociocultural mapping of customer journeys acknowledge the fluctuating and fragmented nature of many consumption cultures, and thus helps companies to incorporate varied and profound knowledge of the customer, consumption experiences, touchpoints, perceptions of importance, and ways of understanding.

The sociocultural mapping of the journey articulates the dynamic experience of the consumption culture that helps to shape it and in which it is embedded. Thus, offering an ultimate customer experience that is satisfying at both functional and emotional levels requires the ability to map out this journey accurately by diving deep into consumption cultures and subcultures to discover what the company is doing well, and what negative elements are potentially damaging the whole customer experience, thereby creating a *decalage* (mismatch) between the company and the customer, and between different touchpoints in the customer journey.

Summary

This chapter has examined one of the components of the experiential marketing mix "E" as "Emic/etic process" that substitutes the "P" of (Process) in the 7Ps of the traditional marketing mix. It has explained how the customer experience can be designed as an iterative process to avoid disconnections by better understanding the hidden meanings related to consumption experiences in each culture or subculture of consumption. In this chapter, I explored two main aspects of the customer experience design: the emic/etic perspective applied to customer journey and the sociocultural mapping of the journey. These two aspects can help companies to design suitable consumption experiences that allow them to connect, deliver, and share values with their customers.

PART III

Future challenges in customer experience design

11

PHYGITAL CUSTOMER EXPERIENCE
Definition, characteristics, types, and key success factors

Purpose and context

The digital revolution began with the transformation and transposition of many activities and functions of "real life" into corresponding digital entities. Today, the trend is reversing in a more and more obvious way; the virtual begins to reveal itself in the real. In terms of experience marketing strategy, phygital suggests the multiplication of bridges thrown between two worlds, physical and digital, to give consumers a more fluid and richer experience.

The alliance of the physical and the digital ("phygital") allows customers to live a new experience of purchase in the store and online. This is the reason why companies and retailers have to offer customers the possibility of optimizing their experiential journey on the shelves according to their running list (indoor location), and of reducing their waiting time at checkout thanks to self-scanning and payment technologies contact, or the use of a promotional program or dematerialized loyalty, etc. In this chapter, I present the future challenge that companies face in designing a customer experience with a continuum offline and online. I introduce and explain in this chapter the concept of phygital customer experience, its characteristic and typologies, and the key success factors.

Learning outcomes

At the end of this chapter, you will be able to understand the origins of the concept of "phygital" and its application to customer experience and experience marketing. This chapter will also provide you with the analysis of different works and empirical examples that will help you to determine appropriate phygital strategies and critically evaluate different approaches to using technologies in designing the ultimate phygital customer experience, which involves combining the reassuring side of physical place contact with the informational, commercial, and interactive aspects of the digital space.

What does phygital customer experience mean?

A contraction of the terms physical and digital, phygital explains the unstoppable digitization of society over-all and particularly of business and trading. It is disseminated by e-commerce stores that have had to reinvent themselves to meet the needs of more and more connected, mobile, and demanding customers. Phygital forces companies to rethink the relationship between real and virtual in order to meet the evolving expectations of their customers.

Today, new hybrid consumer experiences are flourishing thanks to the ubiquity of digital technologies in our daily lives. According to Castelli (2016), the characteristics of these consumption experiences are not exclusively physical, nor fully digital, but they merge the characteristics of the two worlds – digital and physical – which give rise to a third context of consumption: phygital, which is the result of the approximation of physical and digital contexts. Therefore, the phygital customer experience will be a major challenge for companies in the years to come. In fact, companies need to understand its components and typologies to create phygital customer experiences that are continuous, coherent, and satisfying at all levels: technical, functional, emotional, and social.

THEORY BOX 11.1 PHYGITAL, WHAT IS IT?

The term phygital appeared in the marketing field in 2013. It was developed by the Australian Marketing Agency Momentum whose signature is: "An Agency for the Phygital World." This word that could have been an ephemeral buzzword, however, is being rooted in our vocabulary as it perfectly reflects a reality that no one disputes.

Phygital refers to the transformation of physical stores within the digital era: concepts are completely redesigned to offer a new customer experience and use digital tools as sales support. Phygital logic has given rise to a series of equally evocative terms from marketing jargon, such as connected commerce and responsive retail.

Phygital refers to the idea that today's e-commerce and retail stores should be flexible, attentive, and able to respond to the instantaneous and interpret the paradoxes inherent in consumption experiences. Phygital is then the ultimate solution to adapting to smart purchasing behaviors and responding quickly in a multi-channel way to the expectations of impatient and zapper consumers.

The phygital environment is a context of consumption integrated gateways set up by companies between different physical (offline) and digital (online) channels so that customers can pass from one to the other without any difficulties by guaranteeing consistency in the experiential journey from physical to digital context and vice versa. For businesses, it is essential to create effective and high-performance phygital customer experiences that are firmly rooted in consumers' daily habits both offline and online. Yet, designing thematic points of sale equipped with touch pads or other screens giving access to the brand's website, as is available to any other consumer at home, is only a minimalist solution that will only provide a small in-store phygital purchase experience. The transformation of physical stores involves the use of digital tools to support the customer throughout his/her experiential journey – and it starts well before the customer opens the door of the store. Companies should then combine different tools and strategies to offer the ultimate phygital customer experience and enhance the continuum between the real place and the virtual space and vice versa. Amongst the tools and strategies that can help companies create a phygital experience, the following can be considered:

- Mobile and mobile payment. The mobile phone has become an essential object in commercial relationships. First, because the connection technologies now allow companies to establish a close contact with the customer, to identify and log his/her data, and to personalize the messages that are addressed to him/her. But also, in terms of payment technologies, the phygital concept will revolutionize the act of purchasing products and services, allowing, for example, customers to pay for their purchases at any time, or as soon as they enter the store.
- Click and collect and e-booking. With click and collect, customers can buy online at home or on the go, and retrieve their item in-store without paying shipping costs. With e-booking, the customer reserves an article before going into the store, without obligation of purchase. In the first case, the customer ensures that the product is available before purchasing and retrieving it. In the second, the customer comes into physical contact with the product he/she intends to buy, something that is not possible in e-commerce until the receipt of the product ordered is in the hand of the consumer.
- Range extension and the break. The customer orders from the store an article that is not available on site, or that is out of order. This new practice can be either in the form of a catalog extension that enriches the still limited supply of the physical store, or in the form of product customization, as is the case in luxury items. But the most important thing about this approach is that it restores the value of the sellers, who take their place in the heart of the relationship with the customers, to advise and guide them.

- Shopper-centric focus. One of the main differences between traditional marketing, sales, and phygital, is that the company has to think not in "consumer-centric" terms, but in "shopper-centric" terms, that is, to focus not on the customer, but on the buyer. The idea here is that digital marketers should put themselves in the customer's shoes and offer him/her digital solutions that are useful to him/her, enrich, and streamline his/her experience.

MINI-CASE 11.1 PHYGITAL IN THE RETAIL EXPERIENCE: TIMBERLAND'S FIRST PHYGITAL STORE IN NEW YORK

Timberland opened its first flagship phygital store in 2016 in the heart of Manhattan, New York, with a new kind of non-intrusive digital solution. Inside the flagship, a kiosk offers customers the use of a mini tablet that helps them to collect the same product information as those available online, by simply tapping the label. The mini tablets are all equipped with NFC chips, a near field communication technology. The customer is then able to create a list with his/her preferences and send it to him/herself by email. Customers, who choose to enter their email contact information or not, have no obligation to use it.

With the phygital store, Timberland's objective is to reengage the customer at the exit of the store. Once the door of the store is passed, Timberland will be able to re-engage with its clients by sending e-mails to customers who have registered to receive their personalized list of items. Thus, Timberland will be able to offer suggestions, recommendations, and ultimately, push its customers to download the application. Additionally, the iBeacon technology is added to the device to directly communicate with the customer.

The phygital asset is then an extension of the e-shop in store. Timberland also offers a digital wall to its customers who can use it as an extension of its e-shop that also allows them to propose products not available in-store. By placing the tablet on the wall, customers can add the products to their list of preferences. The phygital store allows Timberland to maintain the bridge with its e-shop and engage its clients without appearing intrusive since customers can also simply do their shopping, as in any of the brand's 240 other stores.

Characteristics of phygital experiences

Companies can use numerous technologies, such as iBeacon, quantified-self apps, connected objects, and augmented reality amongst others to connect real places to virtual spaces, thus designing suitable phygital customer experiences.

- The use of the iBeacon technology is a good example that illustrates the importance of merging physical and digital spheres. iBeacon technologies enable digitalization of the physical customer experience at the points of sale. It is a small box with Bluetooth technology that allows the company to interact with its customers in the store, or provide them with contextual information through their smartphones. Introduced by Apple in 2013, iBeacon technology works on the principle of micro-location. It estimates the proximity of a smartphone to a given point represented by a tag. Two conditions are necessary before the reception of the signals: 1) the possession of the dedicated application; and 2) the activation of Bluetooth by the holder of the device. The technology of iBeacon and other indoor location services have become commonplace. In 2016 and 2017, brands mainly used iBeacon systems to send coupons or geolocalized messages. In the oncoming years, brands will use this technology beyond simply pushing brands to the customers. Here are the three examples of how brands can use iBeacon technologies to increase sales, improve customer experience, and guarantee customer loyalty.

MINI-CASE 11.2 "SUE BEE HONEY" USES iBEACON TO INCREASE SALES AND REVENUES

The campaign of American honey producer "Sue Bee Honey" has mainly focused on location in its targeting procedures. It is also generally used in response to the tracking pixels generated by the interests of users' online browsing. As part of this iBeacon campaign, the "moving moments" in bricks and mortar stores were used to expose consumers to location-based advertising. The focus was on targeting consumers precisely when they are about to make a purchase decision. This is a very different approach from most untargeted or poorly targeted ads.

"Sue Bee Honey" has been able to do this in partnership with a platform specializing in local advertising with iBeacon technology. This partnership allowed the company to exploit iBeacon technologies in 100,000 locations. The goal was to energize store applications. This simply appears on the device of potential users when they enter the store by sending a useful message. These helpful messages vary depending on two main focuses: 1) the type of store in which the user is currently located; and 2) the type of application that is used to provide a hyper-relevant message. For example, a user enters a bricks and mortar store with a shopping list app on his/her device, branded content could simply say "Add Sue Bee Honey to your list."

The campaign was a great success. It has enabled "Sue Bee Honey" to increase its overall brand awareness by nearly 50% and its purchase goal by 450%.

MINI-CASE 11.3   XEROX USES iBEACON TO IMPROVE CUSTOMER EXPERIENCE

A lot of iBeacon campaigns in the early stages were aimed primarily at boosting sales. In the final stages, most campaigns and brands aimed to improve the consumer experience. Such a campaign has been led by Xerox, a global US company that sells business services and document technology products. Xerox used iBeacon to customize and personalize transactions. This offer was intended for Hoboken (suburb of New Jersey) users from merchants alongside their travel routes through an app called "Shop and Ride." The iBeacon provided Xerox with an overview of preferred travel times for travelers and transit centers. They were able to ensure that the agreements put in place were fully customized to these travel patterns.

Having seen the growing demand for mobile ticketing, Xerox decided to use the opportunity to its fullest. Xerox sent bids to commuters as part of their transit experience. To achieve this, the "Shop and Ride" app allowed users in Hoboken to receive personalized offers. For example, merchants and restaurants could communicate directly, thanks to iBeacon technologies installed in bus shelters and windows. In order to disseminate relevant offers to users, they should establish a personal profile. The more they use the app, the more the app adds targeted offers. Users are even allowed to save a mobile coupon for immediate or future refund.

To begin, Xerox worked with 35 merchants in the Hoboken area to send offers to New Jersey transit customers. As part of the iBeacon campaign, each participating merchant shared two weekly mobile coupons with "Shop and Ride" users. Thanks to this data, merchants have been able to use important information: for example, anonymous data that displays the number of people who open, record, and exchange transactions. But also, tracking real-time Xerox conversion rates to make more informed decisions about their future deployments. Merchants have been able to decide what kind of offers should be introduced and when they should be deployed.

MINI-CASE 11.4   FRAGRANCE OUTLET USES iBEACON TO ADVANCE CUSTOMER LOYALTY

Fragrance Outlet, a chain of perfumes and cosmetics, launched a campaign of iBeacon technologies that aimed to build on the current loyalty program and attract new buyers. As part of the campaign, the cosmetics chain worked in partnership with an iBeacon awards platform to pilot its rewards programs by adding fragrance samples to the rewards. To start, tags have been deployed in approximately 100 Fragrance Outlet stores.

When customers enter the store, the application activated by the beacons welcome them through the door. They are then rewarded with a "kick" (rewards on app-activated beacons) for the visit. These "kicks" can then be exchanged for discounts. For Fragrance Outlet, the "kick" can lead right to samples of products for brands, such as Calvin Klein, Lacoste, Escada, Hugo Boss, etc.

The cosmetics chain has also adopted Shopkick's associated credit card program. This program offers cash rewards to customers paying with a Visa or a MasterCard. Thus, iBeacon technologies helped Fragrance Outlet to establish brand image and loyalty. Further, pedestrian traffic has been driven to stores by attracting new customers and offering rewards. By coming to the stores, customers have generally had a rewarding experience.

- The use of "quantified-self" applications is another example of the phygital customer experience that highlights self-quantified experiences. Consumers value these experiences when they use applications and connected objects to monitor, control, optimize, and improve their own behaviors.

MINI-CASE 11.5   FITBIT OFFERS A "QUANTIFIED-SELF" ENTERTAINING SPORTS EXPERIENCE

The quantified-self (QS) or "measurement of oneself" became popular in 2007 in the United States with the idea of integrating sensors and wireless technology in wearable products to offer e-training experiences related to fitness and health control. With the launch of a wearable bracelet, Fitbit aims to help customers lead a healthier and a more active life. Fitbit products and their use integrate seamlessly into the life of individuals to help them achieve their workouts and fitness goals whatever they are.

Fitbit offers a quantified-self phygital experience and allows individuals to measure data about their body, health, and activities (e.g., number of steps, distance traveled, number of calories consumed, weight tracking, sleep monitoring, etc.). Furthermore, Fitbit sensors allow recording, conservation, analyzing, and even the sharing of personal data in order to have better control over individuals' well-being and maintain the motivation to exercise or lose weight.

- The use of connected objects: in the years to come, connected objects will be an integral part of all consumption experiences whether they are domestic (home) or extra-domestic (shop). Connected objects can help companies in different industries design optimized and highly customized experiences tailored to the needs of their customers.

MINI-CASE 11.6 AMAZON DASH BUTTON: THE USE OF CONNECTED OBJECTS TO DESIGN OPTIMIZED EXPERIENCES

Amazon has recently opened its third-party vendor automatic refill program. Launched almost three years ago on the American market, Amazon Dash Buttons are connected with Wi-Fi to allow the customer to buy in one click the order previously programmed in the application of Amazon. Each brand has its own button and each button refers to a product of the brand (e.g., Colgate, Red Bull, Nivea, Ariel, Tide, etc.).

A very simple functioning – each button is linked to a brand of everyday products, such as Ariel laundry, Lipton teas, or Gillette razors. Pressing the button starts the order of the product corresponding to the indicated brand. The desired products are set in the Amazon application, which is compatible with iOS and Android. Once the order has been placed, it is delivered to the customer on a business day.

- Augmented reality: the acceptance and rejection of augmented reality or virtual reality shows that some consumers adopt these technologies because they find in them new, exciting, and useful phygital experiences, while others reject them or regard them as useless tech gadgets. However, companies today have to develop knowledge of what makes these phygital experiences useful to consumers. More specifically, companies should focus on the following main issues:

  o What are the values associated with phygital experiences?
  o What are the digital devices, technologies, and tools that contribute to creating a valuable and meaningful phygital customer experience that generates value for the company and its customers?
  o How does the value perceived by the consumer vary through the different stages of the phygital experience?

In a phygital context, digital tools create distinct and unique experiences because of the socio–material characteristics of this context. On one hand, digital contexts immerse consumers in a world in which the functioning is different from the physical sphere:

  o Geographic boundaries are not relevant;
  o Past events can be reactivated by accessing archived data;
  o Impossible dreams can become real by creating virtual objects;
  o Digital contexts allow for high levels of interactivity so that consumers can play a proactive role in designing valuable experiences.

As a result, consumption cultures specific to the digital environment have emerged giving rise to phygital consumption experiences peculiar to this environment. As digital technologies become ubiquitous, companies need to generate a "phygital value proposition" to design consumption experiences that are relevant to the context in which they are experienced. In the marketing field, some researchers, such as Chaffey and Ellis-Chadwick (2012), have examined the characteristics of consumer experiences in the phygital environment by identifying the benefits consumers derive from the use of digital technologies in their consumption experiences. Overall, the results of these studies show that the use of digital technologies in phygital consumption practices improves the relational, hedonistic and aesthetic aspects of the customer experience (e.g., Punj, 2012). Though, these studies do not highlight how these phygital experiences differ from experiments in the physical environment.

o   In terms of utility, studies in the marketing field indicate that consumers are looking for products and services and buying them online because it is more convenient. Going online is more time efficient, and it is also cognitively and physically less demanding than offline shopping.
o   Digital consumption is perceived as more efficient, allowing consumers to make good decisions at their convenience. Consumers believe that they are able to find the product or service that best suits their needs, as they have much more information available and access to a wider variety of choices.
o   Consumers believe they can get the best price for a product through price comparison tools.

The digital sphere offers phygital experiences that are quantitatively different from their offline physical counterparts (higher or lower experiential value, more positive or negative experience).

Typologies of phygital experiences

Phygital customer experiences can be classified according to six main categories (Figure 11.1). Each category brings together specific digital tools tailored to the phygital customer experience and aims to generate value for the company and its customers.

Connected experience

According to McKinsey's study (2015), by 2025 the economic value of the Internet of Things (IoT) will be more than $11 trillion a year. Connected

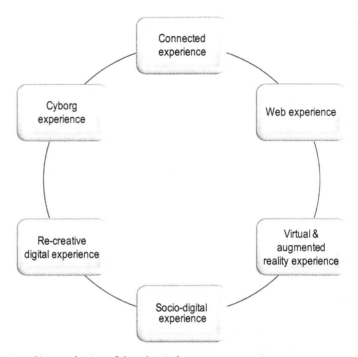

FIGURE 11.1 Six typologies of the phygital customer experience

objects will become part of everyday life for each consumer. According to the Gartner study conducted in January 2017, there are 8.4 billion connected objects in 2017, and there will be more than 25 billion in 2020. Connected objects then represent an integral part of the customer experience and companies should integrate them into the development of their digital strategies at the center of the customer experience. They should also use connected objects as a channel of direct communication with their customers. Therefore, the connected experience made possible by the integration of the IoT technology creates a link between the digital world and the real world while guaranteeing interactions between individuals who share the same consumption practices and have similar values.

Beyond allowing customers to collect real-time data, connected objects become a lever for the continuous improvement of the object itself through a better understanding of its use by consumers in their consumption experiences. Today, connected objects offer businesses the possibility of a quantified return on the customer experience. This information needs to be complemented by other types of more immersive information and made more available to the consumer in order to be able to produce an in-depth analysis of the real experience and its tangible and intangible dimensions.

Web experience

In order to create a satisfying functional and emotional web customer experience, companies need to go beyond the logic of e-commerce sites that do not bring any differentiation from the competition. They should, in fact, turn them into immersive websites through the adaptation of the five sensory elements of the web. The adaptation of sensory components to the specificities of the web can be achieved by using several techniques and digital tools to create web experiences and not just web pages.

- Visual aspects in the web experience. Adapting the visual content of the web to create memorable and satisfying customer experiences can be achieved through:

  o The proposal of a homepage with strong visuals. It should have a strong visual impact from the first visit of the site;
  o Including a concept or design specific to the brand and its DNA;
  o Proposing harmonized colors and HD images with a coherent graphic;
  o Improvement of the editorial style and the font;
  o The integration of interactive or 3D avatars.

- Touch in the web experience. Touch can be adapted to the brand's website through the following actions:

  o Offering a global view with a selective zoom;
  o Incorporating quality slideshows and full screen videos;
  o Proposing a 3D display of objects – a 360-degree and hyper-real visual components;
  o Integration of interactive and alternative views with demos.

- Sound in the web experience. It is a crucial element in the immersion of customers in phygital web experiences. It can be created and enhanced through the following actions:

  o Propose a specific sound signature linked to the identity of the brand;
  o Differentiate the music on the site and offer several options for the visitor to choose from;
  o Propose sound control tools;
  o Offer a soothing sounding background;
  o Integrate the sound with the click;
  o Propose a choice for vocal narration;
  o Use a balanced tone;
  o Provide an opportunity for storytelling in multiple languages.

- Smell in the web experience. To adapt the sense of smell, companies can set up two main actions:

  o Propose an olfactory signature;
  o Integrate broadcasters into connected objects in stores or broadcast screens.

- Taste in the web experience. It is a very important element of the web experience, but it is difficult to adapt. Nevertheless, some actions can be considered:

  o Provide a detailed description of the product;
  o Offer storytelling and strong content;
  o Propose tasting events in which the site and the universe of the brand are associated with a taste;
  o Engage partnerships with chefs and offer taste references to describe products;
  o Communicate on taste through high quality images.

Virtual and augmented reality experience

The phygital customer experience can be created using virtual or augmented reality technologies to extend the actual experience in-store to the virtual world and vice versa. The goal of projecting the virtual into the real world through an augmented reality, is to bring the virtual world into our daily lives using connected objects, such as Google Glass – glasses that allow the projection of digital realities into the real world. These technologies, and in particular that of virtual reality, allow consumers to be immersed in a digitally created, artificial world. It can be a replication of the real world or a totally imaginary universe. The phygital experience is visual, auditory, and sensory. When the person is equipped with the appropriate interfaces, such as gloves or electronically connected devices, he/she may experience some sensations related to touch or certain actions.

MINI-CASE 11.7 PEPSI MAX OFFERS A PLEASURABLE PHYGITAL EXPERIENCE THROUGH THE USE OF AUGMENTED REALITY

The AMV BBDO agency in London has set up a surprising bus shelter for Pepsi Max through a series of "Unbelievable" promotional campaigns. In London, a screen has replaced the glass of a bus shelter. This displays the image of the street in real time, as if it was a transparent window, but some events will be added to the augmented reality image and make pedestrians and motorists react to the people at the bus stop. Using a hidden camera, the trapped people will, for example, discover alien flying saucers in the sky, a meteorite that falls from the sky, a giant robot that fires lasers out of its eyes, or a tiger in the city. With its virtual and real creative campaign, Pepsi Max reveals the slogan "Unbelievable," in the image of its taste, which promotes the absence of sugar and demonstrates a creative ability that combines the real with the virtual by creating an immersive phygital experience.

Socio-digital experience

Social networks (Snapchat, Facebook, Twitter, Periscope, etc.) have an important role in the customer experience. According to the Gartner study conducted in January 2017, 85% of exchanges with a customer will be without human interaction on the brand side by 2020. Thus, in the digital age, where more and more exchanges with customers occur online, social networks should be taken into account by companies in the development of their digital strategies centered on the customer experience. Marketing and communication managers need to understand the expectations of their customers on social media and identify the typologies of experiences specific to each social network in order to adapt the experiential social mix and provide a satisfactory social experience.

MINI-CASE 11.8   TIPP-EX SHARES VALUES WITH ITS CUSTOMERS THROUGH AN INTERACTIVE SOCIO-DIGITAL EXPERIENCE

Tipp-Ex, a leading European producer of correction products and other related products owned by the French company Bic, launched, in August 2010, a viral campaign by posting interactive videos on YouTube called "A hunter shoots a bear!" The hunter, who did not want to kill the bear, was proposing to rewrite the story using the Tipp-Ex correction tape.

The brand staged a hunter and a bear imagined by the Buzzman agency, which was the subject of a quiz game, the Big Tipp-Ex Quiz. Thanks to this game, the fans of the two famous characters, the hunter and the bear, were able to test their knowledge and prove that they were undefeatable by these characters by responding to 50 questions.

This campaign that created an immersive socio-digital shared experience amongst the brand's fans and others has generated more than 50 million views on YouTube. The goal of this viral and participatory campaign was to encourage Internet users to participate in games and develop their creative potential through the proposals they can make. In the video "A hunter shoots a bear," the words and story can change, thanks to the use of the correction tool "Tipp-Ex" displayed throughout the action. The user can change the verb action content in the title, and thus change the end of the story. Dozens of scenarios have been imagined by the Buzzman agency. The impact on sales has been almost immediate. The first two campaigns were broadcast only in English and did not target French consumers directly; however, the Internet has no borders and ultimately even the French customers of the brand have taken to the game.

Re-creative digital experience

The phygital customer experience can also bring together digital creation technologies. These digital tools can serve three main purposes:

- Strengthen the creation: it is about creating objects starting from the virtual universe and migrating towards the real one (e.g., 3D printing of objects designed online);
- Enhance existing creation using Artificial Intelligence (AI)-based technologies;
- Control creation: this is reflected in the use of applications that control consumption in a quantified-self logic.

THEORY BOX 11.2   WHAT IS ARTIFICIAL INTELLIGENCE (AI)?

Artificial intelligence uses algorithms inspired by human intelligence. It is a field of computer science aimed at creating intelligent engines that function and respond like humans. Some of the tasks that artificial intelligence computers can accomplish include: language and visual identification, learning, planning, fixing a problem, etc. AI becomes very interesting in a highly competitive marketplace that features identical products and services; one way for brands to stand out is to provide a different, unique, highly personalized experience that goes beyond the expectations of their users and surprises them.

MINI-CASE 11.9   BURBERRY USES AI TO LIMIT COUNTERFEIT LUXURY PRODUCTS

Burberry uses AI to fight against counterfeiting. It is a technology based on image recognition that is able to determine from a single image of a small section whether the product is authentic or not with 98% accuracy. To launch this technology, Burberry developed a partnership with Apple to use its augmented reality tool, in addition to using its data and AI, to develop its sales. Burberry is also interested in collecting data about the way its products are used to design suitable experiences, products, and services. The brand's 500 stores in 50 countries are equipped with radio-frequency identification (RFID) technology that transmits information to customers on their mobile phones: for example, their mode of production or how to wear them.

Cyborg experience

It is a domestic or extra-domestic customer experience integrating humanoid robots. Humanized robots are becoming more prominent in corporate events and are becoming part of the phygital experience. There are several categories of robots and their use depends on the role the company would like to give to them. For example, the host robot in Japan is used as a hostess in luxury stores.

Therefore, to create or reinvent the phygital experience, all technologies and digital tools should be utilized: 3D and 4D, 360-degree technologies, IoT, humanoid robots, augmented and virtual reality, etc. Today, digital transformation represents a great challenge of connecting the real world to the virtual one while guaranteeing fluid, sensory, emotional, continuous, and satisfying phygital experiences. Delivering a memorable and enjoyable phygital customer experience requires the integration of technological tools and devices, such as smartphones, tablets, connected objects, etc., that also fulfill three main functions of the phygital experience:

- Function 1: create a contextualized, functional, emotional, and sensory phygital customer experience;
- Function 2: strengthen the link between the virtual and real experience on several media and devices (laptops, tablets, apps, website, etc.);
- Function 3: offer engaging experiential content using storytelling techniques. The video can be used to tell stories. This technique is very effective and requires no reading effort and, above all, it is easily shared on social media.

Tools to design phygital experiences

There are three main tools that allow the creation of the customer experience in a phygital environment. All these tools (web 3.0, interactive devices, and immersive tools) convey the brand's values and create a strong emotional bond with the targets. Figure 11.2 presents the tools that companies can use to create meaningful and entertaining phygital experiences.

Web 3.0

To create a satisfying and continuous phygital customer experience, marketers and brand managers can use web tools that are available to them to deliver memorable online experiences. Web 3.0 is an Internet of connected objects in which aggregated data makes more sense based on three essential elements: semantics, mobile objects, and connected objects. Web 3.0 marketing enables companies to use Internet-connected objects, database-enabled devices, intelligent sensors, and an instant responsiveness to the real world. In marketing 3.0, there are four main elements: data, objects (connected hardware), social interactions, and software. Connected objects represent a fast-growing market in all areas of activity: sports, well-being, home equipment, work, etc. Amongst the main trends in connected objects that

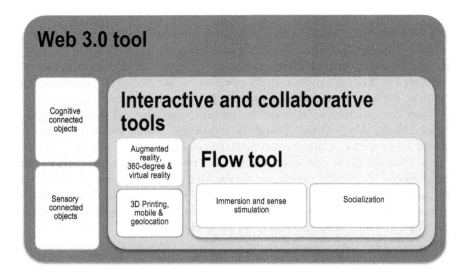

FIGURE 11.2 Tools of phygital customer experience

companies can consider in creating a phygital customer experience, there are two categories: cognitive connected objects and sensory connected objects.

- **Cognitive connected objects.** These objects that collect data about their users, analyze them, and provide them with the results are in great demand by consumers who want to know more about their behavioral patterns, to control them, to share them, or to compare them with other users. Health and well-being are two sectors that are very attracted to this technology. Other examples of connected objects that can use analyzed data to make everyday life easier, include devices that control the entrances and exits of a house via a connected and accessible handle following the daily movements of the user.

- **Sensory connected objects.** These objects are designed to detect the emotion that the user expresses when using the product or practicing a given activity. These objects have sensors for an emotional reading; they also offer options for adapting to the mood of the moment.

Interactive and collaborative tools

To create a phygital customer experience, it is important for marketers and brand managers to involve the user in the co-creation of the product or the service. Interactivity and co-creation should be at the heart of the device for developing an effective and satisfying, functional and emotional phygital experience. There are several technologies that allow interactivity and collaboration with users. Amongst these technologies, four digital tools are needed to adapt the customer experience to the phygital environment.

- **Augmented reality.** It is one of the technological tools that companies can use to optimize the phygital experience by combining real and virtual realities. In an augmented reality, virtual objects are presented in realistic form in a three-dimensional (3D) video.
- **3D printing.** It is a rapid prototyping technology that allows consumers to manufacture three-dimensional objects using a 3D printer, a digital file (often accessible free of charge and open sourced), and some materials depending on the size and composition of the product/object to be printed (plastic, metal, resin, etc.). 3D printing is becoming increasingly attractive to more and more businesses as well as to the public, and anyone else who is curious to explore all the possibilities offered by 3D printing. The technology allows consumers to create and personalize objects, such as smartphone cases, cups, figurines, jewelry, etc.
- **Mobile technologies.** They are widely distributed and consumers are highly equipped with smartphones. This has contributed to the spread of mobile technology and its incorporation into the phygital experience. In terms of functional interactivity, smartphones offer the opportunity for users to obtain product information through QR (quick response) codes that allow consumers to be in both the real world and the virtual space.
- **Geolocation.** It is another form of technology marketers and brand managers can use for its effective targeting. Geolocation allows companies and brands to geographically locate and target the recipients of their marketing messages on a smartphone-like mobile terminal or on a website.

The flow tool

The concept of flow appeared in psychology research with the work of the pioneering psychologist Csikszentmihalyi (see Chapter 3). There is a multitude of elements related to the appearance and intensity of the flow in an optimal experience linking the physical and digital environment. Figure 11.3 presents the elements of flow in the phygital experience.

The two American authors Hoffman and Novak, experts in online behavior, proposed in 1996 a flow definition applied to an online navigation experience. For Hoffman and Novak, flow is a pleasant emotional state that appears during navigation, characterized by fluid communication, facilitated by interactivity, and accompanied by a loss of self-awareness and self-empowerment. In addition, the flow can be facilitated by the characteristics and the type of media used during the online experience. Thus, making the consumer experience a satisfying cognitive

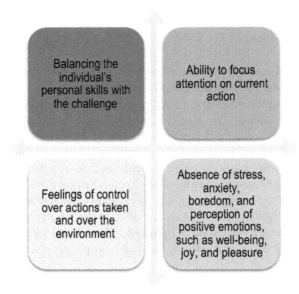

FIGURE 11.3   Elements of flow in the phygital experience

and emotional phygital experience can be achieved by the rapid evolution of digital technologies and immersive tools that can reach the consumer in his/her experience of browsing on a commercial site. Immersion experienced, as part of an experiment in a phygital environment, has several advantages (Table 11.1).

Immersion is an essential element for companies to design the ideal phygital experience and re-enchant their customers. To do so, immersion should include six essential elements: atmospheric, functional, cognitive, human/social, symbolic, and identity (Table 11.2). To make immersion online optimal during a browsing experience, these factors are not enough to bring online customer experiences into a continuum with real-world phygital experience. It is, indeed, essential for brand managers and marketers to take into account the degree of intensity of the digital experience.

Key success factors

How do we design and stimulate the customer experience in a phygital environment? The implementation of an experiential digital strategy guaranteeing a continuum between the physical and digital contexts have to take into consideration two key elements: immersion and functionality.

TABLE 11.1 Advantages of digital immersion

ADVANTAGE 1	Immersion can influence the online behavior of the user
ADVANTAGE 2	Immersion enhances memorization of brand and product information
ADVANTAGE 3	Immersion can effectively involve the user
ADVANTAGE 4	Immersion generates pleasure and stimulation of the senses
ADVANTAGE 5	Immersion promotes exchanges and socialization

TABLE 11.2 Key factors of immersion in digital experience design

Atmospheric factors	They are linked to the website and include the technical elements related to the site's atmosphere and design (colors, sounds, style of writing, iconography, navigability, accessibility, speed of download, zoom quality, etc.)
Functional factors	They are related to the information needed to facilitate the purchase (information on the objects, mode of delivery, price, functionality, etc.)
Human and social factors	They used to establish links and gather spaces for exchanges between customers and the brand via virtual agents, or between customers through discussion forums
Cognitive factors	They are related to the expertise of the consumer related to the use of the Internet. A user with a high level of knowledge and a rich browsing experience will be more easily immersed in the virtual universe of the brand, and therefore, will live a satisfying phygital experience that is both functional and emotional
Symbolic factors	They refer to the need of the individual to assign a meaning to his/her online activities
Identity factors	They are related to the identity quest process undertaken by the individual during his/her experiences of browsing and buying on different websites and platforms

The use of virtual agents for immersion and interaction

In order to make users live phygital experiences, immersive and interactive technological tools linking the brand's physical environment and virtual context should be considered in the experiential design. Both of these elements bring a realistic dimension to the online phygital experience. Thus, customers can experience virtual experiences that are almost identical to real-world experiences (e.g., in-store, hotel, etc.) because they can interact with virtual agents and physical agents (e.g., staff, salespeople, etc.) of the brand. The active participation of consumers is also essential for improving phygital customer experiences.

In fact, brands have to involve customers, not only in the process of co-creating the product or service, but also in the marketing strategy and the communication actions of the brand. Consumers can give their opinions and customize the products and services according to their needs.

The importance of efficiency

The phygital experience should provide a cognitive answer (convenience, time savings, assessment, personalization, etc.) and emotional reply (hedonism, pleasure-seeking, online exchange, etc.) to the requirements of consumers that emerge in the physical context and express themselves in the digital world. For example, the need for human assistance with skills or cognitive response to provide a solution, and empathy skills (emotional response) when the user encounters problems during his/her online purchase and browsing experience.

By applying an experiential phygital strategy linking the physical and digital context, the company will be able to offer these customers the opportunity to experience browsing and buying on commercial sites with creative, innovative, and participatory content that generates a particular emotion, such as joy, admiration, surprise, etc. The emotion generated during this browsing experience is beneficial for the brand, which is attracting users to its physical shops because they have been seduced by the brand's phygital experience on social media platforms, on the brand's commercial website, on the brand's app, etc.

Thanks to the democratization of access to digital technologies and the proliferation of virtual reality tools, companies are now able to offer users new experiences of browsing and buying online. However, companies that set up a phygital experience on their websites are rare. The websites exist primarily, and exclusively, for the purchase of the company's products, and little else. At best, it enables interactions amongst consumers via social media platforms provided by the companies, but fails in creating memorable phygital experiences.

Summary

Creating a customer experience in a phygital environment is a winning strategy that allows companies to ensure the attractiveness of their goods (products and services) while making them accessible to everyone on the Internet. By offering a high quality phygital customer experience, the company reinforces the feeling of the creativity and uniqueness of its products despite their dissemination and accessibility made possible by the Internet.

Beyond its functional dimension, the phygital experience allows brands to spread dreams via digital storytelling and other immersive technologies to attract new customers, but always with a sense of exclusivity through the art of creating multisensory and creative phygital experiences that generate shared values. Values depend mainly on customer perceptions. This chapter emphasized the urgent requirement for companies to prioritize "phygital" aspects of the customer experience in their marketing and digital strategies. It also emphasizes the necessity for marketers and brand managers to converge online and offline experiences in order to ease the buying process and assist the customer throughout the consumption and the browsing process, from pre-purchase to after-sales service. The phygital component ultimately highlights companies' needs to innovate, rethink, and extend the store to implement an omnichannel experience, gather and combine customer data to tailor its offerings, incorporate mobile setting devices to inform, instruct, and involve clients, and finally, to spread the purchase experience on social media and, thus, support connections with the company's products and services.

12

STORYLIVING, THE FUTURE OF CUSTOMER EXPERIENCE DESIGN

From story to action and storyliving strategies

Purpose and context

In this chapter, I introduce storyliving as the future of customer experience design. A story is built in the heat of the moment, then is recounted a posteriori, as an extension of this action and invitation to other actions. It is the experience created by brands for and with their customers that generates the best stories. History has meaning and value only if it is lived first, if it reflects an emotion, or if it is an exchange between the brand and its customers.

Without this unique breath, the story, beautiful as it is, remains an empty shell. And that is the difference between companies that "tell" stories (without real foundation), and those that "make live" their story, those that create shared experiences so rich that the customer wants to live and to extend the experience. Thus, companies should allow their customers to live their stories as it creates for them emotions and the desire to belong and share with the brand's community members. Each company has its own story and should make it livable and sharable with its customers. This chapter provides a framework along with implementation tools, strategies, and illustrative examples of how brands are using storyliving to design and improve customer experiences in different sectors.

Learning outcomes

After reading this chapter, you will be able to define storyliving, which is a future challenge for experiential marketing and customer experience implementation. You will be able to make the difference with storytelling, identify the tools, and strategies that marketers and brand managers can set up to engage customers in memorable experiences by making the stories of their brands livable and sharable amongst the brand community members and other customers.

From story to action

Unlike "storytelling," which consists of imagining stories to appeal to consumers, storyliving combines story and action through lived experiences in order to place customers at the heart of the story of the brand. In fact, while engaging customers is an effective strategy, telling a story is not enough to build customer loyalty. Brands should also engage in "storyliving" projects where they can engage their consumers by turning the brand's storytelling into concrete actions. The term storyliving is derived from anthropology (e.g., Emigh, 1996), which uses the term of "lived-story" to define the social practices of people.

Storyliving or the experience of living a story is an ongoing experience narrated in real time. It could, in any case, be closer to "storybuilding" or even to "storydoing," since there is something that is played in the present. Storytelling and storyliving do not have to be opposed since storyliving is a form of lived storytelling. It is in the field of virtual reality (VR) that storyliving has flourished.

Storyliving gets rid of any element of contextualization in relation to the brand, and immerses its targets in the present time. The idea is to involve customers in a strong relation to the brand. Far from being a new trend amongst advertisers, storyliving logically follows the growth of new methods of communication and content creation on the Internet. Social networks play a major role in the expansion and the success of storyliving. The heart of the transformation lies in living experiences with brands. With Snapchat, Instagram, Facebook, Periscope, or even the YouTube video platforms, more and more creators and influencers are turning to live video to reach their subscribers. It is here that the complete deconstruction of storytelling is based on a short, or even medium-term, reflection towards an ideal of spontaneity that seduces a rather young target heart. The storyliving takes place more in a sort of permanent duration considered as a present (at least that of an event), such as the Periscope function that broadcasts live the moment allowing people to interact and add comments.

The primary goal of storyliving is to share the experience with users, rather than just let them read and comment on the messages they view. The first brands to have started the storyliving trend immediately adopted virtual and augmented reality, videos where the user/customer is the hero, and, of course, a host of live tools: participative debates, tutorials, challenges, etc., with contents likely to attract the user, to involve him/her, to make the buzz, and in return, to attract the curiosity of the whole world. By consolidating its affective community base, storyliving is undoubtedly the major challenge for marketers and brand managers in designing the ultimate customer experience.

The storyliving refers to the brand's ability to bring its values and history to life by offering customers immersive and interactive experiences. These experiences can be shared in the real space (e.g., shops, events, etc.), as well as in the digital world (e.g., e-commerce site and social media). This guarantees a continuum between the "offline" and "online" customer experiences. Storytelling is then the starting point of any successful storyliving, that has to include the following elements:

- Covering all the actions of the company and engaging its various functions (e.g., marketing, communication, HR, R&D, etc.);
- Putting the customer and his/her expectations at the center of the brand's story.

It is obvious that brands that have storyliving approaches will perform better than those that limit their actions to storytelling. The example of Montblanc illustrates it very well. Since its birth in 1906, the German luxury brand has been linked to the culture of writing. With its commitment to Unicef since 2004, Montblanc writes history through concrete actions. These are based on a strategy of "storyliving" in order to promote writing by making it accessible to the greatest number of people.

MINI-CASE 12.1 NESCAFÉ CREATES STORYLIVING THAT MAKES PEOPLE SOCIALIZE

With the rise of the use of social media, one is more often on the phone than face-to-face when conversing. And for Nescafé, there was no way that this should continue. In Italy, the famous brand of coffee collaborated with the Publicis agency to set up the storyliving campaign "The Hello Bench."

Nescafé had the idea of creating a bench that retracts little by little when two people sit on it, thus creating a feeling of closeness that encourages them to meet and talk. It was an excellent initiative that worked in perfect harmony with the values and the communication of the brand. Developing new relationships is much harder than it looks, even if we are in the midst of a crowd of hundreds of thousands of people. For Nescafé, to do that, people need a trigger, an opportunity, and a good coffee – because coffee is even better when it is shared. Here, Nescafé, once again, offers a remarkable storyliving marketing operation.

Storyliving strategies

Storyliving is an effective and vital strategy that allows brands to differentiate themselves from their competitors, and to be more successful in the long run. In order to implement a storyliving strategy, marketers and brand managers should follow seven essential steps. These steps are summarized in Figure 12.1.

Further, marketing and communication managers can use five fundamental strategies: instructive, social and emotional, immersive, experiential, and ideological (Figure 12.2) to establish the transfer of the brand's story to lived action by

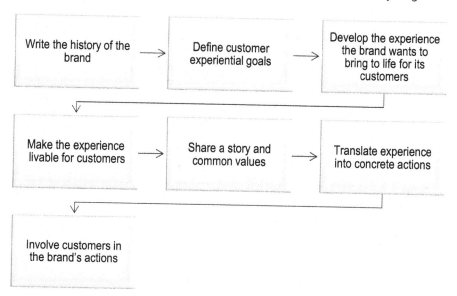

FIGURE 12.1 Seven steps of storyliving

FIGURE 12.2 Five main strategies of storyliving

implementing effective storyliving strategies that customers will connect to as they feel they are at the center of these actions.

- Instructive storyliving is a strategy that focuses on the product and its related information with practical, functional, and educational approaches.

MINI-CASE 12.2   EXPEDIA'S INSTRUCTIVE STORYLIVING THROUGH A VIRTUAL 45 MINUTES RAILROAD JOURNEY IN NORWAY

Different traveling desires? Want to travel lost railroad lines? Are you tempted to explore unknown railway landscapes? Unfortunately, people lack time or resources. To solve this problem, the Norwegian subsidiary of tour operator Expedia, in partnership with the tourist office of the city of Flåm in Norway, has created an unbelievable, online, virtual reality journey to the coastal town Bergen. A journey completed in less than an hour, it takes place on one of the steepest normal gauge lines in the world.

   This virtual immersion and instructive experience offers a unique opportunity to discover this mythical railway line as if we were at the controls of the locomotive. It is a memorable storyliving rail experience. The specialists of Lonely Planet tour guides stated in 2014 that the virtual journey is the most incredible train journey in the world. It is not the longest, certainly, but it allows crossing unquestionably unique landscapes, a southern nature that is hard and beautiful at the same time. The virtual will not replace the actual experience, but it is a good start and most importantly, it is free and instructive in that one does learn a lot about the country and shares his/her lived virtual experience, thanks to Expedia.

* Social and emotional storyliving includes interactive actions the brand implements in order to create an enjoyable social context and interactions amongst its customers and others. Emotional storyliving can be achieved when brands can translate their emotions into actions for many reasons: reaching out to consumers, establishing a strong bond with them, involving them and engaging them, etc. All emotions are to be considered (negative, positive, or neutral).

MINI-CASE 12.3   MCDONALD'S OFFERS SOCIAL AND EMOTIONAL STORYLIVING EXPERIENCES

As part of the release of "The Angry Birds Movie," Rovio partnered with McDonald's to create a storyliving experience. The video features 3D representations of the characters of the famous mobile game, embedded in video captures displayed in the restaurant to reach out to customers and engage them by generating emotions related to the lived story amongst parents, their kids, and the brand, which is funny, entertaining, and playful.

- Immersive storyliving requires involving the consumer through content that utilizes real or virtual interaction.

MINI-CASE 12.4   OREO USES IMMERSIVE STORYLIVING FOR THE LAUNCH OF A NEW PRODUCT

Cupcake Flavored Oreo Cookies developed a remarkable virtual reality and a 360-degree animation video that was introduced as a short animated film with the objective of immersing customers in the incredible and imaginative Oreo cookie-making factory. The virtual reality and the animated video take the user through the incredible journey traveled by cookies throughout the production process. It features a magical world of 360-degree, incredible machines, rivers of milk, chocolate walls, and a real sensory and entertaining storyliving.

- Experiential storyliving aims to project the consumer into a real or virtual world that presents the product in an ordinary or extraordinary environment. This strategy anchors the brand in the consumer's life or mind.

MINI-CASE 12.5   HOW DOES GOOGLE DO EXPERIENTIAL STORYLIVING?

"360 Google Spotlight Story: HELP" is a virtual reality animation video created by Google Studios. It is a real animation film that is purely action-based. The video, an output of the search engine studios, is of very high quality and experiential in nature. A shower of meteors falls on the city of Los Angeles. Panic in the city center ensues, especially when locals realize that an alien is there. We can also follow the adventures of a policeman and a woman who try to flee the monster with the appearance of a gigantic dinosaur. The courage of the young woman and her understanding of the monster offers a surprising end, and a captivating story-lived experience.

- Ideological storyliving is the commitment of the brand to a cause (fight against discrimination, combating violence against women, actions in favor of eco-responsibility, etc.).

MINI-CASE 12.6 TOMS CREATES IDEOLOGICAL STORYLIVING EXPERIENCES

Toms is a socially engaged shoe company that has offered a storyliving experience by taking its customers to a distant village in Peru where they could go on a real and authentic trip. Kids then appear in the video, glad and grateful for the arrival of the volunteers. The children were not just happy about the shoes; they were also happy that the volunteers played with them, interacted with them, and got to know them. The immersive storyliving experience has enhanced the emotional aspect of the brand, and created a strong connection based on commonly shared values with its customers.

Summary

This chapter introduced storyliving as a challenge for the future of customer experience design strategies. Today, marketing professionals and brand managers need to bring the stories of their brands into action by developing creative and innovative strategies using the principles of storyliving. In this chapter, I introduced the framework of storyliving, its main strategies, tools, approaches, and several examples of true, lived stories that show how companies can transform their way of connecting with their customers, and create new business opportunities.

13

CUSTOMER EXPERIENCE RESEARCH METHODS

Experiential and e-experiential research methods

Purpose and context

It is frequently thought that science tells us how things function and that there is no more exhaustive a science than that of quantitative scholarships. Scientific works are quantitative in numerous ways, but every field of knowledge has a qualitative facet in which the individual's experience, subjectivity, perception, and skepticism function together with others' philosophies to support the construction of and experimentation on theories. Distinct from the quantitative method, which trusts direct aspects, and statistical modeling, the qualitative methods are mainly related to individuals' perception and definition of their own world. While together quantitative and qualitative methods have their own value, I decided to discuss in this chapter alternative research methods that are qualitative, immersive, and well adapted to study and analyze customer experience.

The questioning of the research methods used to examine customer experience highlights the challenge for companies to have capabilities that go beyond traditional tools, such as quantitative (e.g. use of questionnaires and surveys) and qualitative techniques (e.g. focus-groups, face-to-face interviews, etc.) by adapting alternative experiential research methods to better understand consumers, their consumption experiences, and the meanings related to their practices. By using immersive creative tools, allowing an exhaustive analysis of the customer experience offline and online, and studying its subjective, paradoxical, symbolic, and emotional dimensions, companies can be able to innovate and design suitable experiences, and thus create a strong competitive advantage. This chapter introduces experiential and e-experiential research methods, as an alternative to studying customer experience, as well as new approaches for understanding and analyzing the customer experience and its functional, social, and emotional dimensions.

Learning outcomes

At the end of this chapter, you will be able to understand how companies and scholars can use alternative methodologies to explore customer experiences and develop a better understanding of the functional and symbolic needs of the consumers. The experiential (projective techniques, Qualitative Diary Research (QDR), ethnography, and subjective and personal introspection) and e-experiential research methods, such as netnography and mobile self-ethnography, will help you to understand the importance of using immersive and exploratory tools offline and online, such as the Internet and multimedia devices, to decode the paradoxes that emerge in the real lives of consumers.

Experiential research methods

Experiential research methods employ a range of immersive and qualitative methodological tools for advancing scientific awareness in the social sciences. There are areas and themes inclusive of all the topics of customer experience that have the potential to lead meaningful understandings, results, and insights of consumers by using an experiential research method, such as ethnography.

The main experiential research method by which information about consumers, their experiences, and the meanings they assign to their consumption practices and brands can be obtained includes four qualitative techniques, as shown in Figure 13.1.

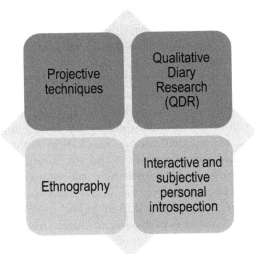

FIGURE 13.1 Experiential research methods

Projective techniques

When a researcher is leading an in-depth interview or conducting a survey through the use of questionnaires as a tool, he/she might face difficulties in the form of language obstacles, a communication gap with the respondent.

- The researcher might come across illiterate respondents, especially in social research and in rural areas;
- Researchers may also face social barriers whereby respondents are too uncomfortable to talk about a subject.

Other psychological obstacles might also occur when consumers feel uncomfortable when recalling special events or feelings, therefore, they might try to avoid certain questions or answers. In order to overcome such difficulties encountered during an interview process, the researcher can substitute the use of a questionnaire for projective techniques. In the marketing field, Haire's research (1950) on consumers' image of the new coffee product Nescafé instant coffee, was the first that uses projective techniques as a research method to collect data. This research had been conducted at a time when instant coffee was considered as a product of innovation and when most households still used traditional drip coffee.

MINI-CASE 13.1   NESCAFÉ USES PROJECTIVE TECHNIQUES TO REVEAL THE TACIT MEANINGS OF ITS INSTANT SOLUBLE COFFEE

This study was the starting point for the use of projective techniques in marketing. The launch in the United States in the late 1940s of the first instant soluble coffee "Nescafé" was a commercial failure even though the pre-tests of blind tasting had been satisfactory. The housewives then questioned said it was the taste they did not like.

Haire then proposed to use projective techniques by testing two identical purchase lists with the exception of one item: the traditional grain coffee was replaced by instant soluble coffee "Nescafé" in one of the lists. The housewives having to describe the profile of the woman who had bought the products on their list, presented the purchaser of traditional coffee grain as a good wife, good housekeeper, thrifty, and that of the other list as a bad wife, poorly organized, and spendthrift.

The respondents do not speak for themselves but of others: that is, in fact, since they were only subconsciously attributing to the others their own frame of reference, their personal feelings, their own motivations, it is likely that they would not have expressed face-to-face with the person what they had so candidly expressed in the testing process.

Following Haire, many researchers in the marketing field (e.g., Westfall et al., 1957; Hill, 1968; Fram and Cibotti, 1991) used replications and extensions to test the usefulness of the projective method in different consumption fields. Other researchers have addressed the use of projective techniques to emphasize the following subjects:

- The need for marketers to make a connection with consumers (e.g., Day, 1989);
- The need to evaluate the measurement competencies of lifestyle typologies (e.g., Lastovicka et al., 1990);
- The need of projective approaches in examining the meaning of gift giving (e.g., McGrath et al., 1993).

The advantage of projective techniques is to get individuals to express feelings that they would otherwise not express verbally. In order to obtain a response from the respondent without asking a direct question, the researcher will create a situation where the respondent projects his/her feelings on to some other person or object. For instance, a researcher might ask respondents to comment on a situation represented as a cartoon and ask them to describe what the cartoon characters think. Alternatively, they could be provided with a list describing an individual's choice of tourist destinations and ask respondents to describe the person who is likely to have formulated this choice.

THEORY BOX 13.1 PROJECTIVE TECHNIQUES TO REVEAL THE MEANINGS OF CONSUMPTION EXPERIENCES

Projective techniques pursue the objective of revealing hidden thoughts of consumers and understanding the tacit meanings of their behaviors. These qualitative techniques are open and indirect approaches that encourage respondents to project their motives, opinions, attitudes, or hidden feelings about a particular consumption situation or experience (e.g., Boddy, 2005; Ereaut et al., 2002).

In projective techniques, participants have to interpret the behavior of others rather than describe theirs, which leads them to indirectly project their own feelings into the situation. Thus, respondents' attitudes are revealed by analyzing their reactions to deliberately unstructured, vague, and ambiguous scenarios. The more ambiguous the situation, the more respondents project their emotions, needs, motives, attitudes, and values. This has been demonstrated by the clinical psychology studies (e.g., Zaltman, 1996; 1997) on which projective techniques are based.

In consumer research, projective techniques are a method for researchers to surpass oral communication obstacles and discover characteristics of consumer experience that respondents may find challenging to voice. Researchers are then able to investigate people's feelings, thoughts and experiences, and encourage respondents to discuss personal issues or motives that the respondent may not be aware of, and without them feeling threatened by the direct approach (Haire, 1950). These techniques are used to overcome the obstacles inherent in explicit consumer attitude measures. Respondents, with or without consciousness, are inclined to provide answers that are socially acceptable when placed in the role of the subject in a research experiment. If this technique is used properly, it will help researchers to go beyond the "common social barriers that inhibit the respondents' expression of attitudes and behaviors" (Steinman, 2009: 2). As in psychology, we can identify four main projective techniques: association, elements to be completed, construction, and expression.

- In association techniques, a stimulus is presented to a participant who is asked to answer the first thing that goes through his/her mind. The association of words is the best known of these techniques. It consists of presenting a list of words, one by one, that the participant should answer using the first word that comes to mind. Interesting words, called test words, are scattered throughout the list, which also contains neutral words to hide the purpose of the study. Thus, in the example of a restaurant experience, some of the test words could be food, quality, location, service, or price. The association technique allows respondents to reveal their deep feelings about their consumption and purchase experiences. Responses are analyzed by calculating the occurrence with which a word is specified as an answer, the time that intervenes before the answer, and the number of people who do not reply at all to a test word in a reasonable time. The schema and details of a participant's responses are used to determine an individual's hidden attitudes or feelings about the subject being studied.

MINI-CASE 13.2   THE USE OF ASSOCIATION TECHNIQUES FOR THE LAUNDRY DETERGENT MARKET

The association of words can be used to study the attitudes of women towards detergents. Given a list of stimuli words (e.g., family, dirty, laundry, time, smell, etc.), the responses of two women of a similar age and social status can be very different depending on the association they will make between the stimuli words and their own perceptions, which are shaped by their personalities and attitudes about the household. For example, answers can show the associations "dirt with food habits" and "dirt with pollution." The associations

(continued)

(continued)

made by the two women show that they regard dirt as part of the location and food practices in the family.

These results suggest that the laundry detergent market could be segmented on the basis of these two moments of life that generate dirt, and thus offer efficient detergents to solve this problem. Companies like Procter & Gamble could then benefit from the positioning of different brands within the lived experiences in different segments of the market.

- Elements to be completed. In this technique, the respondent should find the end of an incomplete sentence or story. The sentences to be completed are similar to word associations. Respondents are offered sentences whose end is missing and which they are asked to finish. They are usually asked to use the first word or phrase that comes to mind. Completing sentences can provide more information about the consumer's feelings than word associations. However, this technique is not so hidden, and respondents can guess what it is. In the technique of stories to be completed, respondents are offered a part of a story, sufficient to draw attention to a particular subject, but without any hint at the end. They are suggested to conclude it with their own words. The end of the story as told by the participants will reveal their hidden feelings and emotions.
- Construction techniques are similar to completed sentence techniques. Participants are asked to construct a response in the form of history, dialogue, or description. The story proposed by the researcher is less developed than with the previous technique. The two main construction techniques include the response to an image and the comics test:

  o Image response technique. The origin of this technique can be traced back to the thematic apperception test (TAT), which shows a series of images of ordinary or unusual events. In some of these images, people or objects are clearly represented, while in other images they are relatively blurred. The respondent is asked to tell stories about these images. The interpretation he/she makes gives indications of his/her personality. For example, an individual can be characterized as impulsive, creative, unimaginative, and so forth.

  o Comics test refers to comic characters that are presented in a particular situation related to the problem. Respondents are asked to indicate what a character might say in response to the comments of another character. This helps to identify respondents' feelings, opinions, and attitudes about the situation. Comic tests are easier to pass and analyze than picture response techniques.

MINI-CASE 13.3 THE USE OF CONSTRUCTION TECHNIQUES TO IDENTIFY A CONSUMER'S EXPECTATIONS ABOUT FOOD

In the United States, the desire for a healthy and lean diet seems to be declining in some segments of the population. When questioned directly, consumers are reluctant to admit that they like to eat what is not good for their health. However, this result appeared in an image response test in which respondents were asked to describe an image of people consuming high fat and high-calorie foods.

A significant number of respondents defended the behavior of these people. They explained that the increased stress of everyday life meant that they were turning away from tasteless cakes to so-called comfort foods. Many marketers have used this result to introduce products that are high in fat and calories (cookies, for example).

- Expression techniques. In these techniques, a verbal or visual situation is presented to the respondents; they are then asked to describe the feelings and attitudes of others about this situation. Respondents do not express their own feelings or attitudes, but those of others. The two major techniques of expression are role-playing and third-person technique:

  o   Role-playing. Respondents should play the role or adopt the behavior of someone else. The researcher assumes that respondents will project their own feelings into the role. These can then be detected by analyzing the responses.
  o   Third-party technique refers to a verbal or visual situation that is presented to the respondent; he/she is then asked to describe the opinions and attitudes of a third person rather than directly expressing one's own opinions and attitudes. This person can be a friend, a neighbor, a colleague, or a caricature of a person. The researcher assumes again that respondents will reveal their own opinions and attitudes by describing the reactions of a third person (speaking on behalf of another person reduces social pressure). Thus, the role-play technique assumes that the individual sees his/her creative spontaneity stifled by the constraints imposed by social life and by physical and mental habits. The role-play will free the individual by making him/her play the role of another.

Projective techniques can then provide verbal or visual stimuli through their indirection, and encourage respondents to reveal their unconscious feelings and attitudes without being aware that they are doing so. Therefore, projective techniques, as a tool to examine customer experience, are fundamental to researchers for capturing the meanings and dimensions related to consumption practices. They are mainly used for answering the "how," "why," and "what" questions that arise in consumer behaviors. Thus, projective techniques can provide a deeper understanding of what consumers truly think and feel about their consumption and shopping experiences.

Although projective techniques are indirect approaches that seek to reveal the opinions, motivations, feelings, attitudes, or even the values of the consumers within their own experiences, this type of technique is used very little in marketing, but has significant advantages in certain situations. Unlike focus groups or in-depth interviews, the purpose of projective techniques is not known to the individuals in the sample studied. When using a projective technique, participants are asked to analyze the behavior of others, not theirs. This method allows researchers to bring out, indirectly, the emotions of the participants, and even more when the staged situation is vague and ambiguous. Thanks to this technique, companies will be able to collect deep and interesting data about the tacit meanings and habits of consumers' experiences.

Qualitative Diary Research (QDR)

Qualitative Diary Research (QDR) is an innovative way to capture rich insights into customers' experiences, their processes, relationships, settings, products, and rituals (e.g., Patterson, 2005). A diary is a personal record of daily events, observations, and thoughts that inform marketers and brand managers about the way consumers see and talk about their everyday consumption practices. We can then argue that QDR is particularly suited to exploring complex aspects (functional, social, emotional, spiritual, ideological, etc.) of individuals' ordinary and extraordinary experiences from their own perspective. So far, very few studies have been carried out using qualitative diaries as the main method of investigating consumption experiences, although the first study was conducted in the early 1940s (e.g., Allport, 1942), some authors, such as Arnould (1998), argue that diaries could add previously unexplored dimensions to consumer research methods. In fact, the use of consumer diaries as an alternative methodology in marketing could yield promising directions in the field of customer experience studies. However, few studies have taken advantage of a diary-centered approach even though this approach, in particular, allows researchers, as stated by Patterson (2005), to capture a "thick description" of the complexities and the dynamics of the customer experience.

QDR is an individual documentation of everyday events, observations, thoughts, and feelings, which can be used as a self-reported tool by consumers to report and explore ongoing consumption and shopping experiences with their tacit (hidden meanings) and explicit (behaviors) dimensions. The use of QDR allows customer experience researchers to accomplish three main objectives:

- The diary method captures little experiences of everyday life that fill most of an individual's working time and occupy the vast majority of his/her conscious attention;

- Diary research is a suitable tool to reveal experiences and thoughts that are often hidden since events are recorded in their natural environment;
- Everyday diaries offer the opportunity for marketing and consumer researchers to study social, psychological, and physiological processes within everyday situations.

MINI-CASE 13.4 THE USE OF QUALITATIVE DIARY RESEARCH TO UNDERSTAND CHILDREN'S CONSUMPTION EXPERIENCES

From birth, children live and grow immersed in the culture of consumption. As consumers, buyers, and influencers, they participate actively in the marketplace and this is why they garner great attention from businesses as well as from social and political actors. In the marketing field, researchers have mainly used quantitative methods to describe the child's reactions to marketing actions. With the evolution of societies and the rise of digital practices at an earlier age, researchers need to think about redefining the scope of their work and to imagine new methodologies.

Thus, the idea of a qualitative diary approach, based on a comprehensive approach to social phenomena, is a way to explore and to enrich the study of kids as consumers, which can contribute to a better understanding of children's consumption experiences. For example, asking children to write on a topic of consumption, explain their prior purchase and consumption experiences, or nourish diary-type activities in the family sphere are amongst relevant techniques that the researcher can use in studying children's consumption experiences in their environment and in their own words.

Qualitative diary research can also be used to examine family consumption experiences (e.g., Chitakunye, 2012). Children can be asked to fill a diary by taking photographs in the different environments where they have their meals with their families or friends to help companies understand children's representations of family consumption experiences related to food, leisure activities, TV practices, etc.

QDR takes place immediately after the event in its natural and spontaneous context. As Gould (1991) acknowledged, this method can have a retrospective shortfall and could potentially be overwhelmed with biases by the limited ability of participants to recall their experiences (Wallendorf and Brucks, 1993). In the consumption field, QDR is also used as a methodology to understand why young people send each other text messages (e.g., Batat, 2014). Another study conducted by Patterson (2005) used real diaries as an alternative methodology to explore relationships between products and consumers. Other consumer researchers, such as Wohlfeil and Whelan (2012), used diary techniques to explore the life of a movie actress's fan from his/her own perspective.

Ethnography

Ethnography is an exploratory, interactive, and immersive methodology that enables marketers, ethnographers, and researchers to understand the social interactions between consumers and market actors as well as the internal interactions within each consumption culture. The aim of ethnography is to analyze the symbolic and emotional dimensions of consumption experiences, behaviors, and practices of consumers from their own point-of-view. Ethnography allows marketers and brand managers to:

- Go beyond the cognitive and rational vision of consumer behaviors by adopting a symbolic and sociocultural perspective;
- Study how consumers build and develop attitudes towards brands and products in their consumption culture, and how the latter contributes to the formation of consumers' attitudes and consumption patterns;
- Use visual and verbal data through the recording of behaviors in real consumption situations;
- Allow researchers to stay in the natural surroundings of the group they are studying. It is up to the ethnographer to make efforts to "become invisible" and "indispensable" within the group.

For companies, ethnography is a source of innovation because it provides a deep knowledge of consumers, which can help companies to identify, categorize, and analyze cultures, subcultures, countercultures, micro-cultures of consumption. In these different cultures, marketers and brand managers will be able to identify typologies of behaviors according to shared norms amongst consumers who belong to the same consumption culture, and thus better adapt their offerings as well as marketing and communication campaigns.

MINI-CASE 13.5   EDF, THE LEADING FRENCH ELECTRICITY PROVIDER, USES ETHNOGRAPHY TO KNOW ITS CUSTOMERS BETTER

In EDF's Research and Development department, several sociologists and anthropologists work together for a better knowledge of the customers with the aim of rethinking electricity services by addressing issues, such as how to introduce sustainable energies. Or, what is the reception of the customers towards new energy offers that can be introduced to them? To address these questions, ethnographers went into the real field to examine how customers or users manage their energy, how they talk about it, etc., in order to identify operational segmentations.

Ethnographers thus intervene, based on fieldwork, on the technical problems that the engineers encounter: the duration is short, but the multiplicity of the fields allows a comparative approach, which is at the base of the anthropological approach. In energy consumption, we can note that energy tools and policies are often created in terms of the "impact of information" (a stimulus, a response), a behavioral mode; however, customers do not always choose the most efficient answer from a technical or economic point-of-view in their daily choices. It is these less accessible and less visible elements that the ethnographers encounter in their day-to-day work on energy consumption.

Given the sociocultural dimension of consumption, the use of ethnographic techniques appears to be the most appropriate tool in understanding the customer experience. In fact, ethnography is used to uncover, interpret, and understand the consumer's point-of-view shaped by his/her sociocultural environment. The study of customer experience through ethnography requires immersive and longitudinal methods for working with, rather than on, consumers; and for discovering meaning in, rather than imposing meaning on, consumer behaviors (e.g., Eckert, 1988). According to McCracken (1988), ethnography allows researchers to access customer experience dimensions imbued with social meaning that is otherwise tacit and made in day-to-day consumption practices, and thus researchers can gain a thick description of experiences from the perspective of consumers to attain an understanding of consumer's view in context. In order to develop a better understanding of customer experiences and uncover the explicit and tacit meanings, Batat (2015) suggests that researchers can familiarize themselves with the consumption culture of the group they are studying, and thus collect rich data by following three main stages: socialization, collaboration, and auto-confrontation.

- Socialization. In the socialization stage, researchers can use observation and informal conversations to work with participants. This stage can be extended over a period of three or six months and allows researchers to be fully immersed within the consumption culture of the informants. Participating in formal and informal conversations and social activities amongst consumers, observing their behaviors and reactions, and informally interviewing as many individuals as possible can help researchers to accomplish the socialization task. As the researcher might become more involved and the group members start to trust him/her and consider him/her as a member of the group sharing the same interests and in turn, regard him/her less as an outsider researcher, data collection becomes more systematic and easy to conduct. This phase allows the researcher to access deep insights about consumer consumption culture and meanings that cannot be obtained by any other means.
- Collaboration. In the collaboration stage, researchers can conduct a participatory study using a model with principles of Participatory Action Research (PAR) similar to that proposed by Ozanne and Saatcioglu (2008). The researcher can invite participants to engage in collective and individual in-depth interviews and workshops on consumption experiences.

- Auto-confrontation. In this stage, the researcher can ask participants to comment on primary results describing their own consumption experiences and other's experiences.

The three steps and the path of exploration can lead the researcher to build a full picture of consumers' perceptions and definitions of their own experiences that are shaped by a particular consumption culture within a marketplace in which they interact with other market actors (e.g. institutions, industry, other consumers, etc.). Furthermore, companies and ethnographers can have the choice between two ethnographic approaches: multi-site and "quick & dirty." Figure 13.2 summarizes the differences between these two approaches.

Therefore, using ethnography (multi-site and "quick & dirty") allows the ethnographer to delve deeply into a consumer's meanings as perceived within a particular subculture in which the experience takes place. Various methods can be used to bring the ethnographer and/or the company close to day-to-day consumer consumption experiences and meanings. Amongst the existing tools that marketers can use when conducting an ethnographic study, we can mention the following: observation, photographs, and narratives.

- **Observation.** Observational research is traditionally associated with an ethnographic and anthropological approach. Observation methods can be a good tool for obtaining information about consumer experiences. This method is used for recording behaviors, objects, and events. Informal observations are extensively used for observing customer buying patterns and the impact of advertisements on buying products or services. The observation technique is

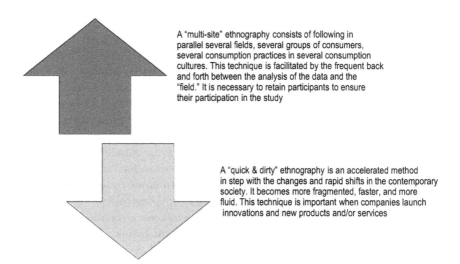

A "multi-site" ethnography consists of following in parallel several fields, several groups of consumers, several consumption practices in several consumption cultures. This technique is facilitated by the frequent back and forth between the analysis of the data and the "field." It is necessary to retain participants to ensure their participation in the study

A "quick & dirty" ethnography is an accelerated method in step with the changes and rapid shifts in the contemporary society. It becomes more fragmented, faster, and more fluid. This technique is important when companies launch innovations and new products and/or services

FIGURE 13.2 Multi-site ethnography vs. "quick & dirty" ethnography

usually used in addition to other research techniques. A specialized form of observation called participation observation occurs when a researcher joins a group for an extended period of time and observes the behaviors of the group members (e.g., Easterby-Smith et al., 2002). Adapted from anthropology, this type of research is growing in popularity, especially when the researcher needs an honest and behind the scenes peek into consumers' lives (e.g., Churchill and Iacobucci, 2005).

THEORY BOX 13.2   THE PERCEIVE FRAMEWORK TO ANALYZE OBSERVATION DATA

Observational research may usefully be guided by a framework, such as PERCEIVE. PERCEIVE stands for (spatial) Proximity, (facial) Expressions, Relative orientation (in space), (physical) Contact, Eyes, Individual gestures, Voice (vocal gestures), and Existence of adapters (small mood accommodating behaviors).

Such a framework draws explicit attention to participants, interactions, routines, rituals, temporal elements, and the setting, as well as elements of a small social organization. This framework points to the importance of nonverbal communication. The advantage of this observation technique is the fact that this method does not rely on the willingness of the respondent to cooperate and provide information, and can discover behavior patterns that a respondent is not necessarily aware of. This information can be recorded by observation only, such as facial expression of a consumer while examining a new product or a service.

However, by using the observation method one cannot observe the consumer's beliefs, feelings, awareness, etc., and the observed behavior pattern should be of short duration and should occur frequently in order to qualify for observation. By replacing humans with mechanical devices, such as video cameras, the accuracy of observation increases, observer bias is reduced, and so are the observation costs.

The immersion in the consumption culture of the informants allows observers to collect data from several observational sources:

o   Direct observation in the field by sharing the life and consumption activities of people at work, with friends, on holiday, at home, at the supermarket, with their families, etc;

o   Comprehensive in-depth interviews through occasional field conversations and formal/informal exchanges related to consumption experiences;

o   The analysis of personal "diary, blogs, and social media" documents in which informants reveal in their own words their point-of-view about their consumption experiences and the world around them.

- **Photographs.** Taking photographs is a way of involving participants in the data collection process. In fact, having participants in the field who are offered the possibility of expressing their practices of consumption through photographs taken by them, and which are representative of the consumption objects and practices that constitute their universe allows researchers to get access to a visual representation of consumers' consumption cultures.
- **Narratives.** This technique refers to the life story and tales of people as a qualitative method that originated in the social sciences, and can be used in marketing to understand consumers and their consumption experiences that are socially constructed in a particular consumption culture. The narrative discourse of consumers provides knowledge about their sociocultural sphere and their interactions with other people, companies, parents, and other social agents.

Interactive and subjective personal introspection

The method of data collection through interactive introspection is closely related to action research and was introduced to the social sciences by Rambo-Ronai (1992) in a sociological study of exotic/lap dancers. In this method, the researcher engaged in an interactive dialogue with other informants who shared their private experiences and insider knowledge (Ellis, 1991). In marketing, Holbrook (1997) introduced Subjective Personal Introspection (SPI) more than 25 years ago as a research methodology that has an extreme form of participant observation. For Gould (2012), there are two approaches that marketing and consumer researchers can use to explore consumer experiences:

- The first approach refers to the use of introspection by taking into account multiple researcher perspectives (e.g., Minowa, Visconti, and Maclaran 2012).

MINI-CASE 13.6 ETHNOGRAPHY: A TOOL FOR CREATING LUXURY BRAND STORYTELLING

Today many brands are using storytelling for reasons of fashion and/or necessity without having clear theoretical and methodological references. Even the most emblematic brands in storytelling have recently shown that telling a story is anything but an easy job.

For methodology and the field of study, the research of Visconti and colleagues is based on ethnography applied to luxury marketing professionals. These researchers also collected the storytellings created by luxury brands in a variety of industries: jewelry, cosmetics, design, fragrances, luxury department stores, luxury hotels, fashion, high-end food, and restaurants. From a methodological point-of-view, the qualitative data were thematized according to the principles applied in the field of interpretative studies. The quantitative data were analyzed through a meta-analysis that gathered in a single database the previous studies conducted by all the researchers who were interested in narrative transportation.

The main results of the study highlighted three important levels related to the art of luxury brand story creation: (1) the storymaking, which represents the design phase of a brand story (What elements are needed for the story? What principles are needed to write a more effective story? Where can narrative sources for a brand be found?); (2) storytelling, which involves the phase of proposing a story (who to target, which media to use, which storytellers, what effect do we want to achieve through a story, etc.); and (3) the "story-receiving," which assesses the effects of a story on its audience (what is the narrative's need for such an audience, what form of persuasion is obtained, etc.). Second, the results of the ethnographic study also allowed the researchers to propose recommendations to luxury brands. For example, simplifying, for a more powerful storymaking it is necessary to bring together four elements: 1) characters to identify with; 2) a story that is imaginable; 3) a crescendo in the story; and 4) a moral, which allows one to learn and memorize the meaning of the luxury brand story and history.

- The second approach, however, uses a personal perspective, in other words, the way the researcher can tell a story in his/her own way (it implies looking inward at oneself) (e.g., Batat and Wohlfeil, 2009).

According to Holbrook (1997), SPI is an experiential, private, and self-reflection approach on the joys and sorrows related to consumption found in one's own everyday participation in the human condition. This is an extreme form of participant observation, which focuses on impressionistic narrative accounts of the writer's very own personal life experiences from the privileged position of the real insider as primary data (Wohlfeil and Whelan, 2008). Thus, Gould (2012) states that unlike any other research methodology in qualitative research, the researcher often takes on the dual role of both researcher and informant.

One of the major advantages of this research method is its possibility to allow researchers to observe an unlimited 24-hours access to an insider's everyday lived experiences with the research phenomenon without having to wrestle with ethical concerns regarding the informant's privacy. Furthermore, SPI enables the researcher to explore the subjective nature of human feelings, daydreams, sensations, and streams of consciousness related to consumption, which could not be identified with traditional qualitative research methods.

There are four different approaches for collecting introspection data as stated by Wallendorf and Brucks (1993) in their review of auto-ethnographic literature: researcher introspection, interactive introspection, guided introspection, and syncretic introspection.

- **Researcher self-introspection.** This auto-ethnographic technique is the most controversial introspective data collection approach. It was introduced to consumer research by Holbrook (1986) and advanced by Gould (1991). The research context is about the researcher's private life experiences so that he/she acts as the expert and the sole informant in a sample of one. The latest study using researcher introspection has been done by Wohlfeil and Whelan (2012) in "*Saved!' by Jena Malone*." This study portrayed an introspective investigation of a consumer's fan relationship with a film actress in *Pride and Prejudice*. In this study, the first author, who is a fan, explored celebrity fandom as a holistic, lived experience from a fan's insider perspective. The lead author (Wohfeil) used SPI to provide insights into his private fan relationship with the actress Jana Malone.

MINI-CASE 13.7 USING SELF-INTROSPECTION TO UNDERSTAND HOW THE EXPERIENCE OF CHANGING PLACES FORMS A PATCHWORK CONSUMER IDENTITY

The purpose of the study conducted by Batat (2015) is to draw on a subjective personal introspection (SPI) approach and Breakwell's (1992) identity process theory (IPT) principles to show how elements from different cultures are performed by an individual to form a unique patchwork identity, and how this patchwork identity will contribute to deepen consumer immersion and, thus achieve and maintain authentic place experience.

The study uses SPI to explore the construction process of a patchwork identity by acculturating and combining multiple ethnicities amongst three consumption cultures through the use of a subjective consumer-centric approach within different cultural settings. This approach goes beyond consumer narratives and uses individual perspectives based on a long-term personal subjective travel experiences of a researcher who is French and based in France, for instance, but brought up abroad within three main cultural contexts (European, North American and North African) where the researcher lived with her family and friends, experienced consumption cultures and social interactions in different cultures, traveled, worked, visited, socialized, etc. The use of subjective introspection gives the researcher easy access to data collected on her own private everyday lived experiences related to consuming different cultural places for unlimited 24-hour access, from an insider's ongoing lived experiences.

The results show that the patchwork consumer identity encompasses the individual's ability to cross different social and symbolic boundaries when experiencing different destinations. Each cultural context contributes to the *bricolage* and the assemblage of the individual patchwork identity revealing one or more IPT dimensions. The practical implications serve to emphasize the importance of SPI-based research to patchwork identity construction in understanding the impact of cultural identity on consumer immersion. This approach can help marketers and tourism professionals to understand how consumers select the cultural elements that fit their identity, and how the patchwork identity formed will contribute to deepening the tourist's gaze and destination experience of authenticity.

- **Interactive introspection**. This technique has been used in recent works focusing on interactive introspection through a narrative transportation approach. In their research on film experience perception, Batat and Wohfeil (2009) used interactive introspection to examine consumers' movie enjoyment (see Mini-case 13.8). In so doing, the two authors wrote, exchanged, compared, and interpreted retrospective essays of their personal movie consumption experiences with special reference to the film *Into the Wild* (US 2007), which they both watched at the same time.

MINI-CASE 13.8   INTERACTIVE INTROSPECTION AND UNDERSTANDING CONSUMERS' MOVIE EXPERIENCES

In order to truly understand movie consumption as a holistic, phenomenological experience from an insider perspective, the focus has to be on the consumer experience in the way it presents itself to consciousness. In their study, Batat and Wohfeil (2009) used the subjective personal introspection approach that could be broadly described as interactive introspection and involves subjective insights through comparing, contrasting, and interpreting introspective essays produced by the two researchers.

Both researchers wrote independently for each other an extensive introspective essay on their personal experiential consumption of the movie *Into the Wild* (Director: Sean Penn, US 2007), which, by coincidence, they have both watched recently. Based on Jon Krakauer's bestselling book, the movie

(continued)

(continued)

retells the true story of Christopher McCandless, a young college graduate who decided to abandon his worldly possessions and leave his perfectly planned life behind in order to escape the trappings of a society he despised by experiencing natural life in all its immediacy in the Alaskan wilderness. While his journey and view of life touched a number of people along the way, his romantic idealism ultimately leads to his doom at the unforgiving hands of Mother Nature.

The two authors then exchanged the two essays and each researcher compared and analyzed them for both common emic themes and individual differences. Finally, they compared their two personal interpretations of the introspective essays for similarities and/or differences and summarized them accordingly.

The study's findings clearly prove that movie enjoyment should be understood as a private lived consumption experience that depends on a holistic tapestry of interrelated factors and, subsequently, should be studied in its entire complexity. Subjective personal introspection offers the potential for gaining interesting insights into the private domain of movie consumption that is less accessible than traditional methods, which focus mainly on the collective domain. The findings show that an individual's personal emotional engagement with the narrative, its characters, and underlying philosophy, which allow for the temporary immersion into the movie's world, is of particular importance for one's movie enjoyment. The level and nature of a consumer's experienced immersion into the movie narrative is determined less by age or gender, and more by one's very private motives and interests.

The managerial implication of these findings is for film producers to stop heeding the calls of consultants for mass-produced, family-friendly, made-by-standard-formula movie packages that serve the smallest common denominator. As consumers want to enjoy the feeling of losing themselves in the movie experience for diverse personal and intimate motives, the narrative has to be challenging and stimulate personal engagement from a variety of different angles. This would require each movie to be created again as an artistic product rather than as an interchangeable commodity. The point seems to be supported in particular by the recent global success and the growing popularity of both independent films and world cinema movies that tend to provide audiences with unique, interesting, involving, challenging, and much more demanding narratives than Hollywood's current standardized and family-friendly blockbuster-diet.

- **Guided introspection.** This data collection approach is becoming increasingly popular in market research practices as an alternative to traditional in-depth interviews and focus groups. Indeed, it is relatively easy, convenient, and cost-efficient to implement. Informants are asked to write a detailed introspective essay on their personal lived experiences with regard to a phenomenon of interest (Brown, 1998a). This approach has been used in consumer research by Brown (1998b) in "Romancing the market: Sex, shopping and subjective personal introspection." This type of data collection method can provide some potential innovative consumer insights for scholars as well as marketers and brand managers.
- **Syncretic introspection.** It is essentially a mixed method approach that involves a combination of the other three introspective methods: researcher self-introspection, interactive, and guided introspection. It was suggested by Wallendorf and Brucks (1993) as a way to introduce more scientific rigor into introspective research, but it has not been applied in any study so far.

E-experiential research methods

Marketing research methods are regularly renewed to adapt to emerging consumer behaviors while capturing the opportunities offered by information technologies, the Internet, and social media. Conventional face-to-face interviewing and in-situ observation techniques are thus enriched by the use of online qualitative data available on the web, particularly on discussion forums and social media platforms, such as Facebook, Instagram, Twitter, etc. This is how netnography appeared in the late 1990s and mobile ethnography/self-ethnography arose later in the early 2010s.

Netnography

Netnography is an online immersion technique on social networks and specialized blogs whose main objective is to analyze the discourses and exchanges between people on the Internet. As the world is changing, netnography, or online ethnography, certainly can be and has been applied to research questions regarding many social scientists' interests, from consumption experiences to game playing and disabled groups. In marketing and consumer studies, Robert Kozinet was the first researcher who introduced, in 1997, the use of netnography as a tool to explore, collect, and analyze consumption practices.

THEORY BOX 13.3 THE STAGES OF NETNOGRAPHY ACCORDING TO ITS FOUNDER ROBERT KOZINETS

Netnography (which is a combination of the words network and ethnography) is a research method applied to virtual environments and online communities. Its founder Robert Kozinets published his first research in 1997 followed by a book on netnography published in 2006. The goal of netnography is not only to understand, but also to share the common passion that drives community members online and offline. This method takes the classic steps of ethnography and adapts them to the study of the behaviors of online communities. In order to implement netnography, the investigator/researcher should follow four main stages, as described by its founder, Robert Kozinets (2015):

- Step 1: entry. The first step of netnography is to make an "entry," where the interviewer has to prepare the groundwork before selecting the community to study and beginning its analysis. First, it is important to set a clear goal and question. Then, using the Internet, the communities that correspond to the defined objective are identified. This approach is used to filter the groups that are most relevant to the objective of the study. It is, therefore, essential to carefully gather as much information as possible about the chosen community and its participants.
- Step 2: data collection. Several types of netnography data can be considered during the collection process. There are data available within the virtual community in the form of texts written by the members of the group, as well as other data related to the external elements of communication with subjects, such as voice, silences, etc. Other data are also considered, such as the data produced by the researcher: notes, reflections, and remarks written by the researcher during the observation process. In the situation where the researcher adopts a participatory attitude, contact can be established with the members in order to conduct individual interviews or engaging in new discussions.
- Step 3: data analysis and interpretation. This step refers to the analysis of messages using a message classification system to identify off-topic messages. Then, the researcher performs an analysis using the constant comparative method. During this process comes the coding of the data with variables that reflect the behaviors of the participants. The researcher should adopt an "emic" approach to achieve a profound level of understanding of the consumption culture. Then, a so-called "ethical" approach is necessary in order to conceptualize the results.

- Step 4: validation by participants and ethics of the process. Netnography is a method that facilitates data validation by involving the participating members. The members of the virtual community can be contacted and the results of the netnography research presented to them in order to collect their comments and show transparency. Feedback is important because it allows members to qualify the results, which improves the investigator's understanding of the behaviors and the situations.

This new form of ethnography is also popular in the study of worldwide online or virtual communities. From relatively humble beginnings of individuals' web pages, blogs have now gained considerable popularity as a form of individual self-expression and as an alternative to large media depictions of the news. As an offshoot of the personal web page, the blog remains acutely and deeply personal. The surveys and experiments are, however, unable to reveal the rich cultural worlds that are being created and experienced through online communities. More recently, other sources of information, such as consumer rating sites (for accommodation, destinations, etc.), have also provided a very useful source of information. Netnography, therefore, relies on the collection of qualitative and quantitative data on the Internet that is generated by online communities and other connected objects. Like ethnography, netnography is interested in the study of brand communities on the Internet. The setting up of a netnography approach can appeal to several methodological tools: online interviews, participant observation on the Internet, and a narrative account of consumer practices.

Netnography is, therefore, an adaptation of the qualitative and quantitative methods often used to study consumer cultures and experiences in a real context in order to match them to the online context with some adjustments. Overall, netnography can be conducted through participant or non-participant observations. Therefore, the advantage of using the Internet for exploratory studies, such as netnography, is to allow people to express themselves freely without fear of judgment. This allows investigators to collect more personal information because of the lack of physical maintenance.

Mobile self-ethnography

Mobile ethnography allows companies to ensure easy and low-cost implementation for "in-situ" approaches. In these approaches of self-ethnography, the observer-investigator is replaced by a portable device (smartphone or mini-camera) that accompanies the consumer or the buyer in all the moments of his/her daily life. The observation is made "in-situ" (where the product/service is consumed/used or purchased). Unlike focus groups or in-depth interviews, mobile ethnography leaves the field of study open, widening the scope to elements that appear a priori outside the field of study for the product or for the brand, including conversations/discussions about all other aspects of respondents' lives: their values, beliefs, motivations, and behaviors.

MINI-CASE 13.9 L'OREAL USES MOBILE SELF-ETHNOGRAPHY TO BETTER UNDERSTAND WOMEN'S BEAUTY EXPERIENCES

The observation and understanding of women's beauty routines and strategies is a crucial and constantly renewed source of inspiration for the development of new insights and new products at L'Oreal. The morning and evening routines are now quite well known and documented through "classic" observation techniques at home or in stores. But the beauty routines performed during the day are less so. This is where mobile self-ethnography comes into play.

The main objectives of the system put in place are the following: 1) capture the moments of truth, "care and makeup," of women throughout the day; 2) understand the beauty habits of women at different times; 3) identify the strategies (e.g., tips for "staying beautiful;" 4) demonstrate the benefits of smartphone mobility and the ability to follow women non-intrusively, including in the workplace and on the road; and 5) demonstrate that the quality of the material obtained is good, and that the richness of information collected allows a profound analysis and relevant recommendations.

In the end, the 12 participants transmitted 295 recordings: videos (112), images (117), audio comments (52), and texts (100). The analysis of extreme richness allowed the brand to meet all the objectives above, and much more. The benefits of this method were: a collection of data without any bias in the implementation, an economic alternative to ethnography with access to less frequent behaviors that occur outside usual hours or over long periods of time, and a live experience of sharing from an online platform and an intuitive and dynamic application.

Thanks to new technologies and their rapid adoption by consumers, mobile ethnography now allows companies to ensure easy implementation of studies complemented by the reduced costs of "in situ" approaches. Such a collection methodology allows participants to record their experiences via their mobile phones, without the presence of a researcher, by transmitting the data on a platform in a format of their choice, such as videos, photos, texts, or audio. Participants have the flexibility to discuss their motivations and provide insights, while researchers can re-launch and guide participants to gain insights on certain points of view.

The device can easily be used in multiple locations over the course of a day or weeks, reducing the need for travel. Content is hosted and analyzed from an online platform where the project is managed, enabling real-time interactions with participants. The content is then available live for all stakeholders. The multimedia material produced by the participants then enhances the final report.

Summary

Unlike quantitative research methods that aim to measure variables related to the purchasing process, experiential (projective techniques, Qualitative Diary Research, ethnography, and subjective and personal introspection) and e-experiential research methods, such as netnography and mobile self-ethnography, are, by their nature, exploratory and provide avenues for reflection in order to better understand customer experiences within a particular consumption culture. The immersive and exploratory aspects of these alternative methodologies allow marketers and brand managers to better anticipate the motivations and attitudes of consumers regarding the expected satisfying experiences.

CONCLUSION

The several chapters in this book have offered a strategic framework of customer experiential marketing and a practical tool provided by the 7Es as controllable components of the experiential marketing mix (Experience, Exchange, Extension, Emphasis, Empathy capital, Emotional touchpoints, and Emic/etic process) that companies can use to design and offer suitable, emotional, and profitable customer experiences offline and online within diverse markets and sectors.

This book has attempted to provide a better understanding of the experiential approach to marketing and management. As I have demonstrated throughout different chapters, experience is a rich and complex notion that can be addressed from diverse approaches and perspectives (consumer, company). The main focus of this book has been to recall the broad conceptual models within which the thinking of the experiential marketing mix and the customer experience have emerged. For companies, the understanding and the implementation of a successful experiential offering needs to be integrated into the comprehensive framework of customer experiential marketing provided by markers, drivers, and outcomes of the experience as well as its translation through the 7Es of the experiential marketing mix, which extends the marketing, communication, and management practices. In this progression, the experiential perspective is particularly relevant since it provides scholars and professionals with a structured and coherent approach to understanding customer experience, which is rather fuzzy, abstract, and difficult to grasp. At the time this book was written, these sociocultural and technological evolutions were still ongoing. It is definitely a very exciting time in research and practice since companies and marketing scholars are increasingly developing corresponding definitions and strategies to offer the ultimate customer experience within a phygital context.

REFERENCES

Abbott, L. (1955). *Quality and Competition*. New York: Columbia University.

Addis, M. and Holbrook, M. B. (2001). 'On the Conceptual Link between Mass Customisation and Experiential Consumption: An Explosion of Subjectivity'. *Journal of Consumer Behaviour* 1, no. 1, pp. 50–66. doi: 10.1002/cb.53.

Addis, M. and Podestà, S. (2005). 'Long Life to Marketing Research: A Postmodern View'. *European Journal of Marketing* 39, no. 3/4, pp. 386–412.

Agar, M. (2011). 'Making Sense of One Other for Another: Ethnography as Translation'. *Language & Communication* 31, no. 1, pp. 38–47. doi: 10.1016/j.langcom.2010.05.001.

Akrich, Madeleine. 1992. 'The De-Scription of Technical Objects', in *Shaping Technology / Building Society: Studies in Sociotechnical Change* (Bijker, Wiebe Eco and Law, John), pp. 205–224. Cambridge: MIT Press.

Alba, J. W. and Hutchinson, J. W. (2001). 'Knowledge Calibration: What Consumers Know and What They Think They Know'. *Journal of Consumer Research* 27, no. 2, pp. 123–56. doi: 10.1086/314317.

Alderson, W. (1957). *Marketing Behavior and Executive Action: A Functionalist Approach to Marketing Theory*. Homewood, IL: Richard D. Irwin.

Ali, S. H. S. and Ndubisi, N. O. (2011). 'The Effects of Respect and Rapport on Relationship Quality Perception of Customers of Small Healthcare Firms'. *Asia Pacific Journal of Marketing and Logistics* 23, no. 2, pp. 135–51. doi: 10.1108/13555851111120452.

Allport, G. W. (1942). *The Use of Personal Documents in Psychological Science*. New York: Social Science Research Council. doi: 10.1037/11389-000.

Anderson-Cook, C. M. (2005). 'Review of *Practical Genetic Algorithms* (2nd ed.) by R. L. Haupt and S. E. Haupt'. *Journal of the American Statistical Association* 100, pp. 1099–1099.

Anderson, J. A., and Meyer, T. P. (1988). *Mediated Communication: A Social Action Perspective (Current Communication)*. Thousand Oaks, CA: Sage.

Arnould, E. J. and Price, L. L. (1993). 'River Magic: Extraordinary Experience and the Extended Service Encounter'. *Journal of Consumer Research* 20, no. 1, pp. 24–45. doi: 10.1086/209331.

Arnould, E. J. (1998). 'Daring Consumer-Orientated Ethnography', in *Representing Consumers, Voices, Views and Vision*. London: Routledge.

Arnould, E. J. and Thompson, C. J. (2005). 'Consumer Culture Theory (CCT): Twenty Years of Research'. *Journal of Consumer Research* 31, no. 4, pp. 868–82. doi: 10.1086/426626.

Babin, B. J., Darden, W. R., and Griffin, M. (1994). 'Work and/or Fun: Measuring Hedonic and Utilitarian Shopping Value'. *Journal of Consumer Research* 20, no. 4, pp. 644–56. doi: 10.1086/209376.

Baddeley, A. D. and Logie, R. H. (1999). 'Working Memory: The Multiple-component Model', in *Models of Working Memory* (Miyake, A. and Shah, P.), pp. 28–61. Cambridge, UK: Cambridge University Press.

Bandura, A. (1977). 'Self-Efficacy: Toward a Unifying Theory of Behavioral Change'. *Psychological Review* 84, no. 2, pp. 191.

Bandura, A. (1980). 'Gauging the Relationship between Self-Efficacy Judgment and Action'. *Cognitive Therapy and Research* 4, no. 2, pp. 263–268.

Bandura, A. (1986). *Social Foundations of Thought and Action: A Social Cognitive Theory.* Englewood Cliffs, NJ: Prentice-Hall, Inc.

Bardhi, F. and Eckhardt, G. M. (2017). 'Liquid Consumption'. *Journal of Consumer Research* 44, no. 3, pp. 582–97. doi: 10.1093/jcr/ucx050.

Batat, W. and Wohlfeil, M. (2009). 'Getting Lost "Into the Wild": Understanding Consumers' Movie Enjoyment Through a Narrative Transportation Approach'. *Advances in Consumer Research* 36, pp. 372–77.

Batat, W. (2014). 'How Do Adolescents Define their Own Competencies in the Consumption Field? A Portrait Approach'. *Recherche et Applications en Marketing* 29, no. 1, pp. 25–54. doi: 10.1177/2051570714526326.

Batat, W. (2015). 'Changing Places and Identity Construction: Subjective Introspection into Researcher's Personal Destination Experiences'. *International Journal of Culture, Tourism and Hospitality Research* 9, no. 4, pp. 379–87. doi: 10.1108/ijcthr-08-2015-0084.

Batat, W. and Hammedi, W. (2017). 'Collaborative Consumption as a Feature of Gen-Y Consumers: Rethinking Youth Tourism Practices in Sharing Economy', in *Advances in Social Media for Travel, Tourism and Hospitality: New Perspectives, Practice and Cases.* London: Routledge.

Bate, P. and Robert, G. (2007). 'Toward More User-Centric OD: Lessons from the Field of Experience Based Design and a Case Study'. *Journal of Applied Behavioral Science* 43, no. 1, pp. 41–6. doi: 10.1177/0021886306297014.

Batson, C. D. (2009). 'These Things Called Empathy: Eight Related but Distinct Phenomena', in *The Social Neuroscience of Empathy* (Decety, J. and Ickes, W.), pp. 3–16. Cambridge, MA: MIT.

Baudrillard, J. (1970). *The Consumer Society: Myths and Structures.* Thousand Oaks, CA: Sage. doi: 10.4135/9781526401502.

Baudrillard, J. (1983). *Simulations.* Los Angeles, CA: Semiotext(e).

Bauman, Z. (2000). *Liquid Modernity.* Cambridge, UK: Polity.

Belk, R. W. (1988). 'Possessions and the "Extended Self"'. *Journal of Consumer Research* 15, no. 2, pp. 139–68.

Belk, R. (2007). 'Why Not Share Rather than Own?'. *Annals of the American Academy of Political and Social Science* 611, no. 1, pp. 126–40.

Belk, R. (2014). 'You Are What You Can Access: Sharing and Collaborative Consumption Online'. *Journal of Business Research* 67, no. 8, pp. 1595–600. doi: 10.1016/j.jbusres. 2013.10.001.

Benkler, Y. (2004). 'Sharing Nicely: On Shareable Goods and the Emergence of Sharing as a Modality of Economic Production'. *Yale Law Journal* 114, no. 2, pp. 273–358. doi: 10.2307/4135731.

Bennett, J. (2010). *Vibrant Matter: A Political Ecology of Things*. Durham, NC: Duke University.

Berry, L. (1995). 'Relationship Marketing of Services: Growing Interest, Emerging Perspectives'. *Journal of the Academy of Marketing Science* 2, no. 4, pp. 236–45. doi: 10.1177/0092070395.

Berry, L. L. (1996). 'Retailers with a Future'. *Marketing Management* 5, no. 1, pp. 39–46.

Berry, L. L. and Parasuraman, A. (1991). *Marketing Services: Competing Through Quality*. New York: Simon & Schuster.

Bitner, M. J. (1992). 'Servicescapes: The Impact of Physical Surroundings on Customers and Employees'. *Journal of Marketing* 56, no. 2, pp. 57–71.

Bitran, G. R. and Hoech, J. (1990). 'The Humanization of Service: Respect at the Moment of Truth'. *Sloan Management Review* 89, no. 2, pp. 89–96.

Boddy, C. (2005). 'Projective Techniques in Market Research: Valueless Subjectivity or Insightful Reality? A Look at the Evidence for the Usefulness, Reliability and Validity of Projective Techniques in Market Research'. *International Journal of Market Research* 47, no. 3, pp. 239–54. doi: 10.1177/147078530504700304.

Bonnemaizon, A. and Batat, W. (2010). 'How Competent are Consumers? The Case of the Energy Sector in France'. *International Journal of Consumer Studies* 35, no. 3, pp. 348–58. doi: 10.1111/j.1470-6431.2010.00937.x.

Boulanger, C. and Lançon, C. (2006). 'Empathy: Reflexions on a Concept'. *Annales Médico-psychologiques* 164, no. 6, pp. 497–505. doi: 10.1016/j.amp.2006.05.001.

Bourdieu, P. (1979). *La Distinction: Critique Sociale du Jugement*. Paris: Editions de Minuit.

Brakus, J. J., Schmitt, B. H., and Zarantonello, L. (2009). 'Brand Experience: What Is It? How Is It Measured? Does It Affect Loyalty?'. *Journal of Marketing* 73, no. 3, pp. 52–68. doi: 10.1509/jmkg.73.3.52.

Brandt, E., Messeter, J., and Binder, T. (2008). 'Formatting Design Dialogues – Games and Participation'. *International Journal of CoCreation in Design and the Arts* 4, no. 1, pp. 51–64. doi: 10.1080/15710880801905724.

Brentano, F. (1973). *Psychology from an Empirical Standpoint*. London: Routledge and Kegan Paul.

Breakwell, G.M. (1992). 'Processes of Self-Evaluation: Efficacy and Estrangement', in *Social Psychology of Identity and the Self Concept*, pp. 335–55. London: Academic Press/Surrey University.

Brett, J. M., Tinsley, C. H., Janssens, M., Barsness, Z. I., and Lytle, A. L. (1997). 'New Approaches to the Study of Culture in Industrial/Organizational Psychology', in *New Perspectives on International Industrial/Organizational Psychology* (Earley, P. C. and Erez, M.), pp. 75–130. San Francisco, CA: New Lexington Press.

Brown, S. (1998a). *Postmodern Marketing Two: Telling Tales*. London: International Thomson Business Press.

Brown, S. (1998b). 'Romancing the Market: Sex, Shopping and Subjective Personal Introspection'. *Journal of Marketing Management* 14, no. 7, pp. 783–98.

Campbell, J. (1949/2008). *The Hero with a Thousand Faces*. Novato, CA: New World Library.

Carlson, J. P., Vincent, L. H., Hardesty, D. M., and Bearden, W. O. (2009). 'Objective and Subjective Knowledge Relationships: A Quantitative Analysis of Consumer Research Findings'. *Journal of Consumer Research* 35, no. 5, pp. 864–76. doi: 10.1086/593688.

Carù, A. and Cova, B. (2003). 'Revisiting Consumption Experience: A More Humble but Complete View of the Concept'. *Marketing Theory* 3, no. 2, pp. 267–86. doi: 10.1177/14705931030032004.

Carù, A. and Cova, B. (2006). *Consuming Experiences*. London: Routledge.

Castelli, A. T. (2016). 'The New Revolution Will Be Physical, not Digital'. *Advertising Age*. Available at: http://adage.com/article/digitalnext/ revolution-physical-digital/302734/ (accessed 20 June 2017).

Cembalo, L., Migliore, G., and Schifani, G. (2012). 'Consumers in Postmodern Society and Alternative Food Networks: The Organic Food Fairs Case in Sicily'. *New Medit* 11, no. 3, pp. 41–9.

Chaffey, D. and Ellis-Chadwick, F. (2012). *Digital Marketing: Strategy, Implementation and Practice*. London: Pearson.

Chen, Y. (2009). 'Possession and Access: Consumer Desires and Value Perceptions Regarding Contemporary Art Collection and Exhibit Visits'. *Journal of Consumer Research* 35, no. 6, pp. 925–40. doi: 10.1086/593699.

Chitakunye, P. (2012). 'Recovering Children's Voices in Consumer Research'. *Qualitative Market Research: An International Journal* 15, no. 2, pp. 206–24. doi: 10.1108/13522751 211215903.

Choy, D. (2008). 'What Exactly Is Touchpoint?'. *Customer Think*. Available at: www. customerthink.com/blog/what_exactly_is_touchpoint (accessed 20 June 2017).

Churchill, G. A. and Iacobucci, D. (2005). *Marketing Research: Methodological Foundations*. Mason, OH: Thomson South-Western.

Clatworthy, S. (2011). 'Service Innovation Through Touch-Points: Development of an Innovation Toolkit for the First Stages of New Service Development'. *International Journal of Design* 5, no. 2, pp. 15–28.

Costley, C., Friend, L., and Babis, P. (2005). 'Respect in the Marketplace'. *Journal of Research for Consumers* 9, pp. 1–9.

Csikszentmihalyi, M. (1990). *Flow*. New York: Harper and Row.

Csikszentmihalyi, M. (1991). *Flow. The Psychology of Optimal Experience Steps toward Enhancing the Quality of Life*. New York: Harper Collins Publishers.

Csikszentmihalyi, M., Abuhamdeh, S., and Nakamura, J. (2005). 'Flow', in *Handbook of Competence and Motivation* (Elliot, A. J. and Dweck, C. S.), pp. 598–608. New York: Guilford Publications.

Cuff, B. M. P., Brown, S. J., Taylor, L., and Howat, D. (2016). 'Empathy: A Review of the Concept'. *Emotion Review* 8, no. 2, pp. 144–53. doi: 10.1177/1754073914558466.

Day, E. (1989). 'Share of Heart: What Is It and How Can It Be Measured?'. *Journal of Consumer Marketing* 6, no. 1, pp. 5–12. doi: 10.1108/eum0000000002534.

Day, G. S. (1999). 'Creating a Market-Driven Organization'. *Sloan Management Review* 41, no. 1, pp. 11–22.

Day, G. S. (2000). 'Managing Market Relationships'. *Journal of the Academy of Marketing Science* 28, no. 1, pp. 24–30. doi: 10.1177/0092070300281003.

Da Silveira, G., Borenstein, D., and Fogliatto, F. S. (2001). 'Mass Customization: Literature Review and Research Directions'. *International Journal of Production Economics* 72, no. 1, pp. 1–13.

Decety, J. (2002). 'Naturaliser L'Empathie'. *Encéphale* 28, pp. 9–20.

Decety J. (2004). 'L'empathie Est-Elle une Simulation Mentale de la Subjectivité D'Autrui ?', in *L'Empathie* (Berthoz A. and Jorland G.), pp. 53–88. Paris: Odile Jacob.

Decety, J., Bartal, I. B., Uzefovsky, F., and Knafo-Noam, A. (2016). 'Empathy as a Driver of Prosocial Behavior: Highly Conserved Neurobehavioral Mechanisms Across Species'. *Philosophical Transactions of The Royal Society B* 371, no. 1686. doi: 10.1098/rstb.2015.0077.

Deleuze, G. and Guattari, F. (1980). *A Thousand Plateaus*. London: Continuum.

Denegri-Knott, J. and Molesworth, M. (2010). 'Digital Virtual Consumption: Concepts and Practices'. *Consumption Markets & Culture* 13, no. 2, pp. 109–32. doi: 10.1080/ 10253860903562130.

Denegri-Knott, J., Zwick, D., and Schroeder, J. E. (2006). 'Mapping Consumer Power: An Integrative Framework for Marketing and Consumer Behavior'. *European Journal of Marketing* 40, no. 9–10, pp. 950–71. doi: 10.1108/03090560610680952.

Depraz, N. (2001). 'The Husserlian Theory of Intersubjectivity as Alterology. Emergent Theories and Wisdom Traditions in the Light of Genetic Phenomenology'. *Journal of Consciousness Studies* 8, pp. 169–78.

Dewar, B., Mackay, R., Smith, S., Pullin, S., and Tocher, R. (2009). 'Use of Emotional Touchpoints as a Method of Tapping into the Experience of Receiving Compassionate Care in a Hospital Setting'. *Journal of Research in Nursing* 15, no. 1, pp. 29–41. doi: 10.1177/1744987109352932.

Dewar, B. (2013). 'Cultivating Compassionate Care'. *Nursing Standard* 27, no. 34, pp. 48–55. doi: 10.7748/ns2013.04.27.34.48.e7460.

Dewey, J. (1934), *Art as Experience*, Rahway, NJ: The Barnes Foundation Press.

Dewey, J. (1938). *Experience and Education*. Toronto: Collier-MacMillan.

Dewey J. (1964). 'Why Reflective Thinking Must Be an Educational Aim', in *John Dewey on Education: Selected Writings*, pp. 210–28. Chicago, IL: University of Chicago.

De Keyser, A., Lemon, K. N., Klaus, P., and Keiningham, T. L. (2015). 'A Framework for Understanding and Managing the Customer Experience'. *Marketing Science Institute*, pp. 15–121.

Dickert, N. W. and Kass, N. E. (2009). 'Understanding Respect: Learning from Patients'. *Journal of Medical Ethics* 35, no. 7, pp. 419–423.

Dillon, R. S. (1992). 'Respect and Care: Toward Moral Integration'. *Canadian Journal of Philosophy* 22, no. 1, pp. 105–131.

Douglas, M. and Isherwood, B. (1979). *The World of Goods*. New York: Basic.

Dubet, F. (1994). *Sociologie de L'expérience*. Paris: Éditions du Seuil.

Duxbury, N., Garrett-Petts, W. F., and MacLennan, D. (2015). 'Cultural Mapping as Cultural Inquiry: Introduction to an Emerging Field of Practice', in *Cultural Mapping as Cultural Inquiry*, pp. 1–42. New York: Routledge.

Easterby-Smith, M., Thorpe, R., and Lowe, A. (2002). *Management Research: An Introduction*. London: Sage.

Eckert, P. (1988). 'Adolescent Social Structure and the Spread of Linguistic Change'. *Language in Society* 17, no. 2, pp. 183–207. doi: 10.1017/s0047404500012756.

Edvardsson, B., Tronvoll, B., and Gruber, T. (2011). 'Expanding Understanding of Service Exchange and Value Co-Creation: A Social Construction Approach'. *Journal of the Academy of Marketing Science* 39, no. 2, pp. 327–39. doi: 10.1007/s11747-010-0200-y.

Eisenberg, N., Fabes, R. A., Schaller, M., Miller, P., Carlo, G., Poulin, R., Shea, C., and Shell, R. (1991). 'Personality and Socialization Correlates of Vicarious Emotional Responding'. *Journal of Personality and Social Psychology* 61, no. 3, pp. 459–70. doi: 10.1037//0022-3514.61.3.459.

Elliott, R. and Wattanasuwan, K. (1998). 'Brands as Symbolic Resources for the Construction of Identity'. *International Journal of Advertising* 17, no. 2, pp. 131–144.

Ellis, C. (1991). 'Sociological Introspection and Emotional Experience'. *Symbolic Interaction* 14, no. 1, pp. 23–50.

Emigh, J. (1996). *Masked Performance: The Play of Self and Other in Ritual and Theatre*. Philadelphia, PA: University of Pennsylvania.

Ereaut, G., Imms, M., and Cullingham, M. (2002). *Qualitative Market Research: Principle and Practice*. Thousand Oaks, CA: Sage.

European Union Commission. (2011). 'EU 2011 Report on Policy Coherence for Development'. Commission Staff Working Paper. SEC (2011) 1627. Brussels: European Commission.

Felson, M. and Speath, J. L. (1978). 'Community Structure and Collaborative Consumption'. *American Behavioral Scientist* 41, no. 4, pp. 614–24. doi: 10.1177/000276427802100411.

Firat, A. F. and Venkatesh, A. (1993). 'Postmodernity: The Age of Marketing'. *International Journal of Research in Marketing* 10, pp. 227–49.

Firat, A. F., Sherry, J. F., and Venkatesh, A. (1994). 'Postmodernism, Marketing and the Consumer'. *International Journal of Research in Marketing* 11, no. 4, pp. 311–16.

Firat, F. and Venkatesh, A. (1995). 'Liberatory Postmodernism and the Reenchantment of Consumption'. *Journal of Consumer Research* 22, no. 3 (Dec), pp. 239–67.

Firat, A.F. and Dholakia, N. (1998). *Consuming People, from Political Economy to Theaters of Consumption*. London: Routledge.

Fitzsimmons, J. A. (1985). 'Consumer Participation and Productivity in Service Operations'. *Interfaces* 15, no. 3, pp. 60–67.

Fortini-Campbell, L. A. (2003). 'Integrated Marketing and the Consumer Experience', in *Kellogg on Integrated Marketing* (Iacobucci, D.). New York: Wiley.

Fram, E. H. and Cibotti, E. (1991). 'The Shopping List Studies and Projective Techniques: A 40-Year View'. *Marketing Research* 3, no. 4, pp. 14–21.

Freshwater, D. and Stickley, T. (2004). 'The Heart of the Art: Emotional Intelligence in Nurse Education'. *Nursing Inquiry* 11, no. 2, pp. 91–8. doi: 10.1111/j.1440-1800. 2004.00198.x.

Freud, S. (1920). 'Psychologie des Masses et Analyse du Moi', in *OEuvres Complètes, XVI.* Paris: PUF.

Frochot, I. and Batat, W. (2013). *Marketing and Designing the Tourist Experience*. Oxford: Goodfellow Publishers.

Gallese, V. (2003). 'The Roots of Empathy: The Shared Manifold Hypothesis and the Neural Basis of Intersubjectivity'. *Psychopathology* 36, no. 4, pp. 171–80. doi: 10.1159/000072786.

Geertz, C. (1973). *The Interpretation of Cultures*. NewYork: Basic.

Gilmore, J. H. and Pine, J. B. (2002). 'Customer Experience Places: The New Offering Frontier'. *Strategy & Leadership* 30, no. 4, pp. 4–11. doi: 10.1108/10878570210435306.

Gould, S. J. (1991). 'The Self-Manipulation of My Pervasive, Perceived Vital Energy through Product Use: An Introspective-Praxis Perspective'. *Journal of Consumer Research* 18, no. 2, pp. 194–207. doi: 10.1086/209252.

Gould, S. J. (2012). 'The Emergence of Consumer Introspection Theory (CIT): Introduction to a JBR special issue'. *Journal of Business Research* 65, no. 4, pp. 453–60. doi: 10.1016/j. jbusres.2011.02.010.

Goulding, C. (2000). 'The Commodification of the Past, Postmodern Pastiche, and the Search for Authentic Experiences at Contemporary Heritage Attractions'. *European Journal of Marketing* 34, no. 7, pp. 835–853.

Grach, S. S. (2015). 'Making Technology Accessible for Everyone'. *Microsoft*. Available at: https://blogs.microsoft.com/chicago/2015/04/23/making-technology-accessible-for-everyone/ (accessed 10 April 2017).

Greenson, R. R. (1960). 'Empathy and its Vicissitudes'. *The International Journal of Psychoanalysis* 41, pp. 418–24.

Grewal, D., Levy, M., and Kumar, V. (2009). 'Customer Experience Management in Retailing: An Organizing Framework'. *Journal of Retailing* 85, no. 1, pp. 1–14. doi: 10.1016/j.jretai.2009.01.001.

Grönroos, C. (2008). 'Service Logic Revisited: Who Creates Value? And Who Co-Creates?'. *European Business Review* 20, no. 4, pp. 298–314. doi: 10.1108/09555340810886585.

Gummesson, E. (1998). 'Productivity, Quality and Relationship Marketing in Service Operations', in *Handbuch Dienstleistungsmanagement* (eds. Corsten, H. and Roth, S.), pp. 843–864. Wiesbaden: Gabler Verlag.

Habermas, J. (1984). *The Theory of Communicative Action, Volume One: Reason and the Rationalization of Society*. Boston, MA: Beacon Press.

Haire, M. (1950). 'Projective Techniques in Marketing Research'. *Journal of Marketing* 14, no. 5, pp. 649–56. doi: 10.2307/1246942.

Harris, M. (1964). *The Nature of Cultural Things*. New York: Random House.

Harris, M. (1999). *Theories of Culture in Postmodern Times*. Walnut Creek, CA: Altamira Press.

Hawksworth, J. and Vaughan, R. (2014). *The Sharing Economy—Sizing the Revenue Opportunity*.PricewaterhouseCoopers.

Headland, T. N., Pike, K., and Harris, M. (1990). *Emics and Etics: The Insider/Outsider Debate*. Thousand Oaks, CA: Sage.

Hein, G. and Singer, T. (2008). 'I feel How You Feel but not Always: The Empathic Brain and its Modulation'. *Current Opinion in Neurobiology* 18, no. 2, pp. 153–8. doi: 10.1016/j.conb.2008.07.012.

Heinonen, K., Strandvik, T., Mickelsson, K. J., Edvardsson, B., Sundström, E., and Andersson, E. (2010). 'A Customer-Dominant Logic of Service'. *Journal of Service Management* 21, no. 4, pp. 531–48. doi: 10.1108/09564231011066088.

Helfrich, H. (1999). 'Beyond the Dilemma of Cross-Cultural Psychology: Resolving the Tension between Etic and Emic Approaches'. *Culture & Psychology* 5, no. 2, pp. 131–53.

Helkkula, A., Kelleher, C. and Pihlström, M. (2012). 'Characterizing Value as an Experience: Implications for Service Researchers and Managers'. *Journal of Service Research* 15, no. 1, pp. 59–75.

Helkkula, A., Kelleher, C., and Pihlström, M. (2012). 'Characterizing Value as an Experience – Implications for Researchers and Managers'. *Journal of Service Research* 15, no. 1, pp. 59–75. doi: 10.1177/1094670511426897.

Higgs, B., Polonsky, M. J. and Hollick, M. (2005). 'Measuring Expectations: Forecast vs. Ideal Expectations. Does It Really Matter?' *Journal of Retailing and Consumer Services* 12, no. 1, pp. 49–64.

Hill, C. R. (1968). 'Haire's Classic Instant Coffee Study–18 Years Later'. *Journalism Quarterly* 45, no. 3, pp. 466–472. doi: 10.1177/107769906804500307.

Hirschman, E. C. and Holbrook, M. B. (1982). 'Hedonic Consumption: Emerging Concepts, Methods, and Propositions'. *Journal of Marketing* 46, no. 3, pp. 92–101. doi: 10.2307/1251707.

Hoffman, D. L. and Novak T. P. (1996). 'Marketing in Hypermedia. Computer-Mediated Environments: Conceptual Foundations'. *Journal of Marketing* 60, no. 3, pp. 50–68. doi: 10.2307/1251841.

Hoffman, D. L. and Novak, T. P. (2009). 'Flow Online: Lessons Learned and Future Prospects'. *Journal of Interactive Marketing* 23, no. 1, pp. 23–34. doi: 10.1016/j.intmar. 2008.10.003.

Holbrook, M. B. (1986). 'I'm Hip: An Autobiographical Account of Some Musical Consumption Experiences'. *Advances in Consumer Research* 13, no. 1, pp. 614–8.

Holbrook, M. B. (1994). 'The Nature of Customer Value: An Axiology of Services in the Consumption Experience', in *Service Quality: New Directions in Theory and Practice*, pp. 21–71. Thousand Oaks, CA: Sage.

Holbrook, M. B. (1997). 'Borders, Creativity, and the State of the Art at the Leading Edge'. *Journal of Macromarketing* 17, no. 2, pp. 96–112.

Holbrook, M. B. (1999). 'Introduction to Consumer Value', in *Consumer Value: A Framework for Analysis and Research*, pp. 1–28. New York: Routledge.

Holbrook, M. B. and Hirschman, E. C. (1982). 'The Experiential Aspects of Consumption: Consumer Fantasies, Feelings, and Fun'. *Journal of Consumer Research* 9, no. 2, pp. 132–40. doi: 10.1086/208906.

Holt, D.B. (1995) 'How Consumers Consume A Typology of Consumption Practices.' *Journal of Consumer Research* 22, pp. 1–16.

Holt, D. B. (2002). 'Why Do Brands Cause Trouble? A Dialectical Theory of Consumer Culture and Branding'. *Journal of Consumer Research* 29, no. 1, pp. 70–90. doi: 10.1086/339922.

Holt, D.B. (2004). *How Brands Become Icons: The Principles of Cultural Branding.* Boston, MA: Harvard Business School Press.

Holt, D.B and Cameron, D. (2012). *Cultural Strategy: Using Innovative Ideologies to Build Breakthrough Brands.* UK: Oxford University Press.

Howard, J. A. and Sheth, J. N. (1969). *The Theory of Buyer Behavior.* New York: Wiley.

Hunt, S. (2004). 'On the Service-Centred Dominant Logic for Marketing'. *Journal of Marketing* 68, pp. 18–27.

Hunter, G. L. and Garnefeld, I. (2008). 'When Does Consumer Empowerment Lead to Satisfied Customers? Some Mediating and Moderating Effects of the Empowerment-Satisfaction Link'. *Journal of Research for Consumers* (2008), no. 15, pp. 1–14.

Husserl, E. (1931). *Ideas: General Introduction to a Pure Phenomenology.* London: Allen and Unwin.

Iacobucci, D. and Calder, B. (2003). *Kellogg on Integrated Marketing.* New York: Wiley.

Ickes W. (2003). *Everyday Mind Reading: Understanding What other People Think and Feel.* Amherst, NY: Prometheus Books.

Ingwer, M. (2012). *Empathetic Marketing: How to Satisfy the 6 Core Emotional Needs of Your Customers.* Basingstoke: Palgrave Macmillan.

Irwin, M., Klein, R. E., Engle, P. L., Yarbrough, C., and Nerlove, S. B. (1977). 'The Problem of Establishing Validity in Cross-Cultural Measurements'. *Annals of the New York Academy of Sciences* 285, no. 1, pp. 308–25. doi: 10.1111/j.1749-6632.1977.tb29359.x.

Kant, I. (2011). 'Rational Beings Alone Have Moral Worth', in *Food Ethics* (Pojman, P.), pp. 10–12. Belmont, CA: Wadsworth Publishing.

Kapferer, J. N. (2004). *The New Strategic Brand Management: Creating and Sustaining Brand Equity Long Term.* London: Kogan Page.

Kedzior, R. (2015). 'Digital Materiality – A Phenomenological Exploration'. *Advances in Consumer Research* 43, pp. 275–81.

Kelley, S. W., Donnelly Jr, J. H. and Skinner, S. J. (1990). 'Customer Participation in Service Production and Delivery'. *Journal of Retailing* 66, no. 3, pp. 315.

Khan, U., Dhar, R., and Wertenbroch K. (2004). 'A Behavioral Decision Theoretic Perspective on Hedonic and Utilitarian', in *Inside Consumption: Frontiers of Research on Consumer Motives, Goals, and Desires* (Ratneshwar, M. S. and Glen, D. G.). New York: Routledge.

Kleinginna, P. R. and Kleinginna, A. M. (1981). 'A Categorized List of Motivation Definitions, with a Suggestion for a Consensual Definition'. *Motivation and Emotion* 5, no. 3, pp. 263–91. doi: 10.1007/bf00993889.

Kotler, P. (1986). *Principles of Marketing.* Upper Saddle River, NJ: Prentice Hall.

Kotler, P. and Keller, K. (2006). *Marketing Management.* Upper Saddle River, NJ: Prentice Hall.

Kotler, P., Kartajaya, H., and Setiawan, I. (2010). *Marketing 3.0: from Products to Customers to the Human Spirit.* Hoboken, NJ: Wiley.

Kozinets, R. V. (2002). 'The Field Behind the Screen: Using Netnography for Marketing Research in Online Communities'. *Journal of Marketing Research* 39, no. 1, pp. 61–72. doi: 10.1509/jmkr.39.1.61.18935.

Kozinets, R. (2010). *Netnography: Doing Ethnographic Research Online.* London: Sage.

Kozinets R. V., de Valck, K., Wojnicki, A. C., and Wilner, S. J. S. (2010). 'Networked narratives: Understanding Word-of-Mouth Marketing in Online Communities'. *Journal of Marketing* 74, no. 2, pp. 71–89. doi: 10.1509/jmkg.74.2.71.

Kozinets, R. (2015). *Netnography: Redefined*. London: Sage.

Kroner, A. (2017). 'Stakeholder Voices Shaping Community Engagement at b.good', in *Managing for Social Impact: Innovations in Responsible Enterprise* (eds. Cronin, M. J. and Dearing, T. C.), pp. 145–154. Switzerland: Springer.

Lastovicka, J. L., Murry, J. P., and Joachimsthaler, E. A. (1990). 'Evaluating the Measurement Validity of Lifestyle Typologies with Qualitative Measures and Multiplicative Factoring'. *Journal of Marketing Research* 27, no. 1, pp. 11–23. doi: 10.2307/3172547.

Lasswell, H. D. (1948). *Power and Personality*. New York: Norton.

Lee, D. (2016). 'HEALTHQUAL: A Multi-Item Scale for Assessing Healthcare Service Quality'. *Service Business* 11, no. 3, pp. 1–26. doi:10.1007/s11628-016-0317-2.

Lemon, K. N. and Verhoef, V. C. (2016). 'Understanding Customer Experience Throughout the Customer Journey'. *Journal of Marketing* 80, no. 6, pp. 69–96. doi: 10.1509/jm.15.0420.

Lévi-Strauss, C. (1962). *La Pensée Sauvage*. Paris: Pion. 117–24.

Levy, S. J. (1959). 'Symbols for Sale'. *Harvard Business Review* July/August, pp. 117–124.

Liedloff, J. (1975). *The Continuum Concept: In Search of Happiness Lost* (Classics in Human Development). New York: Perseus Books Group.

Lipps, T., (1903). 'Einfühlung, Innere Nachahmung und Organempfindung', *Archiv fürgesamte Psychologie*.

Lyotard, J. F. (1984). *The Post-Modern Condition: A Report on Knowledge*. Minneapolis, MN: University of Minnesota.

Magids, S., Zorfas, A., and Leemon, D. (2015). 'The New Science of Customer Emotions'. *Harvard Business Review* (November 2015), pp. 66–76. Available at: https://hbr.org/2015/11/the-new-science-of-customer-emotions (accessed 20 June 2017).

Maglio, P. P., Vargo, S. L., Caswell, N. and Spohrer, J. (2009). 'The Service System is the Basic Abstraction of Service Science'. *Information Systems and e-Business Management* 7, no. 4, pp. 395–406.

Mahapatra, S. S., and Khan, M. S. (2007). 'A Neural Network Approach for Assessing Quality in Technical Education: An Empirical Study'. *International Journal of Productivity and Quality Management* 2, no. 3, pp. 287–306.

Maslow, A. (1968). 'Some Educational Implications of the Humanistic Psychologies'. *Harvard Educational Review* 38, no. 4, pp. 685–696.

Mathwick, C., Malhotra, N. K., and Rigdon, E. (2002). 'The Effect of Dynamic Retail Experiences on Experiential Perceptions of Value: An Internet and Catalog Comparison'. *Journal of Retailing* 78, no. 1, pp. 51–61. doi: 10.1016/s0022-4359(01)00066-5.

Mathwick, C., Wiertz, C., and de Ruyter, K. (2008). 'Social Capital Production in a Virtual P3 Community'. *Journal of Consumer Research* 34, no. 6, pp. 832–49. doi: 10.1086/523291.

McAlexander, J. H., Schouten, J. W., and Koenig, H. F. (2002). 'Building Brand Community'. *Journal of Marketing* 66, no. 1, pp. 38–54. doi: 10.1509/jmkg.66.1.38.18451.

McCarthy, J. and Wright, P. (2004). *Technology as Experience*. Cambridge, MA: MIT.

McLaren, K. (2013). *The Art of Empathy: A Complete Guide to Life's Most Essential Skill*. Boulder, CO: Sounds True, Inc.

McCracken, G. (1986). 'Culture and Consumption: A Theoretical Account of the Structure and Movement of the Cultural Meaning of Consumer Goods'. *Journal of Consumer Research* 13, no. 1, pp. 71–84.

McCracken, G. (1988). *The Long Interview: A Four-Step Method of Qualitative Inquiry*. Newbury Park, CA: Sage.

McGrath, M. A., Sherry, J. F., and Levy, S. J. (1993). 'Giving Voice to the Gift: The Use of Projective Techniques to Recover Lost Meaning'. *Journal of Consumer Psychology* 2, no. 2, pp. 171–92. doi: 10.1016/S1057-7408(08)80023-x.

McKinsey Global Institute (2015). 'The Internet Of Things: Mapping The Value Beyond The Hype'. Available at: www.mckinsey.com/~/media/McKinsey/Business%20Functions/McKinsey%20Digital/Our%20Insights/The%20Internet%20of%20Things%20The%20value%20of%20digitizing%20the%20physical%20world/The-Internet-of-things-Mapping-the-value-beyond-the-hype.ashx (accessed on July 31, 2018).

McNeal, J. U. (1987). *Children as Consumers: Insights and Implications*. Lexington, MA: Lexington Books.

Merriam, S. B. (2009). *Qualitative Research: A Guide to Design and Implementation*. Hoboken, NJ: Jossey-Bass.

Meyer, C. and Schwager, A. (2007). 'Understanding Customer Experience'. *Harvard Business Review* 85 (February), pp. 117–26.

Mills, P. K. and Morris, J. H. (1986). 'Clients as "Partial" Employees of Service Organizations: Role Development in Client Participation'. *Academy of Management Review* 11, no. 4, pp. 726–735.

Minkiewicz, J., Evans, J. and Bridson, K. (2009). 'Co-Creation in the Heritage Sector', in *ANZMAC 2009: Sustainable Management and Marketing Conference*, pp. 1–10. Melbourne, Australia: ANZMAC.

Minowa, Y., Visconti, L., and Maclaran, P (2012). 'Researchers' Introspection for Multi-Sited Ethnographers: A Xenoheteroglossic Autoethnography'. *Journal of Business Research* 65, no. 4, pp. 483–89.

Morris, M. W., Leung, K., Ames, D., and Lickel, B. (1999). 'Views from Inside and Outside: Integrating Emic and Etic Insights about Culture and Justice Judgment'. *The Academy of Management Review* 24, no. 4, pp. 781–96. doi: 10.2307/259354.

Morrison, S. and Crane, F. G. (2007). 'Building the Service Brand by Creating and Managing an Emotional Brand Experience'. *Journal of Brand Management* 14 no. 5, pp. 410–21. doi: 10.1057/palgrave.bm.2550080.

Moschis, G. P. and Mitchell, L. G. (1986). 'Television Advertising and Interpersonal Influences on Teenagers' Participation in Family Consumer Decisions', in *NA – Advances in Consumer Research Volume* 13 (ed. Lutz, R. J.), pp.181–186. Provo, UT: Association for Consumer Research.

Mossberg, L. (2008). 'Extraordinary Experiences Through Storytelling'. *Scandinavian Journal of Hospitality and Tourism* 8, no. 3, pp. 195–210.

Mourrain, J. A. P. (1989). 'The Hyper-Modern Commodity-Form: The Case of Wine', in *Marketing Theory and Practice* (Childers, T.L. et al.) pp. 318–22. Chicago, IL: American Marketing Association.

Mucchielli, R. (1995). *L'Entretien de Face à Face dans la Relation d'Aide*. Paris: ESF.

Muniz, A. M. and O'Guinn, T. C. (2001), 'Brand Community'. *Journal of Consumer Research* 27, no. 4, pp. 412–32. doi: 10.1086/319618.

Narver, J. C. and Slater, S. F. (1990). 'The Effect of a Market Orientation on Business Profitability'. *Journal of Marketing* 54, no. 4, pp. 20–35.

Ostergaard, P., Fitchett, J. and Jantzen, C. (2013). 'A Critique of the Ontology of Consumer Enchantment'. *Journal of Consumer Behaviour* 12, no. 5, pp. 337–344.

O'Sullivan, E. L. and Spangler, K. J. (1998). *Experience Marketing: Strategies for the New Millennium*. State College, PA: Venture.

Ozanne, J. L. and Saatcioglu, B. (2008). 'Participatory Action Research'. *Journal of Consumer Research* 35, no. 3, pp. 423–39. doi: 10.1086/586911.

Park, C. W., Mothersbaugh, D. L., and Feick, L. (1994). 'Consumer Knowledge Assessment'. *Journal of Consumer Research* 21, no. 1, pp. 71–82.

Parasuraman, A., Zeithaml, V. A. and Berry, L. L. (1988). 'SERVQUAL: A Multiple-Item Scale for Measuring Consumer Perceptions of Service Quality'. *Journal of Retailing* 64, no. 1, pp. 14–40.

Patterson, A. (2005). 'Processes, Relationships, Settings, Products and Consumers: The Case for Qualitative Diary Research'. *Qualitative Market Research: An International Journal* 8, no. 2, pp. 142–56. doi: 10.1108/13522750510592427.

Patton, M. Q. (2010). *Qualitative Research & Evaluation Methods*. Thousand Oaks, CA: Sage.

Payne, A. and Frow, P. (2004). 'The Role of Multichannel Integration in Customer Relationship Management'. *Industrial Marketing Management* 33, no. 6, pp. 527–38. doi: 10.1016/j.indmarman.2004.02.002.

Piaget, J. (1975). 'L'épistémologie génétique'. *Revue Philosophique de la France Et de l'Etranger* 165, no. 3, pp. 337–338.

Pike, K.L. (1954). 'Emic and Etic Stand Points for the Description of Behavior', in *Language in Relation to a Unified Theory of the Structure of Human Behavior*, pp. 8–28. Glendale, IL: Summer Institute of Linguistics.

Pike, K. L. (1967). *Language in Relation to a Unified Theory of the Structure of Human Behavior*. The Hague: Mouton.

Pine II, B. J. and Gilmore, J. H. (1998). 'Welcome to the Experience Economy'. *Harvard Business Review* 76, no. 4, pp. 97–105.

Pine II, B. J. and Gilmore, J. H. (1999). *The Experience Economy: Work is Theatre and Every Business a Stage*. Boston, MA: Harvard Business School.

Pitkin, J. (2011). 'The Power of Persuasion: Effective Use of Influencer Marketing'. *PeerIndex*. Available at: www.scribd.com/document/67287343/The-Power-of-Persuasion (accessed 20 June 2017).

Porter, M. E. (2008). *On Competition, Updated and Expanded Edition*. Boston, MA: Harvard Business School.

Prahalad, C. K. and Ramaswamy, V. (2000). 'Co-Opting Customer Competence'. *Harvard Business Review* 78, no. 1, pp. 79–90.

Prahalad, C. K. and Ramaswamy, V. (2004). 'Co-Creation Experiences: The Next Practice in Value Creation'. *Journal of Interactive Marketing* 18, no. 3, pp. 5–14.

Pullman, M. E. and Gross, M. A. (2004). 'Ability of Experience Design Elements to Elicit Emotions and Loyalty Behaviors'. *Decision Science* 35, no. 3, pp. 551–78. doi: 10.1111/j.0011-7315.2004.02611.x.

Punj, G. (2012). 'Consumer Decision Making on the Web: A Theoretical Analysis and Research Guidelines'. *Psychology and Marketing* 29, no. 10, pp. 791–803. doi: 10.1002/mar.20564.

Rambo-Ronai, C. (1992). 'The Reflexive Self Through Narrative: A Night in the Life of an Erotic Dancer/Researcher', in *Investigating Subjectivity: Research on Lived Experience* (Ellis, C. and Flaherty, G.). Newbury Park, CA: Sage.

Ratchford, B. T., Talukdar, D., and Lee, M. S. (2007). 'The Impact of the Internet on Consumers' Use of Information Sources for Automobiles'. *Journal of Consumer Research* 34, no. 1, pp. 111–9. doi: 10.1086/513052.

Reed, E. S. (1996). *Encountering the World*. Oxford: Oxford University.

Ritzer, G. (2004). 'An Introduction to McDonaldization' in *The McDonaldization of Society*. Thousand Oaks, CA: Sage.

Ritzer, G. (Ed.). (2009). *McDonaldization: The Reader*. Newbury Park, CA: Pine Forge Press.

Rodgers, S. and Sheldon, K. M. (2002). 'An Improved Way to Characterize Internet Users'. *Journal of Advertising* 42, no. 5, pp. 85–94. doi: 10.2501/jar-42-5-85-94.

Rogers, C. (1980). *A Way of Being*. Boston, MA: Houghton Mifflin.

Rogers, C. R. (2004). 'The Necessary and Sufficient Conditions of Therapeutic Personality Change', in *Communication, Relationships and Care: A Reader* (ed. Barrett, S.), p. 179. London: Routledge.

Rosenau, P. M. (1992). *Post-Modernism and the Social Sciences: Insights, Inroads, and Intrusions.* Princeton, NJ: Princeton University.

Rust, R. T., Moorman, C. and Dickson, P. R. (2002). 'Getting Return on Quality: Revenue Expansion, Cost Reduction, or Both?' *Journal of Marketing* 66, no. 4, pp. 7–24.

Schensul, S. L., Schensul, J. J., and LeCompte, M. D. (2013). *Initiating Ethnographic Research: A Mixed Methods Approach.* Lanham, MD: Rowman Altamira.

Schmitt, B. H. (1999). *Experiential Marketing.* New York: Free Press.

Schmitt, B. H. (2003). *Customer Experience Management: A Revolutionary Approach to Connecting with Your Customers.* New York: Free Press.

Schmitt, B. H. (2010). 'Experience Marketing: Concepts, Frameworks and Consumer Insights'. *Foundations and Trends in Marketing* 5, no. 2, pp. 55–112. doi: 10.1561/1700000027.

Schmitt, B. H., Brakus, J. J., and Zarantonello, L. (2015). 'From Experiential Psychology to Consumer Experience'. *Journal of Consumer Psychology* 25, no. 1, pp. 166–71. doi: 10.1016/j.jcps.2014.09.001.

Schor, J. B. and Fitzmaurice, C. (2015). 'Collaborating and Connecting: The Emergence of a Sharing Economy', in *Handbook on Research on Sustainable Consumption* (Reisch, L. and Thogersen, J.). Cheltenham, UK: Edward Elgar.

Schouten, J. W. and McAlexander, J. H. (1995). 'Subcultures of Consumption: An Ethnography of the New Bikers'. *Journal of Consumer Research* 22, no. 1, pp. 43–61. doi: 10.1086/209434.

Schroeder, J. E. and Salzer-Mörling, M. (2006). *Brand Culture.* London: Routledge. doi: 10.4324/9780203002445.

Shah, D., Rust, R. T., Parasuraman, A., Staelin, R. and Day, G. S. (2006). 'The Path to Customer Centricity'. *Journal of Service Research* 9, no. 2, pp. 113–124.

Shaw, C. and Ivens, J. (2005). *Building Great Customer Experiences.* New York: Palgrave Macmillan. doi: 10.1057/9780230554719.

Shostack G. L. (1984). 'Designing Services That Deliver'. *Harvard Bus Rev* 62, no. 1, pp. 133–39.

Sleeswijk-Visser, F. (2009). Bringing the Everyday Life of People into Design. Doctoral Thesis Delft. Sleeswijk-Visser, Rotterdam. ISBN 978-90-9024244-6

Sorofman, J. (2014). 'Agenda Overview for Customer Experience, 2015'. *Gartner.* Available at: www.gartner.com/imagesrv/digital-marketing/pdfs/agenda-overview-for-customer.pdf (accessed 20 June 2017).

Stein, E. (1964). *On the Problem of Empathy.* Netherlands: Springer. doi: 10.1007/978-94-017-5546-7.

Steinman, R. B. (2009). 'Projective Techniques in Consumer Research'. *International Bulletin of Business Administration*, no. 5, pp. 37–45.

Stotland, E., Mathews, K. E., Sherman, S. E., Hannson, R. O., and Richardson, B. Z. (1978). *Empathy, Fantasy and Helping.* Beverly Hills, CA: Sage.

Strathern, M. (1997). 'Prefigured Features: A View from the New Guinea Highland'. *The Australian Journal of Anthropology* 8, no. 2, pp. 89–103. doi: 10.1111/j.1835-9310.1997.tb00179.x.

Sweeney, R. T. (2005). 'Reinventing Library Buildings and Services for the Millennial Generation', *Library Administration & Management* 19, no. 4, pp. 165–75.

Tapscott, D. (2009). *Grown Up Digital: How the Net Generation is Changing Your World.* New York: McGraw-Hill.

Thomas, M. J. (1997). 'Consumer Market Research: Does It Have Validity? Some Postmodern thoughts'. *Marketing Intelligence & Planning* 15, no. 2, pp. 54–9. doi: 10.1108/02634509710165858.

Titchener, E. B. (1909/2014). 'Introspection and Empathy'. *Dialogues in Philosophy, Mental and Neuro Sciences* 7, no. 1, pp. 25–30.

Triandis, H. C., Malpass, R. S., and Davidson, A. R. (1972). 'Cross-Cultural Psychology'. *Biennial Review of Anthropology* 7, pp. 1–84.

United Nations. (2014). 'Our Urbanizing World'. *Population Facts.* Available at www. un.org/en/development/desa/population/publications/pdf/popfacts/PopFacts_2014-3. pdf (accessed 1 October 2018).

Vargo, S. L. and Lusch, R. F. (2004). 'Evolving to a New Dominant Logic for Marketing'. *Journal of Marketing*, January 2004, 68, 1, pp. 1–17.

Vargo, S. L. and Lusch, R. F. (2006). 'Service-Dominant Logic: What It Is, What It Is not, What It Might Be', in *The Service-Dominant Logic of Marketing: Dialog, Debate, and Directions*, pp. 43–56.

Vargo, S. L. and Lusch, R. F. (2008). 'Service-dominant Logic: Continuing the Evolution'. *Journal of the Academy of marketing Science* 36, no. 1, 1–10.

Vattimo, G. (1992). *The Transparent Society*. Baltimore, MD: Johns Hopkins University.

Venkatesh, A. (1992). 'Postmodernism, Consumer Culture and the Society of the Spectacle'. *Advances in Consumer Research* 19, pp.199–202.

Venkatesh, A., Sherry, J. F., and Firat, A. F. (1993). 'Postmodernism and the Marketing Imaginary'. *International Journal of Research in Marketing* 10, no. 3, pp. 215–23. doi: 10.1016/0167-8116(93)90007-l.

Verhoef, P. C., Lemon, K. N., Parasuraman, A., Roggeveen, A., Tsiros, M., and Schlesinger, L. A. (2009). 'Customer Experience Creation: Determinants, Dynamics, and Management Strategies'. *Journal of Retailing* 85, no. 1, pp. 31–41. doi: 10.1016/j.jretai.2008.11.001.

Vischer, R. (1873). 'On the Optical Sense of Form: A Contribution to Aesthetics', in *Empathy, Form, and Space. Problems in German Aesthetics, 1873–1893* (Mallgrave, Harry Francis and Ikonomou, Eleftherios (eds., trans.)), pp. 89–123. Santa Monica, CA: Getty Center for the History of Art and the Humanities. 1994.

Vorhies, D. W. and Morgan, N. A. (2005). 'Benchmarking Marketing Capabilities for Sustainable Competitive Advantage'. *Journal of Marketing* 69, no. 1, pp. 80–94.

Wallendorf, M. and Brucks, M. (1993). 'Introspection in Consumer Research: Implementation and Implications'. *Journal of Consumer Research* 20, no. 3, pp. 339–59. doi: 10.1086/209354.

Ward, S. (1974). 'Consumer Socialization'. *Journal of Consumer Research* 1, no. 2, pp. 1–14.

Watkins, R. (2015). 'Conceptualising the Ontology of Digital Consumption Objects'. *Advances in Consumer Research* 43, pp. 275–81.

Weedon, C. (1997). *Feminist Practice and Poststructuralist Theory*. Oxford: Blackwell.

Wernerfelt, B. (1990). 'Advertising Content When Brand Choice is a Signal'. *The Journal of Business* 63, no. 1, pp. 91–8. doi: 10.1086/296485.

Westfall, R. I., Boyd, H. W., and Campbell, D. T. (1957). 'The Use of Structured Techniques in Motivation Research'. *Journal of Marketing* 22, no. 2, pp. 134–39. doi: 10.2307/1247209.

Willis, J. W. (2007). *Foundations of Qualitative Research: Interpretive and Critical Approaches*. Thousand Oaks, CA: Sage. doi: 10.4135/9781452230108.

Wohlfeil, M. and Whelan, S. (2008). 'Confessions of a Movie-Fan: Introspection into a Consumer's Experiential Consumption of "Pride & Prejudice"'. *European Advances in Consumer Research* 8, pp. 137–43.

Wohlfeil, M. and Whelan, S. (2012). '"*Saved!*" by Jena Malone: An Introspective Study of a Consumer's Fan Relationship with a Film Actress'. *Journal of Business Research* 65, no. 4, pp. 511–9. doi: 10.1016/j.jbusres.2011.02.030.

Woodall, T. (2003). 'Conceptualising "Value for the Customer": An Attributional, Structural and Dispositional Analysis'. *Academy of Marketing Science Review* (2003), no. 12, pp. 1–42.

Yin, R. K. (2010). *Qualitative Research from Start to Finish.* New York: The Guilford.

Zaki, J. and Ochsner, K. N. (2012). 'The Neuroscience of Empathy: Progress, Pitfalls and Promise'. *Nature Neuroscience* 15, pp. 675–80. doi: 10.1038/nn.3085.

Preston, S. D. and de Waal, F. B. M. (2002). 'Empathy: Its Ultimate and Proximate Bases'. *Behavioral and Brain Sciences* 25, no. 1, pp. 1–20. doi: 10.1017/s0140525x02000018.

Zaltman G. (1996). 'Metaphorically Speaking'. *Marketing Research* 8, no. 2, p. 13.

Zaltman G. (1997). 'Rethinking Market Research: Putting People Back In'. *Journal of Marketing Research* 34, no. 4, pp. 424–37. doi: 10.2307/3151962.

INDEX

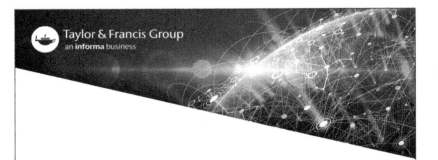